The Seventeenth Degree

The Seventeenth Degree

HOW IT WENT

VIETNAM

HANOI

MEDINA

SONS OF THE MORNING

Mary McCarthy

HARCOURT BRACE JOVANOVICH, INC.
NEW YORK

Printed in the United States of America

Library of Congress Cataloging in Publication Data

McCarthy, Mary Therese, date
The seventeenth degree.

CONTENTS: How it went.—Vietnam.—Hanoi. [etc.]
1. Vietnamese Conflict, 1961-   —Addresses, essays,
lectures.   I. Title.
DS557.A6M2   959.704′3   74-1065
ISBN 0-15-181355-8
ISBN 0-15-680680-0 (pbk.)
BCDEFGHIJ

To Jim and Bill

Contents

HOW IT WENT

Vietnam, Hanoi, and *Medina* were conceived as pamphlets. Each, at the time of publication, I expected to be the last. They were intended in their small way to move public opinion to end the war; hence the pamphlet format: neither a hard cover (too expensive for wide distribution) nor a regular paperback (too great a risk of not being reviewed). As it turns out, the pamphlet format seems to have been a mistake. I should have listened to Harcourt's sales department. The first two books, when they came out, got hardly any reviews (ten of *Hanoi* in the entire United States) and, being the wrong shape —too long, wide, and thin—they did not fit into the paperback racks of drugstores, airports, newsstands, or the paperback shelves of standard bookstores, where the clerks did not know what to do with them, with the result that the general public, to which I hoped I was talking, never saw their outsides, let alone what was in them.

Medina came out in June 1972. One of my friends tried to get it that summer when she was in Idaho (the home state of war critic Senator Frank Church) visiting relations—no luck. When she passed through New York in the fall, same story. No bookstore she went to had heard of it, though a sympathetic clerk at Scribner's directed her to the children's department. In the end, she found it in Rome, on the Via delle Botteghe Oscure, at the bookshop of the Communist party—in Italian. The right place for it, some would say.

I can sympathize with the booksellers. Understandably, there is no slot for a pamphlet, the way the industry is organized; if you have a mass communication to deliver, you should accept mass methods of packaging it. The failure to get reviews is something else. Serial publication, some said: both *Vietnam* and *Hanoi* had come out in large part, though not in their entirety, in the *New York Review of Books.* Yet serial publication did not have that effect in other cases: *The Sea Around Us, The Dead Sea Scrolls, Eichmann in Jerusalem,* and, just recently, *Fire in the Lake*—to name the first titles that cross my mind. Well, those books are longer. True, but *Medina,* extracts from which were published in *The New Yorker,* did get quite a few reviews, though it is the shortest of the three.

The reason cannot have been political: among the journals that did not review either *Vietnam* or *Hanoi* were *The Nation, The New Republic, The New Yorker, Harper's, Partisan Review,* practically the whole liberal establishment, you might say, and all, of course, opponents of the war in Vietnam. Personal, then? But some of the editors of the book sections that were giving my war pamphlets the silent treatment were the very people who were asking me regularly for contributions: "Won't you review X or Y for us? Please say yes." Francis Brown, then editor of the New York *Times* Sunday book section, belonged to that category. Finally I wrote him a letter, since he seemed to be so friendly, asking when he was going to print a review of *Vietnam.* His answer was "Patience!" That was in 1967, and I am still waiting. When *Hanoi* came out the following year, no review in the New York *Times,* daily or Sunday.

The reader may think I am nursing a common author's grievance based on wounded vanity; authors never get enough reviews to suit them. But I have not had this complaint before or since. When a collection of my literary essays, *The Writing on the Wall*, came out the year after *Hanoi*, it was reviewed across the country, and yet those essays—all, incidentally, reprints—were not of burning current interest; if they had been overlooked, it would not have been a great surprise. The surprise was to find that collection being reviewed with such virtual unanimity, after what had happened to the Vietnam publications. So it could not be just me that nobody wanted to hear from. Perhaps me on Vietnam—the combination.

Or some other factor. It has occurred to me that the jealous dislike felt by other editors toward the *New York Review of Books* (sibling envy of a junior?) might have played some part. This could explain why *Medina* got noticed despite the fact that about two-thirds of it had appeared in *The New Yorker*. But maybe editors felt their readers would be more interested in the Medina trial than in what I had observed in South and North Vietnam, where I could be said to be prejudiced as a witness. Still, my reports of those trips, at the time, had a certain pioneering character: in South Vietnam only John Steinbeck and Martha Gellhorn, among American writers, had preceded me, and, in the North, I was the first American novelist to descend at Hanoi airport. Normally the impressions of novelists, whatever their prejudices, are received with some curiosity, since novelists themselves are curious—in both senses—beings.

Unfavorable reviews would have done just as well as favorable, maybe better, in letting the reading public know that those trips to the scene had been undertaken and that a record of the findings was available. As returns poured in from the bookstores and *Vietnam*, long, red, and thin in its durable linen-treated cover, piled up in the warehouse, my publisher and friend William Jovanovich felt that he must be dreaming. He kept saying that never in all his experience had he seen another case like it—where a book by a well-known author on a controversial subject had scarcely been noticed in the press. With *Hanoi*, he was sure it would be different; reparation would be made by *Time, Newsweek, Harper's, The Atlantic*, Francis Brown, et cetera, et cetera. . . . Now he can only scratch his head.

A conspiracy, some eager voices have suggested. No. Who? How? It is a mystery, and I do not know what moral to draw from the experience. Publish in hard covers if you want to be sure of reviews? Or don't publish first in the *New York Review of Books?* I shall be glad to pay a reward to any reader of this volume who can explain to me what happened and why.

ROBERT SILVERS of the *New York Review* asked me to go to South Vietnam for him early in 1966. It must have been shortly after the thirty-seven-day bombing pause, which had begun Christmas Eve and caused a flurry of hope. But let me go back to January 1965. With the coming of the new year, I had become terribly alarmed by the possibility that we would bomb the North. To bring them to the conference table, as it was put. Johnson was starting his second term, and the situation in South Vietnam looked grave; everyone was watching to see what the White House would do. By the end of the month, like

6

many other onlookers, I was feverishly seeking alternatives, in my own mind, to the unthinkable, which was bombing. The intervention of a third party—the UN, India, the Pope? I was unable to believe that we would actually attack from the air a small poor country that had not attacked us—rather than merely *talk* about bombing so as to be overheard by Hanoi. This would surely be one of those crises—like the Cuban missile confrontation, like the Berlin Wall—that would somehow pass. Some solution would be found. My solution (borrowed from a friend) for the Wall crisis had been to move West Berlin to the middle of West Germany and rebuild it: perfectly feasible technically and no more demented than the Wall itself. For Cuba, full recognition of Castro and material aid; then they would not need Soviet missiles.

The fact that my mind in 1965 was still running in search of workable remedies, prescriptions, for U.S. foreign policy showed how wedded I was to a good image of our country despite years of Trotskyist sympathies, anarchist sympathies, of voting for Norman Thomas, though he was part of the good image. Goldwater might bomb, but surely not Johnson. People I knew—friends like Arthur Schlesinger—were *working* in the Administration. I had met George Ball, Humphrey, the Bundy brothers; I knew Adam Yarmolinsky's parents. Such people, whatever I thought of them (not much in a number of cases), were coterminous with my life, even if only for a little piece of the boundary. My own husband worked for the government; he was on loan from the State Department to an international organization, which was why, on the morning of February 8, we were living in Paris.

I saw the headlines at the newspaper kiosk by the Métro station on my way probably to the bakery (or am I confusing it with Hiroshima? I saw that headline while buying Portuguese bread at Mary Snow's store in Truro, on Cape Cod, and wondered what I was taking the loaf home for) and just stood there, swallowing and doing deep breathing, before I bought the papers. We had done it. I turned around and slowly walked home, wanting to be alone to think the unthinkable. The headlines of the next days carried no news of further raids, but that detail did not interest me. I knew we would do it again. When sustained bombing (Operation Rolling Thunder) started the following week, I did not offer myself the consolation of trying to believe that we were hitting only military targets.

The sole thinkable thought left during the next months was that we could be stopped somehow. I did not share the concern expressed by "responsible" editorial writers that our action might bring in Russia and China. If anything, I feared that it wouldn't and wished that it would. Not that I was hoping for nuclear war to descend on us as a punishment. Rather, I hoped that some firm step on the part of the Russians or the Chinese might deter us, if we could not deter ourselves. At least fear of Soviet intervention was keeping our planes away from Haiphong harbor. Yet as our troops began debarking in the South and neither the Russians nor the Chinese moved, I began to have the horrible wish that we would hit a Russian ship by mistake. We were being too lucky in our wicked course. I could not wish we would hit Russian ships deliberately, for that would mean that our policy-makers had become totally reckless, sensing that they had a free hand. This seems to have been Nixon's conviction last * Christmas, when our B-52's struck the Embassy quarter of Hanoi, killing the French Chief of Mission. If the world was shocked by the action—in itself no worse than what we were doing every day to Vietnamese— it was not because of any deep respect for the sanctity of diplomats' lives, but because the raid demonstrated how frighteningly callous to consequences, military or diplomatic, Nixon had become.

In any case, my daydreams of some Russian or Chinese démarche were essentially rescue dreams and the product of despair. In reality, it was better that the Vietnamese should continue to hold us off on their own—no contingents of "volunteers" from China, no Soviet pilots for the MIGs. If we had anybody to thank for saving us from ourselves, that is, from an American victory and its deadly political after-effects, it was the Vietnamese. Ho Chi Minh, the VC, the "fanatical" bonzes who were setting themselves alight. A good deal of the affection felt for representatives of this people by anti-war Americans who met them sprang, surely, from simple gratitude. They were defending our country, as well as their own, against its enemies in the White House, the Pentagon, and Congress.

At home the teach-ins were beginning. Robert Lowell refused Johnson's invitation to a White House festival for the arts. In Paris that summer various acquaintances in the government, posted in Paris or passing through, instructed me not to worry —just give Johnson a little time. McNamara, the gossip ran, was privately against the war. He would soon swing the President around. I doubted that, but the thought that we had a secret

---

* 1972

9

ally in the Secretary of Defense did assuage me for a while. Then we got the announcement that Washington would be sending combat troops—not just Marines to guard air bases. If McNamara was against the war, surely he should be resigning? Like Sister Anne on the parapet, I watched for that headline. But no help, not even a rumor now, came from Defense to hearten the opposition.

As I look back, the chronology of those days telescopes. Nineteen sixty-five blurs with 1966. I thought it was in the summer of 1965 that I did an interview with Edwin Newman in Paris during which I said that if Americans did not act against the war, put down some real stake, our case would not be so different from that of the "good" Germans under Hitler who claimed to have disagreed with the Final Solution, offering as proof the fact that they had taken no active part in it. But my files assure me that it was in 1966. As late as that. So it took me a whole year to say on television what I had been muttering to myself about Vietnam. That is, that talking while continuing your life as usual was not enough. Still, I could not see what else to do.

Vietnam had ensconced itself on my pillow. I *thought* about it just before going to sleep, during intervals of the night, and instantly on waking in the morning, spinning out strategies for opposition that grew baroque and fanciful as I became drowsy. Imaginary dialogues with Johnson's apologists, telegrams to senators and congressmen, Portia-like audiences with McNamara, urging him to make his doubts public. Some of this carried over into waking life. Telegrams were drafted and sent; I incessantly argued with anybody I met who was remotely near the sources of power.

Being practical, I sought means of leverage. Signing protests was just a waste of your name. Why not teach-ins in the factories? It was vital to reach the working class. And tax refusal. If you could get fifteen very well-known people (on the order of Walter Lippmann) to agree to withhold a portion of their income taxes, then, with that nucleus, you could certainly get a hundred to join in a public announcement. That hundred, in turn, could rally fifteen thousand. It would snowball.

Not a bad idea (do you think?), but when I presented it to acquaintances on a brief trip to New York, I could awaken interest in only one person and that a close friend. I was burning with it, but nobody else caught fire. There were a few pacifists, I knew, who were already practicing tax refusal (one a friend, too), but they were not "names." With names, it would be different. And it was no good doing it solo. What was needed was a mass movement of the middle class (maybe in the end you could get a hundred thousand), which would feel itself safe in the company of men like Walter Lippmann. The middle class was the storm center of verbal protest, yet its sons were receiving draft deferment. It was capable of sacrifice. The Abolitionists had been middle-class, too. And the Suffragettes. True, the Treasury could collect your back taxes—and a small fine—by going into your bank account, but think of the manpower it could cost them to pursue a hundred thousand respectable tax delinquents. And if you took the extreme stand of filing no return and they put you in prison, they would have to pay your upkeep there, not to mention the expense of your trial.

Failing to make any headway, I gave up and went back to Paris. At least I had tried. Yet all along, as I urged and

11

reasoned, I had been aware of a considerable problem looming for me. If I were able to convince fifteen well-known people, I, of course, would have to join their ranks. No question about that. This would put me in a delicate situation with my husband, as a U.S. foreign service officer; at the very minimum, we would have to stop filing joint tax returns. I decided to cross that bridge when I came to it. Now I can never know what really I would have done had I found myself on the river's edge face to face with the decision. Maybe I could have persuaded my husband (who, after all, opposed the war himself) to agree to my withholding taxes if I was part of a group. Failing that, maybe I would not be married now. Or I would have welshed, in which case I might not be married now, either, since my welshing would have cast discredit on him, too.

It was a long time, though, before I could fully give up the thought of tax refusal. Despite the fact that I had promised my husband that never, under any circumstances, would I consider doing it alone, it remained in my mind with a mourning band around it, like a lost opportunity, a lost dream. At my desk, I had rather pleasant reveries of going to jail. It would be so peaceful: no telephone. As for teach-ins in the factories, that idea, too, was rejected in New York. My friends said the trade unions would kick out any group that tried it.

YET WHEN Bob Silvers, in early spring 1966, had asked me to go to Vietnam for the magazine, I had refused. I would talk it over with my husband, I told him on the telephone. Or was it a cable I had from him? Anyway, my husband and I did talk it over. Here, we both saw, was my chance to do something. I

wanted to go but knew almost at once that I couldn't. Nevertheless, for a few tense days it hung in suspense. Then one evening
he came home earlier than usual from the office. He sat in an
easy chair, I across from him on the sofa. It was as though we
had made an appointment for the conversation, like a visit to a
doctor or lawyer. We were both very calm.

If I went, he said, he would have to hand in his resignation.
He saw no other recourse. "Are you sure?" I said. "Yes." He
had three children to support, as well as alimony payments to
make, and had spent most of his adult life in government
service, first in the Air Force and later with government agencies. "Well, then, I can't go." I did not feel he was constraining
me, only presenting me with an ineluctable fact. There it was.
I could not invest *his* life in my desire to go to Vietnam. Six
years before, when we had met in Poland, he had been Cultural
Affairs Officer in the Embassy. Now he was fifty-one years old.
After that evening, we did not talk again about my going.
Everything had been said, and there were no bad feelings
between us. Rather, the contrary. It was as if my trip was a
sacrifice we had made jointly: he, too, had wanted it for me.

The following January, three quarters of a year later, Silvers
asked me again. The U.S. now had over four hundred thousand
men in Vietnam. No other correspondent had gone for the
magazine, which had printed many articles on the subject and
was in the forefront of domestic opposition to the war. Again
I told Jim (my husband) and again we considered. Nothing
had changed, so there should have been nothing to discuss.
The war was there; his job was there; the children were there.
Yet we deferred making the decision; we were busy with work

and social life, and no moment seemed to be the right one. Late one morning he telephoned me from his office. "Let's meet after lunch, for coffee, at the Deux Magots." We sat outside; it was a nice day. I knew he had come across town to say yes. What had changed was that three quarters of a year had passed and U.S. policy was the same. "But are you going to resign?" I said. "Hell, no. They'll have to fire me." That was the decision he had come to. "Maybe they won't."

This time we were not at all calm but both very excited. I cried for happiness. We held hands. My eyes were still wet when we saw Henry Moore, the sculptor, come up the street. He sat down at our table, and we told him that he had arrived at a great moment for both of us: we had just agreed that I should go to Vietnam. His appearance there, gray and numinous, like a piece of his own life-enhancing statuary, was an omen, we felt, a heaven-sent blessing on our good action. He seemed pleased to be treated as an omen; we ordered more coffee.

After that, there remained only practical details. Getting shots, a plane ticket. Bringing my summer clothes downstairs. Visas—I would go to Hanoi, too, if they would give me one. Making my will. And the Embassy. That afternoon, when I left the Deux Magots, I decided that I would have to tell Ambassador Bohlen. Jim was not serving under him, being seconded to an international organization, but we had been to their house, and he to ours. As a matter of courtesy, I should let him know. I wrote him a note and at once got back an answer. He asked me to come over to his office; for an hour we debated about Vietnam. It reminded me of school, when you have to listen respectfully to the principal as she carries out her duty, which is to point out to you the errors of your thinking, even though she knows you will do what you have determined to do anyway.

Having executed that formality, he became very nice. I would need permission from the State Department to travel to North Vietnam, which at the time was on Washington's forbidden list. Well, he would take care of that for me; in fact he would telephone. And he wondered about my passport. "You're not planning to use your diplomatic one, are you?" "I hadn't thought about it, to tell the truth." He was amused. "If you go to Hanoi with that, they'll think you're a spy. It could even give you some trouble in Saigon. We'd better get you another passport." It turned out—to my surprise—that I had the right to a second passport, the regular blue one. The next day the consul, on the first floor, was personally issuing me a Mary McCarthy passport, with NORTH VIET-NAM inked out from the list of countries the bearer was not authorized to travel to. Washington's answer had come in less time than it took me to get photos from a studio on Rue Tronchet.

The best qualities of old-fashioned American representatives abroad were being exhibited in "Chip" Bohlen's gay and efficient helpfulness. He also let their people in Saigon know that I was coming as a journalist and asked for the usual courtesies. He sent a message of introduction to Ambassador Lodge. The fact that I was who I was and the wife of a U.S. diplomat (almost like a member of the family) no doubt made a difference, but that is the way the world works everywhere. Or not quite. Had I been the wife of a Soviet official, announcing that I was going abroad to criticize Kremlin imperialism, my husband would have joined me within a matter of days in a camp or a madhouse. . . .

Was Bohlen's co-operativeness designed to make that propaganda point? Was it "policy"? Perhaps, but I don't think so; I think he rather liked me. And he enjoyed the wry humor of harboring a viper in his official bosom. That was very American, too; I had seen it in school, in college, with my grandfather. As for Vietnam, I had the impression Bohlen knew very little about it, which made it easier for him to defend what we were doing there. He let his anti-Communism stretch out to embrace Vietnam as a matter of course, saving him mental effort.

He invited me to come back to the Embassy to hear "our side" before I left. I obeyed and was turned over to their Vietnam expert, who made a routine effort to brainwash me with columns of "confidential" figures on North Vietnamese infiltration and Viet Cong terror. His heart, I felt, was more in it than Ambassador Bohlen's, but his figures were just the old hand-outs, and he could not say how or by whom they had been validated. He was one of the new Americans, tall, thin, youngish, zealous, preoccupied, who gave me the sense that I was wasting his time (true): Vietnam, his manner made clear, was a "field" where only statistics should talk. Yet he gave me the names of men to look up in Saigon, appending in some cases his greetings, and when I had difficulties in getting my visa from the Saigon Embassy, he proved to be very useful; he indicated the right persons there to ask for, he wrote a letter, he telephoned. Unlike Bohlen, he took no relish in it, saw no joke; he simply did it. When I was grateful, he was cold. Still, I have to say that without the facilities provided by the U.S. government both in Paris and on the spot, my report on Vietnam could never have been made. But this was true of all the journalists there. You can say that with the American "image" to sustain, our government could have done no less. Yet in trying to be faithful to that image and permitting a free flow of information, it gave itself a serious handicap in the conduct of the war. One would be insane to argue, though some leftists do, that the reverse of this policy would have been better, more "truthful."

After my return, when my articles began to come out in the *New York Review* and *The Observer* of London, Ambassador Bohlen was no longer so friendly. I had told him and the officials in Saigon exactly what I thought, but opinions look different when you read them in print, I suppose. In June, when I met him at a cocktail party at the house of Bob McBride, the American minister, he seemed affronted and angry. He had just read my first article in *The Observer*. "What does that mean, you were 'looking for material damaging to the American interest'? What *is* the American 'interest'?" I had gone to the party, alone (Jim was away), thinking I must show myself in the official community and stand behind what I had written. But until Bohlen had caught sight of me, on the terrace, I had noticed no difference in my welcome. Now, as we confronted each other, a semi-circle formed, and tactful aides (or so it looked) stood ready to get between us. He had turned slightly red, and I had turned pale, I imagine. I do not remember what I answered, but my position, I knew, was shaky owing to a physical fact: the terrace was covered with several inches of ornamental gravel into which my high heels sank, causing me to lose footing each time I took a step backward or forward or shifted my weight in the course of the exchange. Bohlen, in flat shoes, did not have that disadvantage. After a minute or two, he walked off. Perhaps he had not wanted this debate and had made himself launch on it urged by the same motive that had made *me* come to a party in a U.S. government house. Once he was gone, a few of the Embassy people present came up to tell me they agreed with me and offer their congratulations.

IF NEITHER Jim nor the Embassy put obstacles in the way of my trip or sought to dissuade me, this was not the case with my friends. I had done my best to keep it a secret, but the word had got out, and almost to a man—and a woman—they were against it. Perhaps they were thinking of the danger. But that was something no one dwelt on. Jim and I, so far as I can remember, never even considered it; it had certainly not been high on our list of reasons for saying no to Bob Silvers. For my part, I think I was now too exalted and happy to be bothered about danger. Naturally, making my will, I faced the possibility of my death out there. But I had fun making my will, especially with the bequests of jewelry and art objects. Would the jacinthe and brown topazes be good with Hannah's eyes? And Carmen—the seed-pearl bracelet we had chosen together, with the little insets of sapphires and diamonds. The fire opal? Anjo. Miriam—the diamond-and-pearl earrings from Bucellati. My grandmother's diamond wristwatch with the red and blue figures? Perhaps that should stay in the family. So one of Kevin's daughters? My daughter-in-law, Marcia, would get the Polish lavallière. Jim's daughter, Alison, the thin Polish bracelet with the sapphires. It was like picking out presents, which I

love doing, and the men as usual were harder. Art books, a
clock paperweight, the Arden Shakespeare. . . . To think of my
friends and relations getting their legacies from the lawyer
made me almost look forward to getting killed in Vietnam. I
was forgetting that they would be sad. But in a while they would
not be so sad and would wear the things or have them on their
desks or on their library shelves: "Mary left me that. Just what
I would have wanted. How could she have known?" In short, I
could not take my death seriously—a flaw of character—and
had to see it as a glorious Christmas party with lots of dear
contented guests.

Even when I got to South Vietnam, I had very little fear. The
opposite, as the reader will see, was true of North Vietnam. In
South Vietnam, I can remember moments of slight uneasiness
(the first caused by Têt firecrackers in the hotel garden which
I took for machine-gun fire), but only one instant of real alarm,
when the pilot of a plane I was riding in swerved to avoid
ground fire. Did I feel—senseless as that was—that the Viet
Cong, knowing I was there, would not hurt me? Or, conversely,
that I was protected by the might of the American Army, even
though quite a bit of the time the Army was nowhere nearby?

With Jim, once I was gone, it was different. He was dread-
fully worried all the time I was in South Vietnam, partly
because the mail from there was very slow and because, moving
about so much, I sometimes did not write for days at a stretch.
One morning, in his office, he opened the newspaper and saw a
headline: AMERICAN WRITER KILLED IN VIETNAM. It was Bernard Fall, who had stepped on a land mine on the Street
Without Joy. But there were seconds before Jim lowered his

eyes to the smaller print of the news story. I had been writing him about Fall from Vietnam (just two or three days before, I had met him for the last time, slung with canteens and field gear, at Da Nang airport), and the next morning in Saigon there was a cable of sympathy signed "Jim." I did not know then, of course, in what cruel bold-type form the news had first reached him. In fact, not being frightened myself, I failed to guess that Jim, back in Paris, might be frightened for me. This situation was reversed the following year when I was scared stiff in North Vietnam with the bombers overhead, while he, in Paris, had hardly any fears at all.

But stop, what was I saying just now? Of course, before I went to Saigon, we considered the danger. I promised him that I would not go into combat or—what was worse, according to experts—out on patrol. But, having given the promise, I must have put the danger out of mind. If I fell into a combat situation, *i.e.*, into an ambush while driving in a military vehicle or walking around an installation, that would be something I could not help, and he would have to understand. Once I was on the scene the promise was a limitation for which I felt slightly apologetic ("No, thank you, Major, I can't go along with you to see what that shooting is about. I told my husband . . ."), very much as I had felt as a schoolgirl when I had to tell a boy that my grandparents did not allow me to have dates. But I was also grateful to Jim for insisting. I had no serious wish to tag along into battle as a spectator, supposing that had been permitted; it was bad enough seeing wounded carried into a helicopter. Anyway, the truth I was after in Vietnam would not be found on the battlefront, which would be no different from battlefronts in any other war, but among the people, theirs and ours, in hamlets, hospitals, and refugee camps, on the one hand, in offices and field huts, on the other.

As for going up on a bombing mission which Bernard Fall urged me to do. I thought that would be wicked. Knowing myself, I felt sure that, if we were shot at, I would start empathizing very strongly with the pilot and the bombardiers and the door gunners. If we were not shot at, I would passionately hate them, as they strewed their bombs and napalm around, and hate myself for my complicity—silence gives consent. "But no," said Fall. "That's the point. You must train yourself to go up with them and feel nothing. Be completely detached." Maybe learning to feel nothing could make you strong and proud; I would rather be weak and humble. Or, rather, I *was* weak and humble. For a person like me, a natural civilian, insentience should be the last thing to strive for; detachment would equal indifference. For Fall, who loved war and its implements, it was the opposite; he responded to the thrill of danger, and it was this he had taught himself to curb.

To get back to my friends. The main reason they gave for my not going was my lack of professional competence. If they did not stress the danger, this was probably out of kindness, in case I did go; also an appeal to cowardice is not likely to be persuasive to a romantic kind of person.

I was not a journalist, my friends argued: I did not know the first thing about reporting. Well, I had once done a report on Portugal, for *The New Yorker*, while I happened to be staying there; I had reported on a newspaper strike in Seattle and State of Washington politics, for *The Nation*, while I happened to be staying *there*; I had written about Greenwich Village night life for the New York *Post*. None of these efforts had been an unqualified success: *The Nation* and the *Post* got angry letters from readers disputing what I said; *The New Yorker* was so unhappy about the form of my piece that in the end they cut a whole section out of it—the heart, in my view—which I published, by itself, in *Harper's*. No, I wasn't a professional reporter and (corollary argument) I knew nothing about war. I could hardly tell a grenade from a pomegranate. So why take this on? I would only, they insisted, make a fool of myself and do more harm than good to the liberal opposition by making it look silly, too.

I did not think I was going to make a fool of myself, and, if I did, it did not seem to me important either to my career (something I had never cared about) or to the anti-war movement. John Steinbeck was out there making a fool of *him*self but did not appear to be creating any disarray in the pro-war forces on whose behalf he was traveling. Naturally nobody wants to do a bad job, but what was so hard about describing what you see and what people say to you? "You have to know the right questions to ask. There's a technique to that." Supposing I landed an interview with Ky or General Westmoreland, I would need skill and training to pin them down. But I was not planning to have interviews, certainly not with prominent figures. I had no desire to meet Ky or General Westmoreland; not to have to do so was one of the advantages of not being a professional journalist.

It was true, though: as my friends said, if I got into an interview situation, I would not be able to ask the right questions.

Because I hate embarrassing someone I am talking to. Arguing is one thing. But to sit across a desk, deferential notebook in hand, from some powerful personality you disapprove of, who would start lighting your cigarettes, beaming at you, seeking your sympathy for his difficult position . . . no! I can see parallels with going up in a bomber. I think I would almost rather assassinate such a man, if put to the choice, than fell him with an awkward question. In the few relatively low-level interviews I was forced into while being shuttled from office to office in Vietnam, even when I knew the right, "probing" question, I generally could not bring myself to utter it. Besides, people reveal themselves spontaneously, even behind desks, in offices, and I was more interested in the men than in any factual information —on corruption, civilian casualties, and so on—they might give me if pressed hard enough. The worst would be to watch them lie. Knowing the right question to ask means you know the answer already, and what you want is an *admission.* Once in a while I would hear a distraught official abruptly yield some long-sought estimate, fact, figure; it was always during a group briefing. The other journalists present did not have my inhibitions, that is, did not suffer from vicarious shame.

Just before I left, the telephone one night gave its peremptory long-distance shrieks; it was a woman friend calling. She sounded breathless, as if she had been running. I must not *dream,* she said, of going; what luck that she had heard in time to stop me. "Cancel right away. Mary, I beg you. You're not a journalist, you see." "I know that. Everybody tells me that." But had anybody told me a basic fact of life? The other correspondents. They would be out to get me. She knew cases. (A) I

was a woman. and (B) I was competition. They ran a closed
shop. "You'll be ostracized. They're utterly ruthless. If there's
a news break, they'll just go off together and not tell you.
You'll be on your own, completely. They won't even buy you
a drink." This was the worst news I had had yet. If it was even
partly true, it would be bad.

But I could meet Vietnamese, I told myself. In fact that
would be more interesting. And the French colony. I had better
collect letters of introduction. My doctor, who was giving me
shots, had a brother-in-law with ties in Vietnam, and a dinner
was arranged, which duly bore fruit. A young journalist on the
Monde gave me some names; Frankie FitzGerald, from New
York, wrote to the South Vietnamese Minister of Education, to
a Vietnamese social worker. I had letters to French plantation-
owners, a French banker, the French consul-general, a Vietnamese lady who was in the linen business and had connections
by marriage with a noble French family. I had the feeling that
most of those people would be pretty reactionary, but in one
case, at least, it was not so.

As it turned out, the newspapermen in Saigon were angels.
The Baltimore *Sun* lent me his army jacket and cap (I had
brought only dresses and skirts, not picturing what it would be
like riding in helicopters and striding around military encamp-
ments; the rest of my work wardrobe was made up of a pair
of pants, much too big around the waist but held together by
a long belt, and two shirts, all lent me by a kindly JUSPAO
man, one of Jim's former colleagues in USIA), the New York
Times let me take a hot bath in his bathtub, *Time* organized a
meeting with students, *Newsweek* got me a hotel room and met

me at the airport, Agence France Presse drove me to the airport when I left. The newsmen showed me the ropes, let me in on any leads they had, invited me to meals, parties, drinks, drew up lists of people for me to see when I went to Hue, to Da Nang, put me in touch with some Quakers who were based near Nha Trang. This readiness to help did not stop when I left but went on by correspondence, and today I can count as continuing affectionate friends men I knew in the Saigon fraternity: Tom Buckley, Jon Randal, Bill Tuohy. . . .

Well, I was a new face on the Continentale terrace, and the journalists, in most cases without their wives or girl friends, were bored. But something nicer than boredom was prompting them: a spirit of mutual aid, which was evident in their relations with each other. No doubt this was the product, in part, of the crude salesmanship of the war that was being practiced on the press corps by army and Embassy spokesmen. To help the correspondent of the *New York Review of Books* (a risible idea in itself) find her way through the Vietnamese labyrinth was a proof of solidarity. It did not matter that I was more than *critical* of the war, which was the prevailing press attitude. Some of the same reporters were also befriending an English Tory colonel, who opposed the war, if he did, on the ground that we were conducting it so stupidly. The only thing Colonel Glyn and I had in common was being old enough to be the parents of many of the newsmen who had taken us under their wing. Harrowed by the war, contemptuous of all but a few maverick officers, sick of lies, mistrustful of the Viet Cong, and committed to a monastic rule of objectivity, the Saigon news fraternity must have seen the former Conservative M.P. and

25

the correspondent of the *New York Review of Books* as appealing archaic figures: we belonged to a generation that did not seem to have much trouble in making up its mind.

The objection to my trip that I took most seriously came from an Italian friend. "Why must you go to Vietnam? What is the point? You are a writer, not a journalist. If you want to contribute something, you should stay home and write an article. An essay." In a way, he was right. He had hit on the underlying weakness in my project—my longing for an *action*. But getting on an airplane was not an action; it was just a displacement in space. I knew that. Yet it felt like an action in comparison with sitting down at my desk to write an essay. I protested that I did not know enough about Vietnam to write an essay on it. "Well, then, learn. Study." I groaned. I did not want to study. I wanted to *move*, which I suppose was a way of saying: Move heaven and earth.

But there was one thing he was failing to see: if I stayed home, I would not write an essay. I would not do anything about Vietnam, read and study least of all. He had a philosopher's cast of mind, but mine was concrete. I have never been good at reading up ahead of time about a place I am going to or an event I am about to witness. When I am a tourist, I study the guidebooks *after* I have seen a church or a castle. Or during. The ideal is: look-study-look-study-look. If I do the research in advance, what I read does not stay with me, except for the most general indications. Vietnam would be the same. It was only when I got back from Saigon that I began to bone up on Vietnamese history, past and present. Meeting Bernard Fall in Saigon, I was ashamed to realize that all I had read by him was an article or two in *The New Republic*. Later, when he was dead, I read his books.

So Nicola was right, but I, too, was right. I *could* not write about our involvement in Vietnam unless I went there. Besides, why should anybody want to read a thoughtful essay by me on Vietnam? There were other essays of that kind available that were surely better and more persuasive than anything that would come off my typewriter. But I had one asset that the writers of those essays didn't have. And that reporters didn't have either. My readers. Not the millions—it must be by now—in America that bought or borrowed *The Group*, but some of them. It was unlikely that they kept up with all my writings, yet they would want to know about a month I spent in Vietnam. I have mentioned that people are curious about novelists' impressions. But there was something that went deeper than the mere feeding of curiosity in the reader-storyteller relation. I had the conviction (which still refuses to change) that readers put perhaps not more trust but a different kind of trust in the perceptions of writers they know as novelists from what they give to the press's "objective" reporting or political scientists' documented and figure-buttressed analyses. To hear from a novelist about a trip he has taken through a debated area is like getting a long letter from someone you know well—your son in the Navy on patrol along the Mekong, your sister who is a nurse on a medical mission at Pleiku. Only a columnist is comparable—the kind who writes something close to a journal in self-exposure and tone.

This belief of mine was what was prompting me, like an apostolic "call," to put aside my normal work and go. Did I

27

try to explain that to Nicola? Maybe not, since it sounds a bit cracked, as though you thought you possessed some special truth-seeking apparatus that you had to tote around with you to scenes of national emergency, like a water-witch the populace has been waiting for. Well, I do believe something like that, except, alas, the bit about the populace waiting. And it is not as hubristic as it sounds. In fact everyone must feel he possesses such a divining-rod (how else could he serve on a jury?) and expect to be listened to by his intimates when he recounts some experience he has had. The difference is that the novelist has *more* intimates than the average person—thousands he has never laid eyes on. They have noticed that he has some skill and practice in observation; his fictions "check out" with incidents and characters in their own lives—"I'd almost think you'd *known* my mother." That does not mean they consider him a sage, far from it; he is someone like themselves, as they would be if they only could write.

So I had to board a plane to Saigon, though Nicola could not see the necessity of it. He had a mistrust for action and its theatrics. Other friends worried about Jim. But since he had agreed, there was nothing more to be said on that score. I did not need friends' gently reminding me that it would be hard on him. That was something I did not care to dwell on. For me to grieve over it at this point would be cruel and somehow insincere.

THAT IS HOW I came to go, the first time. In a little over a month I was back, having stopped off in Cambodia to see if my visa for North Vietnam had come. It had not, and, urged by

Jim's cables, I went off for a few days to Angkor Wat and the other temples around Siemreap. This was meant to be my former self, the devoted handmaid of *belles lettres*, art, and architecture, gladly emerging from the temporary metamorphosis of military cap, field jacket, pants, dirt, sweat. As if in confirmation of this round-trip ticket back to myself, in Phnom Penh I met the British ambassador, a keen Ivy Compton-Burnett fan who had just finished reading my article about her in a last year's *Encounter*—a small world, wasn't it? He and his wife had me to an easy-going, civilized luncheon. I was home. Then I took the plane for Siemreap, alone.

There, on the edge of the jungle, I was overcome by terror. For no reason. There was nobody around but inescapable tourists, no wild animals, not even any fierce jungle birds; yet, as night fell, very swiftly, as it does in the Orient, while I swam in the pool of the Villa Princière, I would have an attack of panic. Perhaps it was the vegetation, the sinuous crawling gray tree trunks I had seen during the day, or the long files of smiling Buddha figures, or else it was the fear I had been suppressing, without knowing it, in Vietnam, now burgeoning like some gross luxuriant plant that choked me. In the morning I would "do" the circuit of temples with a local driver, unwilling to linger because I sensed him waiting, full of curiosity, behind me, and because the big tourist groups were always on my heels, telling me to move so that their cameras could take a picture. My solitude made me conspicuous: what was I up to, alone and palely loitering? I felt followed, stalked, and can remember only one instant of undiluted pleasure, when I stood in front of the small, pink, somehow "Renaissance" temple of Banteay Srei and said to myself: "Man is a lintel-building animal."

I never dream of Vietnam, North or South, but I have a recurrent nightmare *concerning* Vietnam but laid in Cambodia or, sometimes, Laos. I am in the midst of unfriendly, excitable people, brown, like the Cambodians, but there are some whites, too, perhaps American officers. I have an important message to carry or a report to make to a court of law. It is something about a war crime I have witnessed, and these people swarming around may try to obstruct me. Then I realize I have forgotten the thing I need to report about. It has slipped my mind, and now—the frontier is closed or there is fighting—I cannot get back into Vietnam to find it. Yet maybe it will come back. Something in the countryside here will remind me of it. I am running around, looking. I see a rural railroad station, an army truck, uniformed men in it. "They . . ." I almost have it. No. Gone. I cannot remember the rest of the sentence. It is a version of the examination dream. I fail.

Probably this is my secret assessment of how I carried out my Vietnam "assignment." Some essential was missing. But I do not know what it was, and indeed that is the plot of the dream: that, being the person I am, I am unable to recover that essential, find the master-switch that will give illumination. I had it once, apparently (in my youth?), and lost it, from sheer distraction.

Still, in Hanoi the following year, when we heard Johnson's "abdication" speech live, on the radio, courtesy the Armed Forces Network, in Wilfred Burchett's hotel room, all of us—foreign journalists and one professor—dancing, kissing, hugging each other, took a bit of the credit to ourselves. A plump French photographer was doing a sort of proud jig with a flower-pot on his head. He took my anti-bomb metal helmet and pretended to kick it like a football. I felt a dazed pride myself. We had helped bring the war to an end—for that of course was our expectation as we drank a toast in a horrible Bulgarian alcohol. It could not last much longer.

So it had been worth it, I thought. Jim in Paris (what time was it?) would have just turned off the radio and would know that the bombing had stopped at least in the part of North Vietnam we were in. He would be rejoicing, and we could both assure ourselves, with a great relieved sigh, that I had done the right thing. Three weeks ago, waiting in Laos for the I.C.C. plane to take us on the last leg of the long journey to Hanoi, I had had awful doubts.

IN PARIS, before I left, there had been reports that the I.C.C. plane—Saigon, Phnom Penh, Vientiane, Hanoi, and return— was failing to meet its twice-a-week schedule. Nobody knew why or how often it was happening. A few travelers bound for Hanoi had thought it wiser to go via Moscow through China. Being Americans, my companion and I could not do that; we had to trust to the vagaries of the I.C.C. plane. Sure enough, when we got to Phnom Penh, we heard that it had been missing flights regularly. It was the weather, thought the British ambassador. On the morning of our scheduled departure, the weather looked all right, yet after breakfast we were informed that the plane would probably not come through from Saigon. And that if it did there would not be room for us, since there was a backlog of passengers waiting from last week's canceled flights. So four days to kill in Cambodia. I had rented a car to go back to Siemreap (this time not alone), when news was brought that the plane was landing and we would be permitted to board. Already loaded with our suitcases, the car turned around and raced for the airport. We were still congratulating ourselves on our luck as we landed in Vientiane. Then the announcement came that it would not proceed any farther; the Control Commission offered no explanation. Something about radar and the control tower, one passenger had heard the pilot say. So we were dumped in Vientiane—without visas. There was a good possibility that we might be sent on to Bangkok, for which we had no visas either. Then what—back to Paris? In the end the authorities at the airport let us go into the town and put up at the hotel for the night. As I checked in, someone cried "Madame West!" It was an American Embassy man, Perry Stieglitz, whom I supposed to be still serving in Paris. Thanks to him, in the morning our situation was regularized. We could stay. Four days or indefinitely—till the next flight for Hanoi came.

I sent Jim a cable to tell him what had happened, and we settled down. Vientiane was not so bad. Two Japanese—a novelist, Seicho Matsumoto, and a journalist—had been dumped there in the same way ten days before. We made friends. It was early March. While we waited, we became fatalistic. The reprieve from Hanoi was only a reprieve. Inevitably we would go, and the bombs would meet us. One morning—I think it was a Sunday—the Bangkok *Post* arrived with a picture, on the front page, of the dread F-111A's. The news story said they were waiting in Thailand, which was just

32

across the river, to start raids next week on North Vietnam. In fact (as we heard later in Hanoi) they went into action the day we got there. That pair of wicked-looking swing-wing planes, supposed then to be invincible and timed, as it were, to coincide with us, still idling in Vientiane, struck the fear of God into me. In Paris, though I did not guess it, Jim, formerly Captain West, navigator, U.S. Air Force, was examining those evil profiles in the *Herald Tribune*. His experienced blue eye measured their capability without pleasure, but, not being literary, he did not conclude that they had a personal appointment with me.

This was not the only coincidence. Invited to dinner by the Japanese at a Chinese restaurant on the river, we discovered that my traveling companion, Professor Franz Schurmann, and I had the same birthday—June 21, the summer solstice—and that Mr. Matsumoto's was December 21, the winter solstice. So our fates were linked; we were all three going to die together in Hanoi. Further, Mr. Matsumoto's daughter's husband—Mr. Watanabe—was on the Japanese delegation to the OECD, where Jim worked. Surely—said Mr. Matsumoto—I must have met his daughter in Paris; they had been stationed there some time. I was not sure, but anyway we felt this was a cheerful omen: those three presences gently touching in Paris were reaching out, like guardians, to touch us and give us their protection. Jim, I told Mr. Matsumoto, was going to Tokyo soon, for his OECD work; he would meet me there when I came from Hanoi. That promise was a guarantee that lightened Mr. Matsumoto's heart. "OECD," he would say to me softly during alerts in the hotel air-raid shelter in Hanoi, his voice fingering those initials like an amulet. "Mrs. McCarthy, take me back to Tokyo."

In the Chinese restaurant that night on the Mekong, Mr. Morimoto, the reporter from the *Asahi Shimbun* and the youngest member of our group, had a different interpretation of the birthdays. He looked up from his food to announce with a grave face that no, it was he who would die, since his birthday, which fell on some irrelevant date in November, was the odd one and therefore unlucky. This seemed much sadder—so lonely. Poor child, I thought. But Mr. Matsumoto took no stock in that junior reading of destiny. He was convinced that *he* was going to leave his bones in Hanoi. I tried to cheer him up. If the F-111A's got really too bad, I said, we could escape from Haiphong on a Polish freighter, and he could get back to Tokyo from Gdansk.

Already I had taken on the role of comforter, since he was showing his fears so candidly, almost mischievously, as if we were children playing a game of who could tell the scariest stories. He was practicing exorcism, I guessed, and I was grateful. In his company I felt stronger.

When I was alone in my room in the Lane Xang ("Million Elephants") Hotel, it was otherwise. The birthdays did not alarm me; that was a joke, like having your fortune told. But I fell prey to a *moral* kind of superstition. The F-111A's were winged retribution figures. I should never have come this far and, if I was not a coward, I would turn around and go home. It was a wrong I was doing to Jim to be in this place, heading for Hanoi. How had I not seen this before? I was a cruel, selfish woman. He had left his family for me. I had not urged it but I had consented. If I got killed, he would never forgive me. And

34

that was *why* I was going to be killed, to show me that my acts were consequent.

Looking back, I can surmise that the waiting and uncertainty had unstrung my resolve, which for months had been bent taut as a bow on the goal of Hanoi. Postponement had forced on me an undesired interval for reflection. Worse, it had hinted to me that I might still be saved from going. But at the time, in that hotel room, it only seemed to me that I had been granted a terrible lucidity. There was not the slightest doubt in my mind that I was going to my death. The certainty of that had been established as guilt fed apprehension. What I saw was that I had no right to die: my stupid, silly life did not belong to me alone; it was in a joint account. Personally (I thought), I no longer cared whether I got killed; it would almost be a relief. I was only agonizing on Jim's behalf. Was this truthful or not? Then, at any rate, I was sure it was. Today, I can wonder whether remorse may not have been the form physical fear was taking in me. But it was remorse in a pure state that I felt. And it was useless to dream now of expiation, atonement: even if by a miracle I escaped death, I had probably killed his love for me.

I paced around my small room. I sat on my bed. I cried. I got hold of myself and tried to read. A wave of panic would hit me, and I would moan. It hurt, like a real pain. I wrote him letters. But as soon as my pen touched paper, a censor interposed. "Careful, my friend. Watch yourself." I could not pour my heart out; that criminal relief was forbidden. If I told him I was sure I was going to be killed, that would finish him. Assuming he still cared about me, and perhaps even if he didn't. Maybe better not to mention the F-111A's? Or touch upon them lightly, in a comical way? Tell about Mr. Matsumoto and our three birthdays and the garden party at the French Embassy. Mention my idea about Haiphong and the Polish freighter. . . . Poland, where we had met, was "our song"; a woman had written that about us in *The Observer*.

Above all, show no weakness or irresolution. This was not a moment for honesty. If I revealed my state, I was likely to elicit a cable: WELL MAKE UP YOUR MIND IF YOU FEEL THAT WAY COME HOME JIM. Or, more probable: MAKE UP YOUR MIND DARLING REMEMBER YOURE FREE TO COME HOME LOVE JIM. Or: COURAGE.

LUCIDITY FADED as the days passed and was replaced by sheer turmoil. I was incapable of deciding what course was the course of weakness or where my duty lay—if I could find one that was distinguishable from frenetic impulse. My bad conscience told me it lay in returning to Jim. If I went on to Hanoi, would it not be from mere force of inertia—since I was three-quarters of the way there, it was the easiest thing to do—or fear of letting the side down? Letting Jim down was easier because he was only one. How horrible if true! On the other hand, might I not be inflating the notion of a duty to Jim simply in order to run away? The reason that had been dictating my trip (to strike a small blow against the war) had not altered; the only new element in the picture was on the front page of the Bangkok *Post*. Yes, but perhaps it had needed that visual aid, like a monitory finger pointing to an exit, to bring me to my senses. Those silhouettes might be telling me to go home, as a penitent, to that man of sorrows while there was still time. . . .

It occurs to me now that you cannot embark on what you think is a good deed without sacrificing someone else to it. Someone close to you, naturally. Or something equally close— an idea, a principle. Good deeds are Molochs. I cannot recall a single instance of pure *self*-sacrifice in my entire history. On a reasonably large scale, I mean. Not skipping a meal to give the money to feed famine victims. But possibly self-sacrifice, by its very nature, since the self has many extensions, includes the willingness to sacrifice your nearest and dearest.

In the letters I wrote him from Vientiane (which Jim had copied and put in a folder labeled "The Laos Letters"), I could not tell him, as I say, how scared and repentant I was, and yet between the lines I tried to put messages, like the tiny "I love you" we used to hide under the stamp when I was a girl in boarding-school, hoping and dreading that the boy we were writing to would know enough to steam off the stamp and find it. I was sending Jim messages of apology, in case I was killed, messages that told him that if he could not forgive me, I would understand, or, rather, had understood while still alive, thinking it was natural and right for him to feel that way. As with those schoolgirl "missives," I have never been sure whether he went under the surface and saw what was hidden for him: my sad, stricken love. Maybe, for all I know (I have not let myself look into the folder), it was transparent.

WHEN, AFTER four days, the I.C.C. plane came and took us to Hanoi, all that torment ceased. Every other day, in the hotel, I wrote out a cable for the North Vietnamese to send so that Jim would know that I was alive. When I understood they would not let me pay for the cables, I made them very short.

37

And Ambassador Bohlen was wrong. The North Vietnamese knew very well that the husband they were telegraphing in Paris was an American diplomat, but they never regarded me as a spy—after the bombing stopped, they even took me to visit a military installation. Nevertheless, as a precaution, so as not to worry them, I avoided any expression that could sound like code.

This is almost the end of the story. Jim was waiting for me in the airport in Tokyo. During the next days he met Mr. Matsumoto and Mr. Morimoto and heard us tell about Laos and little events in Hanoi—the time, for instance, their table was empty in the dining-room for a whole twenty-four hours and I feared they had been arrested because Mr. Morimoto, in the hotel shelter, had played back a tape-recording he had made during the last alert that clearly registered the voices of a Chinese technical delegation; yes, I was just nerving myself for the awful task of pleading for their release when they turned up, having spent the night in Haiphong! Now it was all fun. In a geisha house, we laughed about the F-111A's, which had proved to be such duds. Jim told how furious he had been when he got my letter about the Polish freighter. We visited Mr. Morimoto's paper. Mr. Matsumoto's son-in-law, Mr. Watanabe, materialized from Paris. Francois Pelou, from A.F.P. in Saigon (the one who had driven me the previous year to the airport), we found sitting in our hotel lobby. Then Franz Schurmann . . . It was like the finale of a Mozartian opera with all the cast reunited and lustily singing. Through Mr. Watanabe (here on official business), I was debriefed on my Hanoi impressions by the Japanese Foreign Office, at a luncheon where we sat with our feet in a well. For its part, the State Department never troubled to find out what, if anything, I had learned about the attitude of North Vietnamese officials toward a settlement with the United States. But I had a visit in Paris from the same official Bohlen had instructed—so long ago, it seemed—to give me "our side." He had heard that I had taken out mail for P.O.W.'s families and wanted a list of the names. List? It horrified him to learn that I had just stamped the letters and dropped them in a Japanese mailbox. Jim kept his job.

AT FIRST, after my Vietnam trips, I was less haunted by the war. Of course it was in my mind every day, but, having done something active, I did not have to lie in bed at night casting about for fresh approaches. Moreover, I was writing on the subject and giving occasional speeches and TV interviews. I pretty much forgot about tax refusal. The McCarthy children's crusade, Chicago, Kent State, the shutdown of the universities, draft-card burning—there was no lack of new initiatives. Eventually, though, after the Moratorium and the Mobilization marches, a lull in the protest movement came. Proclaiming Vietnamization, Nixon had started troop withdrawals, and ordinary people were frightened by the Weathermen.

Violence had failed to accomplish the task it had set itself, of ending the war and revolutionizing society. What was left? You could not just go on marching up and down. There had been some talk of a general strike, but as my friend Hannah Arendt said: "We are too weak. If we try that, they will see how weak we are." Once again I was racking my brain. What could I do that was practical? I was tired of listening to myself

39

talk, so I could imagine the effect I must be having on others. Writing about Vietnam was becoming a habit, and not just with me. The law of diminishing returns had begun to operate. You might as well chant slogans or scrawl *"Nixon assassin. FNL vaincra!"* on a wall. It was no good writing unless I could find a new point of contact with the subject: something concrete. In short, I was right back where I had started.

It was out of this near-despair that the Medina book grew. When the Calley trial started, at Fort Benning, I was finishing a novel I had begun six years before. We were in page proofs when the verdict came and I sensed that here had been a way of talking about Vietnam again: I could have covered the trial. I had missed the boat.

Perhaps that regret was still in the back of my mind when I met Gunnar Myrdal at the house of some friends. It was spring, 1971. We talked about the uproar Calley's conviction was causing. On one point we strongly agreed: there was no obligation to choose between Calley's guilt and the Army's. *They were both guilty*. But nobody seemed to be able to say that simple, obvious thing. The insensate discussions that were raging in the press were being faithfully reproduced in private, with the volume turned up. In Paris, whenever Americans sat down at a dinner table and the name "Calley" was pronounced, two minutes later (one night, wearied, Jim looked at his watch and timed it) they were all yelling. "How can he be innocent if he killed all those women and children?" "But he's a *scapegoat*, don't you see?" "Hell, the Cong use women and children to throw grenades." "The Army had no right to try him." "Don't give me that! Calley's a bad apple." "No! They're ALL murderers. The brass, anyway." "Then who ought to try him?" "NOBODY!"

"You should write about this," said Myrdal. "It's important for Americans to hear." He thought they were tending to absolve themselves, juggling the blame back and forth between Calley and the Army. That way, the general guilt was lost sight of. It was the old question of responsibility. Collective shouldn't exclude individual. "It is made up of individuals, no?" "Yes." "Then write an article. Or better a book. It's a big subject." "Thank you," I said. "I'll think about it." "No. Do it!" I hesitated. "Mightn't it be better to wait till Captain Medina—his superior officer, you know—is tried? I could report the trial and bring these questions in." I sensed a disappointment in Professor Myrdal. Like Nicola, he preferred an essay. Book-length; Nicola was more modest. "Well, yes," Myrdal conceded. "You could do that."

The next week I wrote to *The New Yorker* and asked if I could cover the Medina trial for them. I had decided this time to try for a more mainstream audience; the *New York Review of Books'* readers needed no further persuasion to oppose the war in Vietnam. With one slight reservation (by summer would people still be interested in the issues?), *The New Yorker* accepted. I was happy. I would be able to raise my voice again, and from another quarter, where it might not be expected to come from: a military courtroom in Georgia. People might think they were sick of Vietnam, but everybody likes to read about trials. So once more into the breach. Besides, it would be an adventure. I was conscious of some temerity.

There was no sacrificial element in my journey to Fort

McPherson, except that it occurred during August, square in the middle of Jim's vacation. He stayed in our house in Maine while I, having skipped the first week's testimony, flew off to Atlanta. I had hoped the trial would be over by the time his vacation started. The trouble with trying to be a reporter is that events either hurry ahead of you or else lag behind. They do not sit still and wait for you to join them like the characters in a novel. Why couldn't they have court-martialed Medina around Decoration Day when Jim had so much work in the office that he would have hardly noticed that I was gone? No, it had to come out of his vacation.

Bit by bit, Vietnam had altered the pattern of our lives. Not only had I turned into a part-time itinerant journalist, with longish absences, separation, but our summer holidays were now spent in a new geography. Until Vietnam seized us, we used to go to Italy, on the Ligurian coast, for August and early September and, in my case, part of July. But in 1967 we bought the house in Maine. That was right after I had come back from South Vietnam, and one of our motives was the war: if I was going to take a stand against U.S. policy, I ought to have a piece of U.S. ground under my feet. This was not an unconscious factor guiding our decision. We always cited it to ourselves as an argument in favor of buying (sight unseen in my case), along with other arguments—that Jim came from Maine and was homesick for it, that he had to have some place to spend compulsory home leave, that the house was beautiful, that he could pass it on to his children—balancing all these against the cost, the distance, the fact that most years we would be able to occupy it for only a month or six weeks. . . . On the Fourth of July, he showed me into the house.

42

We have never been back to the Ligurian coast since, and that is a loss; I miss it—the dumpy village at the mouth of the River Magra, the white marble mountains above Carrara, the Punta Bianca, where we swam, the purple sea-urchins I used to pay the children a bounty for, and, above all, the circle of friends—Chiaromontes, Levis, Craigs, Grandjacquet—that, beginning that summer, 1967, gradually broke up, scattered, eroded so that now none of them goes there. Like the Punta Bianca, which was swept away in a storm.

Because of Vietnam, then, we lost Italy, and I have pretty well lost Italian. It is strange to think that because of our hateful foreign policy I have been, so to speak, repatriated. Now I share with Jim a cemetery lot overlooking Penobscot Bay. Even my reading has been Americanized. Here in Paris, instead of Italian periodicals, French periodicals, I read *Time* and *Newsweek*, which, before Vietnam, I seldom glanced at, though Jim brought them home. I still read the English Sunday papers but now less for news of art and literature than for what they have to say about Watergate. When Vietnam happened, I had a plan for a book on the Gothic. That too went. On the other hand, I hardly ever—once in a blue moon—see anyone from the Embassy; if you ask me for the present Ambassador's name, it will be a struggle to remember it. Last June, Jim was retired—normally for his category—from the State Department. He is still in charge of information for the organization with the magic initials: OECD.

The last time I lay awake worrying the bone of Vietnam was Christmas, 1972. In the summer there had been the dikes, the mining of Haiphong harbor. But this was the worst yet. I was in Amsterdam, in a hotel bed. Jim was asleep. The "carpet-bombing" had started the week before; in Paris we had known of it on the morning of the nineteenth, when we were about to give our annual Christmas party; we thought of canceling and didn't—the tree, the turkey, the presents. Now, four days later, it was still going on, in spite of world protests. America was strangely quiet; scarcely a demonstration, so far as we could learn. I was mentally composing a telegram to the Pope.

"Holiness, you are a Christian. Is it not your pious duty to share the dangers of the Vietnamese people, many of whom are your brothers in Christ? Holiness, go to Hanoi." The morning threw cold water on this message, which already during the night had gone through a number of variations: "your fellow-Catholics," "Christian duty," "share the sufferings." Montini, *"quell' animaccia nera,"* as Nicola, now dead, might have said, would never answer a call like that. Fat chance. The most that weasel would ever do was "deplore" the breakdown of the peace talks. The next night, Christmas Eve, my thoughts lit on the Bishop of Haarlem, a nice-looking old man I had just seen on Dutch television. Would he be willing, if I went to Haarlem on the train tomorrow and asked him, to join a group to go to North Vietnam and live under the bombs as witnesses? I could surely get a letter of introduction; Holland was a small country where the leading figures all knew each other. From what I had picked up from our Dutch friends, he was a better prospect than the Pope. Off and on during the night, as the church clock sounded, I rehearsed my imaginary call on him. In the morning, though, I could no longer see myself marching up the stairs of the episcopal palace. What about Willy Brandt? No.

The idea of the Pope was the best, alas. And he would be perfectly safe. If he went to Hanoi, Nixon would have to stop bombing. Nixon might not mind about the Bishop of Haarlem, but as long as the Pope stayed in North Vietnam, *everybody* would be safe. I tried to think if I knew anybody in the Vatican. Not a soul, except the curator of the Vatican galleries, the author of a little guide I had. What a tragedy that Pope John was dead. If he could visit the jailbirds in Regina Coeli, he could certainly have flown to Hanoi. He would not have needed a telegram to remind him that he was a Christian. But instead we had Montini! Even if he could be assured that Nixon would not hurt a hair of his pate, he would be too much of a coward politically.

The reader is entitled to a feeling of *déjà vu*. Yes, I now see, this was tax refusal assuming yet a new form, like some mythical monster that, when in appearance you kill it, simply undergoes metamorphosis. Or the nine-headed Hydra or a nine-lived cat. Yes, here are all the old elements: prominent people, a group. Plus a certain economy of design. There a sort of chain-letter principle—tax refusal spreading by arithmetic progression. First fifteen, then a hundred, and so on. Here something even more simple and beautiful: the displacement of only one body (though not *any*body) would be enough. I am surprised nobody else had the idea. There was only one hitch. It depended on the Pope's being a good man. That conjunction probably occurred with something like the frequency of Halley's comet: the last one before Pope John had been Leo XIII, "the working man's pope" (d. 1903).

By Christmas morning, I had given up on both Montini and

the Bishop of Haarlem. These were figments of the night. But behind them, of course, was a daylight project. A group of leading Americans to agree to go to Hanoi and live under the bombs as witnesses—in the Biblical, not the legal, sense of the term. Ever since the previous Wednesday, back in Paris, I had been feverishly making lists of names, crossing some out and adding others. I had been on the long-distance telephone to Washington and New York, collecting advice and suggestions, trying to reach Ramsey Clark, whom I did not know but who seemed to me the right person to head the kind of group I had in mind. Not left-wingers but reasonably solid citizens and in some cases, one could hope, never previously identified with opposition to the war. There ought to be around twenty, from different walks of life and including some prominent Republicans. They would all have to be people respected for their integrity.

While I was busy with these calculations, Stephen Spender had called from London. It was a sympathy call about the bombing. Was there anything one could do? I told him my idea and at once, without hesitation, he asked to be put on the list. Yes, a poet would be good, especially one who looked like an archangel. Maybe a European group could be organized as well. I could work on that in Holland. He was only worried about having enough money for the ticket. Someone else, I said, could pay his fare. "That's fine, then." We had our first volunteer.

Among artists and writers at home, I had been telling myself, there were probably many, like Spender, who would be grateful for the opportunity. But we needed public men, too. Would

Gene McCarthy do it? Father Hesburgh, of Notre Dame? The greatest problem would be to find prominent citizens who had not already taken public stands against the war and who at this desperate juncture would be willing to go. Yet there must be some with private misgivings, in banks and Wall Street law offices, high up in the trade unions, for whom the bombing would have finally tipped the balance. Unthinkable that there would not be.

Ramsey Clark, when I reached him from Paris in the small hours of the morning (my time), had agreed in principle to be the center of such a group. But I must be sure, he said, to clear it with the North Vietnamese in Paris before recruiting anybody else, though it would be all right to take quiet soundings. No public announcement or press conference till visas had been definitely promised; otherwise the Nixon gang could make us look like pharisees.

Thursday morning, the twenty-first, we had held off our departure for Holland while I telephoned the North Vietnamese at Choisy-le-Roi and explained the project to them. They said they would query Hanoi and let me have the answer. How soon? They could not say. When I mentioned the number twenty, Mr. Phan, an old friend of mine from North Vietnam, sounded aghast. He doubted that Hanoi could accommodate so many. But that was the point, I told him. The travel of three or four would not have sufficient "impact." The number had to be in scale with the bombing. And those who came would not mind a little hardship. But even as I pleaded I could see that I was bucking the Vietnamese tradition of hospitality. And if it boiled down to ten?

I had felt rather odd going off to Holland with this grave business pending, but there were Dutch friends waiting for us and another friend, from America—Elizabeth Hardwick—had arrived to join us on the trip. Mr. Phan said he would keep in touch with me. I took down all the delegation's telephone numbers. It would be better if I called *him*, I said, fearful of a mix-up with the hotel switchboard. "Tomorrow morning, then?" He thought the next day would be soon enough. I knew he must understand as well as I did the necessity of our going fast, if we went, but I also knew from experience (just as with their laws of hospitality) that the Hanoi bureaucracy could not be hurried. If I was going to be kept in suspense, I told myself, it might as well be in Holland as in Paris. I could get back in an hour, assuming the answer was positive.

I have said "our going" and "we." There it was again, the old story. The same as tax refusal. I could not rally a group to live under the bombs unless I was willing to be one of them. That was obvious. Hanoi of course might veto me, or the group itself could decide that I did not qualify, not well known enough nationally or insufficiently respected or just not novel enough, having been to Hanoi before. That last could be said of Ramsey Clark, too, but he was essential and I was inessential. If the group decided that I was "wrong" for the trip, I would gladly bow out, but that was up to them, not me. As I had tried to make clear to Clark, I would do whatever the rest thought best. And if Hanoi refused me, that was that. Yet, from Mr. Phan's warm and pleased tone when I mentioned myself as one of the possible components, I got the impression that if any group was let in I would be among them.

That had been both good news and bad news. Jim was not taking kindly to this project. In Paris, during the flurry of departure, I had failed to be aware of his opposition or at least to measure the depth of it. A certain somber expression, a hard set of the jaw I attributed to normal annoyance at being kept awake by transatlantic telephone conversations, at being made to wait, with the car packed, while I let the morning go by, dialing a series of numbers (some wrong) at Choisy-le-Roi —he does not like driving at night. But in Amsterdam, settled in our hotel room, I could not escape the evidence of a total lack of sympathy with what I was up to.

This at first took the form of mutism, absence of any comment on the progress or setbacks of the effort. "While you were out, I talked to Phan. Oh, what a time I had getting him. No news yet." "Oh," or some other dour monosyllable. He was hoping, I imagine, that Hanoi would kill the project with one swift blow. No. That is not quite right. Better would be to say that he wished it had never been thought of. And he detested the brain that had conceived it: mine. This latest chimera had brought me far lower in his esteem than tax refusal. "Do you want people to think you have a suicide urge?" he burst out late one afternoon. This was the first direct allusion he had made to the rancorous thoughts in his mind.

"I don't care," I said. "Do you care if *I* think it?" "Yes, of course. But you're wrong. Honestly, I don't want to be killed. I want to come back to you." This only made him more ireful. "But if you go out there and don't get killed, what's the point? You have to be killed to make your point." "I don't follow that." He was right, though. Today I can follow his thought. My commitment was less than total. In the kind of sacrifice I was imagining there was a ram in reserve somewhere. Offstage. The action I contemplated would be frivolous—a pseudo-action, footlit—unless it had a suicidal constituent. Supposing none of the ten or twenty got killed, what would we eventually do? Go home. And tell the public that bombs were falling? They knew that already. That word "witness" I was using so freely was the same as "martyr" in Greek. Did I want to be a martyr? I don't know.

None of this, however—in so far as I reluctantly took it in— affected my belief that some such gesture was necessary, indeed imperative. I had not had a Catholic girlhood for nothing. Besides, on the practical plane, if David Rockefeller, say, could be stirred up to go to Hanoi, that *would* have some effect; the head of Chase Manhattan would not need to be hit by a bomb to open up a big fissure in Nixon's "solid" majority. Yet for me to stir up somebody to stir up David Rockefeller and/or his equivalents in the Wall Street milieu (my contacts in New York were working on that now) required that my skin, too, be invested, to be paid out on demand. Q.E.D. Jim could not deny that a mission including even one such figure would be worth it, but he declined to understand why *I* should be locked into the plan.

I was not going to debate it with him; let that be my Christmas present. When Mr. Phan said yes, there would still be time. First every morning and then every other morning I called Choisy-le-Roi: no word yet. We were due to leave Holland for England the night of the twenty-seventh, to look at English cathedrals. The thought of carrying this weary load of uncertainty and indecision across the water, up to Lincoln, York, the Border, was almost more than I could bear.

The truth was, I had not made up my mind yet what I would do if Hanoi agreed. It depended on Jim, I thought. I wanted his approval, as with any other project. Yet it looked as if he was not going to give it. Of course, I hoped to be able to win him over at the last moment. Even if argument would be useless, his heart might respond to my misery. Up to now I had not seriously tried to reach him in his softer feelings. But perhaps I was not trying because I too clearly foresaw the result. His stony demeanor already forbade access. It seemed to me days since I had been able to coax a smile from him. I could hardly have expected him to be enthusiastic about a proposition that involved a high risk of my death; yet I am someone who needs enthusiasm. Probably I even demand it. When now it was not forthcoming, I began to wilt like an untended plant. I felt utterly exhausted and in my heart I held it against him that every day, perhaps every hour, I wanted less to go to Hanoi. The reader knows that I am not a stranger to fear, and Jim was making it harder for me. The fact that I less and less wanted to go did not mean I would not do it. But now I faced the prospect of having to do it myself, without consolation or encouragement. I had been making a false assumption; my process of decision, this time, would not have Jim to depend on, which perhaps was only fair, but cruel just the same. Naturally all this led me to hope, shamefully, that Mr. Phan would say no.

I could not flatter myself that Jim's lack of support really showed how much he cherished and valued me. I do not have that kind of vanity, and his behavior was plainly demonstrating the opposite. There in Amsterdam our marriage was dissolving. This was like Laos but even more melancholy, because our disunity, our separation, was a gulf stretching across a twin-bedded hotel room. A continental divide. Worse, too, because on my side there was no remorseful flow of tenderness going out to him. How I could feel remorse when I had not done anything yet? And if his making it so hard were to stop me, in the end, from doing anything, I would not feel any gratitude.

Well, it was a bad time to be in a hotel on a canal hearing Christmas church bells ring while out there the bombs continued to fall. Jim and I were not even friends any more, except when other people were around, which fortunately was most of the time. When other people were around, we could talk about the bombing in one anxious voice; only Lizzie and three Dutch confidants knew that I had any special relation to it in my pending file, but the wider Dutch circle, without knowing that, treated us kindly, with commiseration, as though we were in mourning. Everyone was concerned and rather grave; the fact that we were among liberal and left-wing people, themselves under strain from the bombing, eased the strain of eating, drinking, and joking. I felt great love for our friends there—Cees, Liesbeth, and Harry. When Jim and I were by ourselves, contrary to what might be expected, we did not quarrel; the estrangement was too deep for that and the occasion too serious. Each sensed, I suppose, that if we did we could never make up: the rupture would be definitive.

Yet between two people who have cared about each other,

of course it is not quite like that. There is a memory of former friendship, of how it once was, the *"bei momenti."* I think of an afternoon when we went to Haarlem on the train—not to visit the Bishop; to see the Franz Hals museum. Afterwards, still talking about the pictures, we walked and drank coffee. That was good. Another day, we were driving back from a country house near the German border, where we had had lunch with friends; we passed a road sign "Zutphen," and Jim was pleased, I thought, when I remembered that that was where Sir Philip Sidney, fatally wounded, gave the cup of water to the soldier. Such little things.

Still more inconsistent with what I have been relating is a brief conversation I slowly dredge up and examine. In our hotel room, late one afternoon; could it have been the day after Christmas, the feast of the first martyr? "If you go, I'm going with you," he said, out of the blue. "But you can't," I said. "You mustn't." I was thinking of his children. He insisted, suddenly rather gay, almost insouciant. Half humoring him, I too became merry. "All right, I accept." We swung hands on it. I had no intention of letting that come to pass, but the offer— or was it a threat?—greatly moved me. Then what happened? Did someone come into the room? I don't remember.

If it was the day after Christmas, that explains quite a lot. On the morning of the twenty-seventh, the answer came. It was no. Hanoi reported that the airport had been half destroyed by raids. A group of Americans (including Joan Baez) who were already in the North when the carpet-bombing started were now unable to get out, so there could be no question of another group's flying in. Mr. Phan was full of regrets but firm. That night, at The Hook, we boarded the car ferry for Harwich. We were still low-spirited; the heavy damage to the airport told too awful a tale. But we were relieved of our private uncertainty and at peace with each other. That could hardly have been the case, I conclude, if Jim's "I'm going with you" had not recently sealed a pact. The details of whether he could have walked out on his job (or simply requested leave from the office for "personal business"?), whether he could have got a visa, whether I could have deterred him by invoking his duty as a father to stay alive—all that had become irrelevant now that nobody was going. What mattered was that he had finally let me know that this was something that, in one fashion or another, whoever stayed home or whoever went, we would do together.

We were in the White Hart Inn, in a big double-bedded room facing Lincoln cathedral, when the bombing stopped. We could go on with our tour in a calmer frame of mind. York, Beverly Minster, Durham, Carlisle, Hexham Abbey, Selby Abbey, Southwell. The war was not over, but I must have felt a presentiment, faintly tinted with promise, that it had run its term. A few minutes before midnight, New Year's Eve, in a village near the Roman Wall, I took out my notebook and wrote the first sentence of my book on the Gothic.

MR. PHAN, on the telephone, had asked if I would please come to see the delegation when I got back to Paris. I had agreed. Waiting on my desk, the day I returned, was a letter from the friend I have mentioned who, back in 1965, was practicing tax refusal and who, for all I know, is still doing so. Barbara Deming. The letter, by then ten days old, outlined a project for a group of women to go to North Vietnam as volunteers and live and work under the bombs. Work. The idea of contributing my labor had not entered my head. She wanted my help in getting the North Vietnamese to agree. When, by appointment, I went to Choisy-le-Roi, I had the letter with me. They all knew Barbara Deming. Vy, the deputy head of the mission, received me. As usual, we drank tea. Reading Barbara's letter, he smiled. He smiled, in indulgent retrospect, at my own naïve initiative, now ancient history. *"Je comprends, vous vouliez mourir sous les bombes américaines."* He appreciated our desire to offer our lives. Then he laughed, quite gaily. *"Mais si vous voulez mourir, pourquoi vous ne le faîtes pas devant la Maison Blanche?"* He meant that the place to be effective had been America. It was not so easy, I said, to die in front of the White House. The guards there would not shoot you; at most, they would put you in jail and let you out the next morning. I laughed, too, in a rueful way. *"C'était plus facile de mourir à Hanoi, Monsieur Vy."*

In fact his view of these projects rather resembled Jim's in Amsterdam; they were too death-centered for his taste. Still, he was grateful for the wish to share his people's sufferings. He thanked me and asked me to thank Barbara and her friends. So as to make sure I would not misinterpret his laughter, he took my hand and warmly pressed it. About the failure of Americans at home to rise in protest against the bombing he was bitter. "What could they do?" I said. "Just hold another demonstration. Everybody but a few radicals was busy with Christmas." Our anti-war people were tired, I explained. In North Vietnam, the people had solidarity to strengthen their determination to resist, but in the United States opponents of the war were alone and often discouraged—he had seen how the November election had gone. He both understood and could not understand the discouragement. We said good-bye. As I left, he sent his cordial wishes to my husband.

What I did not tell Vy (perhaps I did not know it yet) was that the group I had been bent on forming had turned out to be even more of a figment than my vision of the Pope, in tiara, flying off to Hanoi. Those Republican bankers. All I could say was that they had not been my idea; New York had dreamed them up. When sounded out by a very dignified intermediary— the father of one of my friends, in fact—not one was even faintly receptive. Consider going to Hanoi as a public duty? Why? With varying degrees of heartiness, they approved of the bombing or, in one instance, disliked it but did not care to rock the boat. My friend's father had been stunned and shaken: he thought he had known those men well. "You spoiled my family's Christmas," she said. In the course of her father's calls, he had met *one* just man, a heavy Nixon contributor who had flown to Key Biscayne to protest and been denied entry.

The other day, rummaging in an old pocketbook, I came upon a small piece of paper, folded and creased and dog-eared, with penciled notes running down it and additions in pen in the margins. For a minute, before I put on my glasses, I took it for a shopping list. Then I recognized the names I had put down December 20 in a tiny restaurant while we ate dinner with Lizzie. Here is how the list looks, misspellings and all.

England:
Wollheim

Wald + Luise
Jas J. William Ward
Jerome Wiesner
Galbraith

Holoman
Taylor
Gene McCarthy
etc
Ramsay Clark
F. Fitzgerald
Hans Morge
Norman Mailer
Francine Gray
Tom Wicker
Francis Plympton
Tom Finletter
Bishop Moore
John Kerry
Ot. Govern

Father Hesburgh
Rabbi Abraham Heschel

THE OTHER SIDE:

Mayor Lindsey
Al Lowenstein
A. Presley
René Dubos
James Baldwin
Roy Wilkins
Coretta King
Margaret Mead
Ed Koller
Robert Lowell
John Knowles
Andrew Young
Ron Dellums
Arthur Schlesinger
Barrington Moore

Garry Wills

James Jones
Wm. Styron

In the right-hand margin of the recto, in ink, are five U.S. phone numbers—which you don't see because I have censored that portion of the holograph—and below, between parentheses, quite small (Vy).

VIETNAM

The Home Program

I confess that when I went to Vietnam early last February I was looking for material damaging to the American interest and that I found it, though often by accident or in the process of being briefed by an official. Finding it is no job; the Americans do not dissemble what they are up to. They do not seem to feel the need, except through verbiage; e.g., napalm has become "Incinderjell," which makes it sound like Jello. And defoliants are referred to as weed-killers—something you use in your driveway. The resort to euphemism denotes, no doubt, a guilty conscience or—the same thing nowadays—a twinge in the public-relations nerve. Yet what is most surprising to a new arrival in Saigon is the general unawareness, almost innocence, of how what "we" are doing could look to an outsider.

At the airport in Bangkok, the war greeted the Air France passengers in the form of a strong smell of gasoline, which made us sniff as we breakfasted at a long table, like a delegation, with the Air France flag—our banner—planted in the middle. Outside, huge Esso tanks were visible behind lattice screens, where U.S. bombers, factory-new, were aligned as if in a salesroom. On the field itself, a few yards from our Boeing 707, U.S. cargo planes were warming up for take-off; U.S. helicopters flitted about among the swallows, while U.S. military trucks made deliveries. The openness of the thing was amazing (the fact that the U.S. was using Thailand as a base for bombing North Vietnam was not officially admitted at the time); you would have thought they would try to camouflage it, I said to a German correspondent, so that the tourists would not see. As the 707 flew on toward Saigon, the tourists, bound for Tokyo or Manila, were able to watch a South Vietnamese hillside burning while consuming a "cool drink" served by the hostess. From above, the bright flames looked like a summer forest fire; you could not believe that bombers had just left. At Saigon, the airfield was dense with military aircraft; in the "civil" side, where we landed, a passenger jetliner was loading G.I.'s for Rest and Recreation in Hawaii. The American presence was overpowering, and, although one had read about it and was aware, as they say, that there was a war on, the sight and sound of that massed American might, casually disposed on foreign soil, like a corporal having his shoes shined, took one's breath away. "They don't try to hide it!" I kept saying to myself, as though the display of naked power and muscle ought to have worn some cover of modesty. But within a few hours I had lost this sense of incredulous surprise, and, seeing the word, "hide," on a note pad in my hotel room the next morning, I no longer knew what I had meant by it (as when a fragment of a dream, written down on waking, becomes indecipherable) or why I should have been pained, as an American, by this high degree of visibility.

As we drove into downtown Saigon, through a traffic jam, I had the fresh shock of being in what looked like an American city, a very shoddy West Coast one, with a Chinatown and a slant-eyed Asiatic minority. Not only military vehicles of every description, but Chevrolets, Chryslers, Mercedes-Benz, Volkswagens, Triumphs, and white men everywhere in sport shirts and drip-dry pants. The civilian take-over is even more astonishing than the military. To an American, Saigon today is less exotic than Florence or the Place de la Concorde. New office buildings of cheap modern design, teeming with teazed, puffed secretaries and their Washington bosses, are surrounded by sandbags and guarded by M.P.'s; new, jerry-built villas in pastel tones, to rent to Americans, are under construction or already beginning to peel and discolor. Even removing the sandbags and the machine guns and restoring the trees that have been chopped down to widen the road to the airport, the mind cannot excavate what Saigon must have been like "before." Now it resembles a gigantic PX. All those white men seem to be carrying brown paper shopping bags, full of whiskey and other goodies; rows of ballpoints gleam in the breast pockets of their checked shirts. In front of his villa, a leathery oldster, in visored cap, unpacks his golf clubs from his station wagon, while his cotton-haired wife, in a flowered print dress, glasses slung round her neck, stands by, watching, her hands on her hips. As in the American vacation-land, dress is strictly informal; nobody but an Asian wears a tie or a white shirt. The Vietnamese old men and boys, in wide, conical hats, pedaling their Cyclos (the modern version of the rickshaw) in and out of the traffic pattern, the Vietnamese women in high heels and filmy ao-dais of pink, lavender, heliotrope, the signs and Welcome banners in Vietnamese actually contribute to the Stateside impression by the addition of "local" color, as though you were back in a Chinese restaurant in San Francisco or in a Japanese sukiyaki place, under swaying paper lanterns, being served by women in kimonos while you sit on mats and play at using chopsticks.

Perhaps most of all Saigon is like a stewing Los Angeles, shading into Hollywood, Venice Beach, and Watts. The native stall markets are still in business, along Le Loi and Nguyen Hue Streets, but the merchandise is, for Asia, exotic. There is hardly anything native to buy, except flowers and edibles and firecrackers at Têt time and—oh yes—souvenir dolls. Street vendors and children are offering trays of American cigarettes and racks on racks of Johnnie Walker, Haig & Haig, Black & White (which are either black market, stolen from the PX, or spurious, depending on the price); billboards outside car agencies advertise Triumphs, Thunderbirds, MG's, Corvettes, "For Delivery here or Stateside, Payment on Easy Terms"; non-whites, the less affluent ones, are mounted on Hondas and Lambrettas. There are photo-copying services, film-developing services, Western tailoring and dry-cleaning services, radio and TV repair shops, air conditioners, Olivetti typewriters, comic books, *Time, Life,* and *Newsweek,* airmail paper—you name it, they have it. Toys for Vietnamese children (there are practically no American kids or wives in Vietnam) include U.S.-style jackknives, pistols, and simulated-leather belts, with holsters—I did not see any cowboy suits or Indian war-feathers. Pharmaceuticals are booming; young Vietnamese women of the upper crust are enrolling in the School of Pharmacy in order to open drugstores; and a huge billboard all along the top of a building in the central marketplace shows a smiling Negro—maybe a long-ago Senegalese soldier—with very white teeth advertising a toothpaste called Hynos.

If Saigon by day is like a PX, at night, with flares overhead, it is like a World's Fair or Exposition in some hick American city.

There are Chinese restaurants, innumerable French restaurants (not surprising), but also La Dolce Vita, Le Guillaume Tell, the Paprika (a Spanish restaurant on a rooftop, serving paella and sangría). The national cuisine no American wants to sample is the Vietnamese. In February, a German circus was in town. "French" wine is made in Cholon, the local Chinatown. In the night clubs, if it were not for the bar girls, you would think you were on a cruise ship: a *chanteuse* from Singapore sings old French, Italian, and American favorites into the microphone; an Italian magician palms the watch of a middle-aged Vietnamese customer; the band strikes up "Happy Birthday to You," as a cake is brought in. The "vice" in Saigon—at least what I was able to observe of it—has a pepless *Playboy* flavor.

As for virtue, I went to church one Sunday in the Cathedral (a medley of Gothic, Romanesque, and vaguely Moorish) on John F. Kennedy Square, hoping to hear the mass in Vietnamese. Instead, an Irish-American priest preached a sermon on the hemline to a large male white congregation of soldiers, construction-workers, newspaper correspondents; in the pews were also a few female secretaries from the Embassy and other U.S. agencies and a quotient of middle-class Vietnamese of both sexes. I had happened, it turned out, on the "American" mass, said at noon. Earlier services *were* in Vietnamese. The married men present, the celebrant began, did not have to be told that for a woman the yearly rise or fall in skirt lengths was a "traumatic experience," and he likened the contemporary style centers—New York, Chicago, San Francisco—to the ancient "style centers" of the Church—Rome, Antioch, Jerusalem. His point seemed to be that the various rites of the Church (Latin, Coptic,

67

Armenian, Maronite—he went into it very thoroughly) were only *modes* of worship. What the Sunday-dressed Vietnamese, whose hemline remains undisturbed by changes emanating from the "style centers" and who were hearing the Latin mass in American, were able to make of the sermon, it was impossible to tell. Just as it was impossible to tell what some very small Vietnamese children I saw in a home for ARVN war orphans were getting out of an American adult TV program they were watching at bedtime, the littlest ones mother-naked. Maybe TV, too, is catholic, and the words do not matter.

Saigon has a smog problem, like New York and Los Angeles, a municipal garbage problem, a traffic problem, power failures, inflation, juvenile delinquency. In short, it meets most of the criteria of a modern Western city. The young soldiers do not like Saigon and its clip joints and high prices. Everybody is trying to sell them something or buy something from them. Six-year-old boys, cute as pins, are plucking at them: "You come see my sister. She Number One fuck." To help the G.I. resist the temptations of merchants—and soak up his buying power—diamonds and minks are offered him in the PX, tax free. (There were no minks the day I went there, but I did see a case of diamond rings, the prices ranging up to 900-odd dollars.) Unfortunately, the PX presents its own temptation—that of resale. The G.I. is gypped by taxi drivers and warned against Cyclo men (probably VC), and he may wind up in a Vietnamese jail, like some of his buddies, for doing what everybody else does—illegal currency transactions. If he walks in the center after nightfall, he has to pick his way among whole families who are cooking their unsanitary meal or sleeping, right on the street, in the filth.

When he rides in from the airport, he has to cross a bend of the river, bordered by shanties, that he has named, with rich American humor, Cholera Creek.

To the servicemen, Saigon stinks. They would rather be in base camp, which is clean. And the JUSPAO press officer has a rote speech for arriving correspondents: "Get out of Saigon. That's my advice to you. Go out into the field." As though the air were purer there, where the fighting is.

That is true in a way. The Americanization process smells better out there, to Americans, even when perfumed by napalm. Out there, too, there is an enemy a man can respect. For many of the soldiers in the field and especially the younger officers, the Viet Cong is the only Vietnamese worthy of notice. "If we only had them fighting on our side, instead of the goddamned Arvin [Army of the Vietnamese Republic], we'd *win* this war" is a sentiment the newspapermen like to quote. I never heard it said in those words, but I found that you could judge an American by his attitude toward the Viet Cong. If he called them "Charlie" (*cf.* John Steinbeck), he was either an infatuated civilian, a low-grade primitive in uniform, or a fatuous military mouthpiece. Decent soldiers and officers called them "the VC." The same code of honor applied in South Vietnamese circles; with the Vietnamese, who are ironic, it was almost a pet name for the enemy. Most of the American military will praise the fighting qualities of the VC, and the more intellectual (who are not necessarily the best) praise them for their "motivation." In this half of the century Americans have become very incurious, but the Viet Cong has awakened the curiosity of the men who are fighting them. From within the perimeter of the camp, behind the barbed wire and the sandbags, they study their habits, half-amused, half-admiring; a gingerly relationship is established with the unseen enemy, who is probably carefully fashioning a booby trap a few hundred yards away. This relation does not seem to extend to the North Vietnamese troops, but in that case contact is rarer. The military are justly nervous of the VC, but unless they have been wounded out on a patrol or have had the next man killed by a mine or a mortar, they do not show hatred or picture the black-pajama saboteur as a "monster," a word heard in Saigon offices.

In the field, moreover, the war is not questioned; it is just a fact. The job has to be finished—that is the attitude. In Saigon, the idea that the war can ever be finished appears fantastic: the Americans will be there forever, one feels; if they go, the economy will collapse. What postwar aid program could be conceived—or passed by Congress—that would keep the air in the balloon? And if the Americans go, the middle-class Saigonese think, the Viet Cong will surely come back, in two years, five years, ten, as they come back to a "pacified" hamlet at Têt time, to leave, as it were, a calling card, a reminder—we are still here. But, at the same time, in Saigon the worth of the American presence, that is, of the war, seems very dubious, since the actual results, in uglification, moral and physical, are evident to all. The American soldier, bumping along in a jeep or a military truck, resents seeing all those Asiatics at the wheels of new Cadillacs. He knows about corruption, often firsthand, having contributed his bit to it, graft, theft of AID and military supplies from the port. He thinks it is disgusting that the local employees steal from the PX and then stage a strike when the manageress makes them line up to be searched on leaving the building. And he has heard that these "apes," as some men call them, are salting away the profits in Switzerland or in France, where De Gaulle, who is pro-VC, has just run the army out.

Of course, all wars have had their profiteers, but it has not usually been so manifest, so inescapable. The absence of the austerity that normally accompanies war, of civilian sacrifices, rationing, shortages, blackouts (compare wartime London or even wartime New York, twenty-five years ago) makes this war seem singularly immoral and unheroic to those who are likely to die in it—for what? So that the Saigonese and other civilians can live high off the hog? The fact that the soldier or officer is living pretty high off the hog himself does not reconcile him to the glut of Saigon; rather the contrary. Furthermore, an atmosphere of sacrifice is heady; that—and danger—is what used to make wartime capitals gay. Saigon is not gay. The peculiar thing is that with all those young soldiers wandering about, all those young journalists news-chasing, Saigon seems so middle-aged—inert, listless, bored. That, I suppose, is because everyone's principal interest there is money, the only currency that is circulating, like the stale air moved by ceiling fans and air conditioners in hotels and offices.

The war, they say, is not going to be won in Saigon, nor on the battlefield, but in the villages and hamlets. This idea, by now trite (it was first discovered in Diem's time and has been rebaptized under a number of names—New Life Hamlets, Rural Construction, Counter Insurgency, Nation-Building, Revolutionary Development, the Hearts and Minds Program), is the main source of inspiration for the various teams of missionaries, mili-

71

tary and civilian, who think they are engaged in a crusade. Not just a crusade against Communism, but something *positive*. Back in the fifties and early sixties, the war was presented as an investment: the taxpayer was persuaded that if he stopped Communism *now* in Vietnam, he would not have to keep stopping it in Thailand, Burma, etc. That was the domino theory, which our leading statesmen today, quite comically, are busy repudiating before Congressional committees—suddenly nobody will admit to ever having been an advocate of it. The notion of a costly investment that will save money in the end has a natural appeal to a nation of homeowners, but now the assertion of an American "interest" in Vietnam has begun to look too speculative as the stake increases ("When is it going to pay off?") and also too squalid as the war daily becomes more savage and destructive. Hence the "other" war, proclaimed by President Johnson in Honolulu, which is simultaneously pictured as a strategy for winning War Number One and as a top priority in itself. Indeed, in Vietnam, there are moments when the "other" war, for hearts and minds, seems to be viewed as the sole reason for the American presence, and it is certainly more congenial to American officials, brimming with public spirit, than the war they are launching from the skies. Americans do not like to be negative, and the "other" war is constructive.

To see it, of course, you have to get out of Saigon, but, before you go, you will have to be briefed, in one of those new office buildings, on what you are going to see. In the field, you will be briefed again, by a military man, in a district or province headquarters, and frequently all you will see of New Life Hamlets, Constructed Hamlets, Consolidated Hamlets are the charts and graphs and maps and symbols that some ardent colonel or brisk bureaucrat is demonstrating to you with a pointer, and the mimeographed handout, full of statistics, that you take away with you, together with a supplement on Viet Cong Terror. On paper and in chart form, it all sounds commendable, especially if you are able to ignore the sounds of bombing from B-52's that are shaking the windows and making the charts rattle. The briefing official is enthusiastic, as he points out the progress that has been made, when, for example, the activities organized under AID were reorganized under OCO (Office of Civilian Operations). You stare at the chart on the office wall which to you has no semblance of logic or sequence ("Why," you wonder, "should Youth Affairs be grouped under Urban Development?"), and the official rubs his hands with pleasure: "First we organized it *vertically*. Now we've organized it *horizontally!*" He does not say that one of the main reasons for the creation of OCO was to provide a cover for certain CIA operations. Out in the field, you learn from some disgruntled officer that the AID representatives, who are perhaps now OCO representatives without knowing it, have not been paid for six months.

In a Saigon "backgrounder," you are told about public-health measures undertaken by Free World Forces. Again a glowing progress report. In 1965, there were 180 medical people from the "Free World" in Vietnam treating patients; in 1966, there were 700—quite a little escalation, almost four times as many. The troop commitment, of course, not mentioned by the briefer, jumped from 60,000 to 400,000—more than six-and-a-half times as many. That the multiplication of troops implied an obvious escalation in the number of civilian patients requiring treatment is not mentioned either. Under questioning, the official, slightly irritated, estimates that the civilian casualties comprise between 7½ and 15 per cent of the surgical patients treated in hospitals. He had "not been interested particularly, until all the furore," in what percentage of the patients were war casualties. And naturally he was not interested in what percentage of civilian casualties never reached a hospital at all.

Nor would there have been any point in asking him what happens to the Viet Cong wounded—a troubling question I never heard raised in nearly a month in Vietnam. A very few are in hospitals—some have been seen recently by a journalist in Can Tho—and the mother of a Marine killed in action has made public in a Texas newspaper a letter from her boy telling how he felt when ordered to go back to the battlefield and shoot wounded VC in the head (prompt denial from the Marine Corps). But American officials on the spot are not concerned by the discrepancy between estimated VC wounded and estimated VC in hospitals: 225 being treated in U.S. medical facilities in one week in May, whereas at the end of April an estimated 30,000 to 35,000 had been wounded in action since the first of the year.

But—to return to the "backgrounder"—the treatment of war victims, it turned out, was not one of the medical "bull's-eyes" aimed at in the "other" war. Rather, a peacetime-type program, "beefing up" the medical school, improvement of hospital facilities, donation of drugs and antibiotics (which, as I learned from another source, are in turn *sold* by the local nurses to the patients for whom they have been prescribed), the control of epidemic diseases, such as plague and cholera, education of the population in good health procedures. American and allied workers, you hear, are teaching the Vietnamese in the government villages to boil their water, and the children are learning dental hygiene. Toothbrushes are distributed, and the children are shown how to use them. If the children get the habit, the parents will copy them, a former social worker explains, projecting from experience with first-generation immigrants back home. There is a campaign on to vaccinate and immunize as much of the population as can be got to co-operate; easy subjects are refugees and forced évacués, who can be lined up for shots while going through the screening process and being issued an identity card—a political health certificate.

All this is not simply on paper. In the field, you are actually able to see medical teams at work, setting up temporary dispensaries under the trees in the hamlets for the weekly or biweekly "sick call"—distributing medicines, tapping, listening, sterilizing, bandaging; the most common diagnosis is suspected tuberculosis. In Tay Ninh Province, I watched a Philcag (Filipino) medical team at work in a Buddhist hamlet. One doctor was examining a very thin old man, who was stripped to the waist; probably tubercular, the doctor told me, writing something on a card which he gave to the old man. "What happens next?" I wanted to know. Well, the old man would go to the province hospital for an X ray (that was the purpose of the card), and if the diagnosis was positive, then treatment should follow. I was impressed. But (as I later learned at a briefing) there are only sixty civilian hospitals in South Vietnam—for nearly 16 million people—so that the old man's total benefit, most likely, from the open-air consultation was to have learned, gratis, that he might be tubercular.

Across the road, some dentist's chairs were set up, and teeth were being pulled, very efficiently, from women and children of all ages. I asked about the toothbrushes I had heard about in Saigon. The Filipino major laughed. "Yes, we have distributed them. They use them as toys." Then he reached into his pocket— he was a kindly young man with children of his own—and took out some money for all the children who had gathered round, to buy popsicles (the local equivalent) from the popsicle man. Later I watched the Filipino general, a very handsome tall man with a cropped head, resembling Yul Brynner, distribute Têt gifts and candy to children in a Cao Dai orphanage and be photographed with his arm around a little blind girl. A few hours earlier, he had posed distributing food in a Catholic hamlet— "Free World" surplus items, such as canned cooked beets. The photography, I was told, would help sell the Philcag operation to the Assembly in Manila, where some leftist elements were trying to block funds for it. Actually, I could not see that the general was doing any harm, whatever his purposes might be, politically—unless not doing more is harm, in which case we are all guilty—and he was more efficient than other Civic Action leaders. His troops had just chopped down a large section of jungle (we proceeded through it in convoy, wearing bulletproof vests and bristling with rifles and machine guns, because of the VC), which was going to be turned into a hamlet for resettling refugees. They had also built a school, which we stopped to

76

inspect, finding, to the general's surprise, that it had been taken over by the local district chief for his office headquarters.

The Filipino team, possibly because they were Asians, seemed to be on quite good terms with the population. Elsewhere—at Go Cong, in the delta—I saw mistrustful patients and heard stories of rivalry between the Vietnamese doctor, a gynecologist, and the Spanish and American medical teams; my companion and I were told that we were the first "outsiders," including the resident doctors, to be allowed by the Vietnamese into *his* wing—the maternity, which was far the cleanest and most modern in the hospital and contained one patient. Similar jealousies existed of the German medical staff at Hue. In the rather squalid surgical wing of the Go Cong hospital, there were two badly burned children. Were they war casualties, I asked the official who was showing us through. Yes, he conceded, as a matter of fact they were. How many of the patients were war-wounded, I wanted to know. "About four" of the children, he reckoned. And one old man, he added, after reflection.

The Filipinos were fairly dispassionate about their role in pacification; this may have been because they had no troops fighting in the war (those leftist elements in the Assembly!) and therefore did not have to act like saviors of the Vietnamese people. The Americans, on the contrary, are zealots—above all, the blueprinters in the Saigon offices—although occasionally in the field, too, you meet a true believer—a sandy, crew-cut, keen-eyed army colonel who talks to you about "the nuts and bolts" of the program, which, he is glad to say, is finally getting the "grass roots" support it needs. It is impossible to find out from such a man what he is doing, concretely; an aide steps forward to state, "We sterilize the area prior to the insertion of the RD teams," whose task, says the colonel, is to find out "the aspirations of the people." He cannot tell you whether there has been any land reform in his area—that is a strictly Vietnamese pigeon —in fact he has no idea of *how* the land in the area is owned. He is strong on co-ordination: all his Vietnamese counterparts, the colonel who "wears two hats" as province chief, the mayor, a deposed general, are "very fine sound men," and the Marine general in the area is "one of the finest men and officers" he has ever met. For another army zealot every Vietnamese officer he deals with is "an outstanding individual."

These springy, zesty, burning-eyed warriors, military and civilian, engaged in AID or Combined Action (essentially pacification) stir faraway memories of American college presidents of the fund-raising type; their diction is peppery with oxymoron ("When peace breaks out," "Then the commodities started to hit the beach"), like a college president's address to an alumni dinner. They see themselves in fact as educators, spreading the American way of life, a new *propaganda fide*. When I asked an OCO man in Saigon what his groups actually did in a Vietnamese village to prepare—his word—the people for elections, he answered curtly, "We teach them Civics 101."

The American taxpayer who thinks that aid means direct help to the needy has missed the idea. Aid's first target is economic stability within the present system, *i.e.*, political stability for the present ruling groups. Loans are extended, under the counterpart-fund arrangement, to finance Vietnamese imports of American capital equipment (thus AIDing, with the other hand, American industry). Second, aid is *education*. Distribution of canned goods (instill new food habits), distribution of seeds, fertilizer, chewing gum and candy (the Vietnamese complain that the G.I.'s fire candy at their children, like a spray of bullets), lessons in sanitation, hog-raising, and crop rotation. The program is designed, not just to make Americans popular, but to shake up the Vietnamese, as in some "stimulating" freshman course where the student learns to question the "prejudices" implanted in him by his parents. "We're trying to wean them away from the old barter economy and show them a market economy. Then they'll really *go*."

"We're teaching them free enterprise," explains a breathless JUSPAO official in the grim town of Phu Cuong. He is speaking of the "refugees" from the Iron Triangle, who were forcibly cleared out of their hamlets, which were then burned and leveled, during Operation Cedar Falls ("Clear and Hold"). They had just been transferred into a camp, hastily constructed by the ARVN with tin roofs painted red and white, to make the form, as seen from the air, of a giant Red Cross—1,651 women, 3,754 children, 582 men, mostly old, who had been kindly allowed to bring some of their furniture and pots and pans and their pigs and chickens and sacks of their hoarded rice; their water cattle had been transported for them, on barges, and were now sickening on a dry, stubbly, sandy plain. "We've got a captive audience!" the official continued excitedly. "This is our big chance!"

To teach them free enterprise and, presumably, when they were "ready" for it, Civics 101; for the present, the government had to consider them "hostile civilians." These wives and children and old fathers of men thought to be at large with the Viet Cong had been rice farmers only a few weeks before. Now they were going to have to pitch in and learn to be vegetable farmers; the area selected for their eventual resettlement was not suitable for rice-growing, unfortunately. Opportunity was beckoning for these poor peasants, thanks to the uprooting process they had just undergone. They would have the chance to buy and build their own homes on a pattern and of materials already picked out for them; the government was allowing them 1,700 piasters toward the purchase price. To get a new house free, even though in the abstract that might seem only fair, would be unfair to them as human beings, it was explained to me: investing their own labor and their own money would make them feel that the house was really *theirs*. "The Lord helps those who help themselves"—the social worker's Great Commandment—is interpreted in war-pounded Vietnam, and with relentless priggery, as "the U.S. helps those who help themselves."

In the camp, a schoolroom had been set up. Interviews with the parents revealed that more than anything else they wanted education for their children; they had not had a school for five years. I remarked that this seemed queer, since Communists were usually strong on education. The official insisted. "Not for five years." But in fact another American, a young one, who had actually been working in the camp, told me that strangely enough the small children there knew their multiplication tables and possibly their primer—he could not account for this. And in one of the razed villages, he related, the Americans had found, from captured exercise books, that someone had been teaching the past participle in English, using Latin models—defectors spoke of a high-school teacher, a Ph.D. from Hanoi.

Perhaps the parents, in the interviews, told the Americans what they thought they wanted to hear. All over Vietnam, wherever peace has broken out, if only in the form of a respite, Marine and army officers are proud to show the schoolhouses their men are building or rebuilding for the hamlets they are patrolling, rifle on shoulder. At Rach Kien, in the delta (a Pentagon pilot project of a few months before), I saw the little schoolhouse Steinbeck wrote about, back in January, and the blue school desks he had seen the soldiers painting. They were still sitting outside, in the sun; the school was not yet rebuilt more than a month later—they were waiting for materials. In this hamlet, everything seemed to have halted, as in "The Sleeping Beauty," the enchanted day Steinbeck left; nothing had advanced. Indeed, the picture he sketched, of a ghost town coming back to civic life, made the officers who had entertained him smile—"He used his imagination." In other hamlets, I saw schoolhouses actually finished and one in operation. "The school is dirty," the colonel in charge barked at the alarmed Revolutionary Development director, who claimed to have been the first to translate Pearl Buck into Vietnamese. It was an instance of American tactlessness, though the belligerent colonel was right. A young Vietnamese social worker said sadly that he wished the Americans would stop building schools. "They don't realize—we have no teachers for them."

Yet the little cream schoolhouse is essential to the American dream of what we are doing in Vietnam, and it is essential for the soldiers to believe that in *Viet Cong* hamlets no schooling is permitted. In Rach Kien I again expressed doubts, as a captain, with a professionally shocked face, pointed out the evidence that the school had been used as "Charlie's" headquarters. "So you really think that the children here got no lessons, *nothing*, under the VC?" "Oh, indoctrination courses!" he answered with a savvy wave of his pipe. In other words, VC Civics 101.

If you ask a junior officer what he thinks our war aims are in Vietnam, he usually replies without hesitation: "To punish aggression." It is unkind to try to draw him into a discussion of what constitutes aggression and what is defense (the Bay of Pigs, Santo Domingo, Goa?), for he really has no further ideas on the subject. He has been indoctrinated, just as much as the North Vietnamese P.O.W., who tells the interrogation team he is fighting to "liberate the native soil from the American aggressors"—maybe more. Only, the young American does not know it; he probably imagines that he is *thinking* when he produces that formula. And yet he does believe in something profoundly, though he may not be able to find the words for it: free enterprise. A parcel that to the American mind wraps up for delivery hospitals, sanitation, roads, harbors, schools, air travel, Jack Daniel's, convertibles, Stim-u-dents. That is the moral C-ration in his survival kit. The American troops are not exactly conscious of bombing, shelling, and defoliating to defend free enterprise (which they cannot imagine as being under serious attack), but they plan to come out of the war with their values intact. Which means that they must spread them, until everyone is convinced, by demonstration, that the American way is better, just as American seed strains are better and American pigs are better. Their conviction is sometimes baldly stated. North of Da Nang, at a

Marine base, there is an ice-cream plant on which is printed in
large official letters the words: "ICE-CREAM PLANT: ARVN MO-
RALE BUILDER." Or it may wear a humanitarian disguise, *e.g.*,
Operation Concern, in which a proud little town in Kansas
airlifted 110 pregnant sows to a humble little town in Vietnam.

Occasionally the profit motive is undisguised. Flying to Hue
in a big C-130, I heard the pilot and the co-pilot discussing their
personal war aim, which was to make a killing, as soon as the
war was over, in Vietnamese real estate. From the air, while keeping an eye out for VC below, they had surveyed the possibilities
and had decided on Nha Trang—"beautiful sand beaches"—better than Cam Ranh Bay—a "desert." They disagreed as to the
kind of development that would make the most money: the pilot
wanted to build a high-class hotel and villas, while the co-pilot
thought that the future lay with low-cost housing. I found this
conversation hallucinating, but the next day, in Hue, I met a
Marine colonel who was back in uniform after retirement; having fought the Japanese, he had made his killing as a "devel-
oper" in Okinawa and invested the profits in a frozen-shrimp
(from Japan) import business supplying restaurants in San Di-
ego. War, a cheap form of mass tourism, opens the mind to business opportunities.

All these developers were Californians. In fact, the majority
of the Americans I met in the field in Vietnam were WASPs
from Southern California; most of the rest were from the rural
South. In nearly a month I met *one* Jewish boy in the services (a
nice young naval officer from Pittsburgh), two Boston Irish,
and a captain from Connecticut. Given the demographic shift
toward the Pacific in the United States, this Californian ascend-

ancy gave me the peculiar feeling that I was seeing the future of our country as if on a movie screen. Nobody has yet dared make a war movie about Vietnam, but the prevailing unreality, as experienced in base camps and headquarters, is eerily like a movie, a contest between good and evil that is heading toward a happy ending, when men with names like "Colonel Culpepper," "Colonel Derryberry," "Captain Stanhope" will vanquish Victor Charlie. The state that has a movie actor for governor and a movie actor for U.S. senator seemed to be running the show.

No doubt the very extensive press and television coverage of the war has made the participants very conscious of "exposure," that is, of role-playing. Aside from the usual networks, Italian television, Mexican television, the BBC, CBC were all filming the "other" war during the month of February, and the former Italian Chief of Staff, General Liuzzi, was covering it as a commentator for the *Corriere della Sera*. The effect of all this attention on the generals, colonels, and lesser officers was to put a premium on "sincerity."

Nobody likes to be a villain, least of all a WASP officer, who feels he is playing the heavy in Vietnam through some awful mistake in typecasting. He *knows* he is good at heart, because everything in his home environment—his TV set, his paper, his Frigidaire, the President of the United States—has promised him that, whatever shortcomings he may have as an individual, collectively he is good. The "other" war is giving him the chance to clear up the momentary misunderstanding created by those bombs, which, through no fault of his, are happening to hit civilians. He has *warned* them to get away, dropped leaflets saying he was coming and urging "Charlie" to defect, to join the other side; lately, in pacified areas, he has even taken the precaution of having his targets cleared by the village chief before shelling or bombing, so that now the press officer giving the daily briefing is able to reel out: "Operation Blockhouse. 29 civilians reported wounded today. Two are in 'poor' condition. Target had been approved by the district chief." Small thanks he gets, our military hero, for that scrupulous restraint. But in the work of pacification, his real self comes out, clear and true. Digging wells for the natives (too bad if the water comes up brackish), repairing roads ("Just a jungle trail before we came," says the captain, though his colonel, in another part of the forest, has just been saying that the engineers had uncovered a fine stone roadbed built eighty years ago by the French), building a house for the widow of a Viet Cong (so far unreconciled; it takes time).

American officers in the field can become very sentimental when they think of the good they are doing and the hard row they have to hoe with the natives, who have been brainwashed by the Viet Cong. A Marine general in charge of logistics in I-Corps district was deeply moved when he spoke of his Marines: moving in to help rebuild some refugee housing with scrap lumber and sheet tin (the normal materials were cardboard boxes and flattened beer cans); working in their off-hours to build desks for a school; giving their Christmas money for a new high school; planning a new marketplace. The Marine Corps had donated a children's hospital, and in that hospital, right up the road ("Your ve-hickels will conduct you"—he pronounced it like "nickels"), was a little girl who had been wounded during a Marine assault. "We're nursing her back to health," he intoned—and paused, like a preacher accustomed, at this point, to hearing an "Amen"; his PIO (Information Officer) nodded three times. In the hospital, I asked to see the little girl. "Oh, she's gone home," said the PIO. "Nursed her back to health." In reality the little girl was still there, but it was true, her wounds were nearly healed.

A young Marine doctor, blue-eyed, very good-looking, went from bed to bed, pointing out what was the matter with each child and showing what was being done to cure it. There was only the one war casualty; the rest were suffering from malnutrition (the basic complaint everywhere), skin diseases, worms; one had a serious heart condition; two had been badly burned by a stove, and one, in the contagious section, had the plague. The doctor showed us the tapeworm, in a bottle, he had extracted from one infant. A rickety baby was crying, and a middle-aged corpsman picked it up and gave it its bottle. They were plainly doing a good job, under makeshift conditions and without laboratory facilities. The children who were well enough to sit up appeared content; some even laughed, shyly. No amusements were provided for them, but perhaps it was sufficient amusement to be visited by tiptoeing journalists. And it could not be denied that it was a break for these children to be in a Marine hospital, clean, well-fed, and one to a bed. They were benefiting from the war, at least for the duration of their stay; the doctor was not sanguine, for the malnutrition cases, about what would happen when the patients went home. "We keep them as long as we can," he said, frowning. "But we can't keep them forever. They have to go back to their parents."

Compared to what they were used to, this short taste of the American way of life no doubt was delicious for Vietnamese children. John Morgan, in the London *Sunday Times*, described another little Vietnamese girl up near the DMZ—do they have one to a battalion?—who had been wounded by Marine bullets ("A casualty of war," that general repeated solemnly. "A casualty of war") and whom he saw carried in one night to a drinking party in sick bay, her legs bandaged, a spotlight playing on her, while the Marines pressed candy and dollar bills into her hands and had their pictures taken with her; she had more dolls than Macy's, they told him—"that girl is real spoiled." To spoil a child you have injured and send her back to her parents, with her dolls as· souvenirs, is pharisee virtue, whitening the sepulcher, like "treating" malnutrition in a hospital ward. The young doctor, being a doctor, was possibly conscious of the fakery—from a responsible medical point of view—of the "miracle" cures he was effecting; that was why he frowned. Meanwhile, however, the Marine Corps brass could show the "Before" and "After" to a captive audience. In fact two. The studio audience of children, smiling and laughing and clapping, and the broader audience of their parents, who, when allowed to visit, could not fail to be awed by the "other" side of American technology. And beyond that still a third audience—the journalists and their readers back home, who would recognize the Man in White and his corpsmen, having brought them up, gone to school with them, seen them on TV, in soap opera. I felt this myself, a relieved recognition of the familiar face of America. These are the American boys we know at once, even in an Asian context, bubbling an Asian baby. We do not recognize them, helmeted, in a bomber aiming cans of napalm at a thatched village. We have a credibility gap.

Leaving the hospital, I jolted southward in a jeep, hanging on, swallowing dust; the roads, like practically everything in Vietnam, have been battered, gouged, scarred, torn up by the weight of U.S. matériel. We passed Marines' laundry, yards and yards of dark-green battle cloth, hanging outside native huts like a kind of currency displayed by the fortunate washwoman. Down the road was a refugee camp, which did not form part of the itinerary. This, I realized, must be "home" to some of the children we had just seen; the government daily allowance for a camp family was ten piasters (six cents) a day—sometimes twenty if there were two adults in the family. Somebody had put a streamer, in English, over the entrance: "REFUGEES FROM COMMUNISM."

This was a bit too much. The children's hospital had told the story the Americans were anxious to get over. Why put in the commercial? And who was the hard sell aimed at? Not the refugees, who could not read English and who, if they were like all the other refugees, had fled, some from the Viet Cong and some from the Americans and some because their houses had been bombed or shelled. Not the journalists, who knew better. Whoever carefully lettered that streamer, crafty Marine or civilian, had applied all his animal cunning to selling himself.

The Problems of Success

A short trip by helicopter from Saigon in almost any direction permits a ringside view of American bombing. Just beyond the truck gardens of the suburbs, you see what at first glance appears to be a series of bonfires evocative of Indian summers; thick plumes of smoke are rising from wooded clumps and fields. Toward the west, great blackish-brown tracts testify to the most recent results of the defoliation program; purplish-brown tracts are last year's work. As the helicopter skims the treetops, and its machine guns lower into position, you can study the fires more closely, and it is possible to distinguish a rice field burned over by peasants from neat bombing targets emitting spirals of smoke. But a new visitor cannot be sure and may tend to discredit his horrified impression, not wishing to jump to conclusions. Flying over the delta one morning, I saw the accustomed lazy smoke puffs mounting from the landscape and was urging myself to be cautious ("How do you *know?*") when I noticed a small plane circling; then it plunged, dropped its bombs, and was away in a graceful movement, having hit the target again; there was a flash of flame, and fresh, blacker smoke poured out. In the distance, a pair of small planes was hovering in the sky, like mosquitoes buzzing near the ceiling, waiting to strike. We flew on.

Coming back to Saigon in the afternoon, I expected to hear about "my" double air strike in the daily five o'clock press briefing, but no air activity in the sector was mentioned—too trivial to record, said a newsman. On a day taken at random (Washington's Birthday), the Air Force and the Marine Corps reported 460 sorties flown over *South* Vietnam "in support of ground forces"; whenever a unit is in trouble, they send for the airmen. Quite apart from the main battle areas, where fires and secondary explosions are announced as so many "scores," the countryside is routinely dotted with fires in various stages, so that they come to seem a natural part of it, like the grave mounds in the rice fields and pastures. The charred patches you see when returning in the afternoon from a morning's field trip are this morning's smoking embers; meanwhile, new curls of smoke, looking almost peaceful, are the afternoon's tally. And the cruel couples of hovering aircraft (they seem to travel in pairs, like FBI agents) appear to be daytime fixtures, almost stationary in the sky.

The Saigonese themselves are unaware of the magnitude of what is happening to their country, since they are unable to use military transport to get an aerial view of it; they only note the refugees sleeping in the streets and hear the B-52's pounding a few miles away. Seeing the war from the air, amid the crisscrossing Skyraiders, Supersabres, Phantoms, observation planes, Psywar planes (dropping leaflets), you ask yourself how much longer the Viet Cong can hold out; the country is so small that at the present rate of destruction there will be no place left for them to hide, not even under water, breathing through a straw. The plane and helicopter crews are alert for the slightest sign of movement in the fields and woods and estuaries below; they lean forward intently, scanning the ground. At night, the Dragon-ships come out, dropping flares and firing mini-guns.

The Air Force seems inescapable, like the Eye of God, and soon, you imagine (let us hope with hyperbole), all will be razed, charred, defoliated by that terrible searching gaze. Punishment can be magistral. A correspondent, who was tickled by the incident, described flying with the pilot of the little FAC plane that directs a big bombing mission; below, a lone Vietnamese on a bicycle stopped, looked up, dismounted, took up a rifle and fired; the pilot let him have it with the whole bombload of napalm—enough for a platoon. In such circumstances, anyone with a normal sense of fair play cannot help pulling for the bicyclist, but the sense of fair play, supposed to be Anglo-Saxon, has atrophied in the Americans here from lack of exercise. We draw a long face over Viet Cong "terror," but no one stops to remember that the Viet Cong does not possess that superior instrument of terror, an air force, which in our case, over South Vietnam at least, is acting almost with impunity. The worst thing that could happen to our country would be to win this war.

At the end of February, President Johnson's personal representative announced to the assembled press corps in Saigon that whereas ten months ago the U.S. had confronted "the prommlms of failure" (read "problems of failure") in Vietnam, now it confronted "the prommlms engendered by success." This Madison Avenue Mercury, once a CIA agent, whose lips flexed as he spoke like rubber bands, was concluding a whirlwind tour of the country, and he kept conspicuously raising his arm to study his wrist watch and frown during his brief appearance; in an hour or so he would be airborne to Washington, on a breeze of confidence. One of "the problems of success" he listed was the refugees. This swift conversion of a liability into an asset is typical of the current American approach to Vietnam.

It is true that the French, who failed, did not have the problem. As a blunt Marine colonel said in his battery headquarters: "We created the refugees. There weren't any in the French war. Everybody fought and then went home at night." Today all that has been changed. Early in February an OCO man estimated that 10 per cent of the population are now refugees—a million and a half, he reckoned, since January 1964. With every new American operation the figure of course is revised upward. Yet the technology that is able to generate a record production of homeless persons, surpassing the old norms reached by floods and earthquakes, is able to reverse itself, when a real emergency looms, and use its skills for a salvage or mercy operation in the manner of the Red Cross. The emergency occurred in January with the Iron Triangle victims, originally counted as about 8,000 civilians, who have been finally boiled down to the 5,987 persons in the camp at Phu Cuong.

These people, obviously, are not refugees at all in the dictionary sense of the word ("A person who flees his home or country to seek refuge elsewhere, as in time of war, political or religious persecution, etc."). They did not flee from the B-52's, though they might well have; they were moved by U.S. troops, who were systematically setting fire to their houses. Thanks to world press and television coverage, nobody could claim that they had "voted with their feet" to join the Free World. They did not use their feet; they were packed into army trucks and loaded onto boats. And here begins the story of how with nerve and enterprise you can convert a liability into an asset, not just by word manipulation, but by the kind of action that talks. The Americans moved in squarely to meet unfavorable publicity with favorable publicity. They changed their image, like so many vaudeville artists making a rapid costume change in the wings.

Let me be fair. No doubt humane considerations played a part in the decision to treat this particular group of "refugees" with kid gloves. Surely individuals in the Army were shocked and even sickened by the orders for Operation Cedar Falls coming from "higher up." Possibly Johnson's advisers sincerely regretted what was seen as a military necessity in terms of "shortening the war," "saving American lives," or whatever formula was applied. Anyway, Washington decided to do right by the "refugees."

It is paying off. The camp at Phu Cuong has become a showcase. Newspaper people and other visitors are flown in by military helicopter—a short run from Saigon—to see for themselves. Everything there is open and above board, contrary to what a suspicious person might think. You can interview the évacués through the camp interpreter if you have a mind to. Or you can bring your own interpreter and talk to them alone. Fresh water is brought in daily by army trucks and pumped steadily into reserve tanks. When I arrived, the pump had stopped working, but a colonel of Engineers was there in a trice to fix it, scratching his sandy head and using his American know-how. "These people are river people; they waste a lot of water," said the young camp supervisor. Latrines of a primitive kind had been built. The authorities were trying to teach the people not to squat behind their huts, to collect their garbage at the indicated pickup points instead of throwing it on the paths, not to splash water when ladling it out of the tank. Instructions in Vietnamese were plainly posted.

At noon, a Revolutionary Development cadre, in black pajamas, was supervising the rice distribution. The free market had been introduced—a novelty, it was said, to these peasant women and old peasant men. Merchants from the town came to sell fresh vegetables and buy canned and packaged products accumulated by the camp inhabitants, who received a daily ration as well as welfare payments and cash for what labor they did. In the beginning, the merchants had cheated the camp people, who did not know the fair market price of American surplus products, but the Americans had quickly put a stop to that. The évacués were learning to make bricks out of mud, water, and a little cement for the supports of their future homes, using an American moulding process called Cinvaram—all over Vietnam, wherever the Americans were "pacifying," there was Cinvaram, a singularly ugly gray brick. Six TV sets had been donated by AID; in time, the authorities hoped to get cleaner programs—striptease shows from Saigon were "kind of shocking" for backward peasant families with little kids. And in accordance with the Friendly Forces policy, the ARVN was getting a credit line for putting the camp on its feet; it was they who had done all the construction work, the Americans insisted—they themselves had only advised, supplied some materials, and the daily water delivery.

Any impartial person would concede that conditions were not too bad here, given the inevitable crowding. The "refugees" complained of the heat; in their river villages, there had been shade, and here there was not a tree, just an expanse of baking dust, which was regularly kicked up by arriving helicopters and military vehicles. They complained that their cattle were sick, that some of their hoarded rice had been stolen from them; not true, said the advisers: they had been *told* to mark it carefully and they had only themselves to blame if the unmarked sacks got mixed up in transit. They complained of the arrogance of the Revolutionary Development cadres, who were there to supervise them, one weedy youth to each group hut, and of the fact that spies had been placed among them; an indispensable measure, said the advisers, to prevent agitation and propaganda: after all, these people were Viet Cong dependents, and some troublemakers in their midst were trying to stir up a protest strike, playing on their little grievances. A number of the troublemakers were known to the authorities and would be dealt with; in time, the rest would be picked out.

But the young camp supervisor, a Quaker, was pleased on the whole with how things were going. One hundred and fifty families out of the original camp population had already agreed to go and learn to be rubber workers on a plantation. This had somewhat alleviated the crowding, and some new shelters were being built. To his mild astonishment, the camp had just been "passed" by the World Health Organization. He was keeping his fingers crossed about the strike, which, if it happened, would do the camp no good. The cadres identified as "arrogant" would soon be replaced, he hoped. Women whose husbands were Hoi

Chanh (defectors) in the nearby Chieu Hói camp would eventually be allowed to join them, so that families would be reunited and resettled. It would be great when the school reopened, after the Têt holiday; the kids had already had one day of classes. As he passed, some of the bolder children touched him and ran away, laughing; he was popular. It was only when a military helicopter landed, I noticed, that the pack of children following us suddenly showed fear and retreated, in a rush.

This modest and moderately frank young man did not discuss the policy that had turned these people into camp inmates. That was a thing of the past; he was focused on the present. In his absorption in the task he had not stopped to reflect, evidently— nor had anyone else who was official—on what alternatives, really, the armed forces had had as to what to do with this mass of non-combatants once the decision had been made to clear the so-called Iron Triangle. Could they have been dumped into a field like human garbage and left to starve? *Something* had to be done with them, and quick, in view of public opinion. What *had* been done was not in any way meritorious, except in comparison to an atrocity. Yet seen through official eyes, misted over with sentiment, a cruel action was redeemed (school desks! six TV sets!) because its sequel was not as barbarous as someone might have reasonably expected. The briefing officers, telling the heart-moving "story" of Phu Cuong, showed a chuckling tenderness for the battle-weary American soldiers who had with their own hands helped those unfortunates move their pitiful furniture and animals—a great TV episode, replete with homely, humorous touches, squealing pigs, cackling hens, and a baby being born, surely, with a sergeant acting as midwife.

The hero of the Phu Cuong story is American know-how, American generosity, Uncle Sam with candy in his pockets. And Uncle Sam, like so many benefactors, is misunderstood. At lunch in his house, the local JUSPAO official expressed hurt and bewilderment over a New York *Times* story about Phu Cuong. The reporter had interviewed several refugees and printed what they told him; he quoted one woman as saying that she wished she were dead. "But that's natural," I objected. "Her husband had been killed by the Americans, and she'd lost her home and everything she had." "He ought to have given a cross-section," the man said in injured tones. "It creates the wrong picture of the camp." "If only one woman out of five wished she were dead, you're lucky," I said. But he was not persuaded. The story was unfair, he repeated. He actually wanted to think that the évacués in the camp were *happy*.

This lunatic attitude is widespread, though not always so doggedly stated. In their command posts, where the RVN flag proudly waves over what was recently a VC hamlet, American troops like to see smiling faces around them and hear the hum of reviving crafts and trades. The army band plays during Med Call in a half-reconstructed dispensary, to get the population to march up and take its medicine cheerfully; if no one comes, the Psy-war man is disconcerted. It is taken as a good sign (fortune is smiling) if the market reopens in a hamlet to which the population is inching back, though how the few inhabitants who return could be expected to live at all without a market for the exchange of vegetables, fish, rice, ducks is not clear. But to the men in occupation, the market proves that the hamlet *likes* the Army or the Marines. Not only do the Americans like to be liked

—the major clumping through the marketplace while the kids crowd around him shouting "You Number One," meaning "You're tops"—they want the local people to feel that the Americans like *them*. The Marine Corps recently gave a questionnaire to Marines and to Vietnamese. The results showed that only 46 per cent of the Vietnamese felt that "Americans like them as people," while a much larger percentage—65 or 70 —said they liked Marines. A very sad situation, which the Marine Corps will have to get to work on, using its talent for public relations.

Of course there is a reason for this campaign to win friends. The strategists want the villagers to run and tell the nice captain when a VC attack is planned and to inform on their neighbors who are suspected Viet Cong sympathizers. You will be told by some vibrant officer that the people in his area have begun to "co-operate" with the Americans—the word "collaborate" is avoided—and yet his purpose in telling you this, jubilant and hand-rubbing, is confused. Is he glad that some old man has denounced his neighbor (quite possibly a private enemy) because this shows that security is increasing or because it is a sign that his command is well liked personally? Sometimes the second seems to dominate, especially when the officer is the "sincere" type who sees himself as bringing security to the hamlets he patrols, when practically he ought to be seeing himself as guaranteeing security to his troops. Such complex self-deception goes back perhaps to the old Indian fighting, where an Indian who liked white men was a good Indian: "an outstanding individual."

To some of the men fighting in Vietnam, naturally, there are no good Vietnamese except dead ones. They do not care about smiling faces; they want results—hard information delivered on the line. These are the Marines and other forces who stand by, watching noncommittally, while an ARVN soldier beats a captive girl: such a scene—one was described to me by a veteran artist commissioned to do war sketches who had witnessed it that afternoon—permits the man in uniform, puffing on a cigarette or chewing his cud of gum, to despise *all* Vietnamese equally. But in my experience the average soldier in Vietnam, when not fighting, is rather kindly—at least in those companies working on "pacification." He looks up and grins ("Morning, Ma'am") as he shows two slant-eyed kids how to fill sandbags to protect an artillery installation. It may not occur to him that his little helpers' fathers may be with the VC, 350 meters away, across the bridge from which sounds of a fire-fight are coming; if it does, what the hell? The kids are having fun.

If you tell an American official that the camp at Phu Cuong is a showcase, he is indignant. Of course it is a showcase, but the Americans don't like the word because it seems to impugn their motives. They will not even allow that their motives might be mixed. If you called it a pilot project, they would not mind. They also object if you call Phu Cuong a concentration camp, though that is what it is: these people have been arbitrarily rounded up and detained there, behind barbed wire, subjected to interrogation, and informers have been placed among them. To our officials, the term "concentration camp" has been copyrighted by the Nazis and automatically produces an image of jailers making lampshades of human skin—which they *know* is not happening at Phu Cuong. The barbed wire is there, they explain patiently, to protect the camp from the Viet Cong, but if the "refugees" are Viet Cong dependents, it is hard to imagine why their husbands and fathers would attack them with mortars and hand grenades.

In no respect is Phu Cuong a typical refugee camp, whether our authorities whose job is to deal with refugees are aware of the fact or not. To maintain that it is would be like saying that Mr. Lodge's (now Mr. Bunker's) residence is a typical Vietnamese dwelling. The fresh-water supply puts Phu Cuong in a class by itself, in my experience; so do the latrines, the school, the electricity, the TV sets, the garbage pickup points, the new tin roofing, the relatively substantial food ration, the possibility of earning money by working, the quantity of household furniture, as well as the new American pajama sets the children are wearing and that were probably donated by some voluntary agency. Perhaps there are other refugee camps that have one or two of these features, but I have not heard of them. I can only speak of what I saw, in the north, near Hoi An, where I was taken by a group of German volunteers—the Catholic Knights of Malta—who were eager to have me see what *they* considered, after several months in the field, typical refugee camps. They did not show me what they called "the worst ones," because they were too hard to get to, which suggests that almost nobody sees them but visiting medical teams.

I had met these young Germans at Hue, in the University compound, where they were spending the evening with the German Professor of Medicine, who had organized the Medical School, and his wife—a real German evening, with Vietnamese *schnapps*, fresh sugared ginger, Schumann on the tape recorder, reminiscences of Jaspers (the doctor had been his student at Heidelberg), consultation of art books, to look up examples of Bavarian rococo and Rhineland "double" churches. The next morning, which was Sunday, the young people showed me the leper house in Hue, which they had been trying to clean up and humanize—a one-story structure, surrounded by mud, that may once have been a cow stable or a pigsty and that now housed seventy persons, lepers and their families. The Germans had installed electric lights, paved a dirt passageway directly in front of the hovel, washed the inside walls. You could not do much more, they said, as long as the lepers were living there. A tall, reddish-haired, round-featured electrical engineer from Cologne named Wolfgang surveyed the rusty screens full of holes, the stained walls, the dark dormitory where the women were crowded (one of the electrical fixtures was not working, he noted), the dirty floor; he sighed. Then he took me outside to show me the overflowing cesspool that had been located just outside the small room where the lepers ate. A sickening smell of human excrement came from the regurgitating cesspool and from the latrine a few feet away. Next to the cesspool, outside the kitchen, where some food was being warmed, was a heap of uncollected garbage. A few chickens were stalking around the garbage heap, and some ducks were swimming in muddy water that had collected in a depression in the yard. Wolfgang and his friends were discouraged. The head of the Hue hospital disapproved of their efforts. "Why are you giving things to those lepers?" he had told them. "They are all VC."

The young Knights of Malta, boys and girls, had conceived the project of moving the lepers into a decent building. They had secured an old hospital pavilion the town government had condemned; they had carpentered, wired, painted (the outside was now a pale cream-yellow), installed ventilating equipment, which they had bought in the town, when the head of the hospital tried to sell them the old equipment for much more, it turned out, than what new ventilators were selling for on the market. Then, as soon as they had installed it, the whole ventilating system was stolen, over a weekend—by the hospital electrician, the police reckoned. So it was all to do over, and meanwhile the lepers were still in the filthy old leper house, with their families, including some children who were not lepers, on the Vietnamese live-in system, and including also, Wolfgang confided, one or two that he thought were pseudo-lepers, who lived in the leprosarium and rented their houses—a pitiful case of graft.

They received from the government a daily ration of rice, a little meat, and occasionally bananas. "Not enough," said Wolfgang, shaking his head. In a small workshop, some of them wove on frames the pale, wide, conical hats that are a specialty of Hue, to sell on the market. When we visited, it was Têt, so that no one was working; the men, some lacking a finger, were playing cards, and the women were lying or crouching on their wooden beds, without bedclothes—one was dying. They showed us the little Buddhist and Catholic altars they had decorated for the New Year.

As a supplement, the Knights of Malta gave me a quick tour of the Hue madhouse, known as the "psychiatric wing" of the hospital. Here conditions were more terrible than in the leprosarium. A few sane children of insane mothers were roaming about the dirty, untended female ward; a depressive sat howling on her bed. Rusty torn screens, fly-splattered walls. There was no sign of a nurse; no patient had been washed or combed. At the entrance to the dangerous ward, old tin cans were lying in the mud. A madman stared out of a peephole; the place was locked, and no one could go in because, at least today, there were no attendants. It was worse before, the Knights of Malta said, when the government used to put political opponents here.

Seeing the Hue leper house and this bedlam somewhat readied me for the "temporary" refugee camps I was shown the next day, in Cam Chau, outside Hoi An. The first of these camps was about six months old and contained 1,500 people. As I walked with a German doctor through rows of communal huts, we came to a stagnant duck pond, ten or fifteen feet wide, in which some ducklings in fact were swimming amid floating tin cans and other refuse. This was the water facility—the *only* water for drinking, washing, and cooking, to supply 700 people. On the other side of the camp, which was divided in two by a road, was another duck pond, slightly larger, which served the remaining 800. There were no sanitary facilities of any kind; we saw women and children squatting; garbage was strewn in front of the huts, which had earth floors and inflammable old straw roofing. Yet *The Reporter* dated January 12 was telling its readers in a reassuring article that seems to have sprung, full-blown, from a briefing session that Dr. Que, "a doctor by training" and head of the Vietnamese refugee bureau, has "established standards for sanitation and medical attention in refugee camps." It is true that the writer does not say what the standards are.

The misery and squalor of that first camp is hard to convey.

My eyes in fact had avoided looking too closely at it, as though out of respect for the privacy of those who were enduring such disgrace. The women stood massed in their doorways to watch us pass; some approached the doctor and asked for medicine. But mostly they just watched, defying us, I felt, to watch *them*. Skin diseases were rampant, especially among the children, diseases of the scalp, eye diseases, gross signs of malnutrition, bad teeth, stained by betel-chewing and reduced, often, to stumps. Most of the refugees (as usual women and children and a few grandfathers) were dirty—how could they wash? In contrast to the new American-made seersuckers and ginghams of Phu Cuong, the pajamas of the children here were old, torn, discolored. The daily food allowance of ten piasters per family, supplemented irregularly by a little rice, said the doctor, was below subsistence requirements. Some families had begun straggly little vegetable patches—mainly lettuce plants, cabbage, and mustard—that were growing haphazardly amidst the refuse. This would help a little. And there were a few pigs, chickens, and the ducklings. But except for this spasmodic gardening, there was no work for these people—no fields they could plant, nothing. The Knights of Malta had procured a mechanical saw, in the hope of giving work to the able-bodied older men and teaching a trade to the boys, but owing to Vietnamese bureaucratic stubbornness, the young carpenter, who had left his job in Germany to come here, like the others, for a year, had not been authorized to take apprentices. This tall pale embodiment of German conscientiousness was working alone in his "shop" in province headquarters, sawing perfect boards, like some woodcut figure in a folk tale from the Black Forest, while outside the window an idle company of Popular Forces, in black pajamas, watched him all day long and giggled. The Knights of Malta were disgusted. "Maybe I will just *draft* some of the refugees," said the baron from the Rhineland, a graduate in agriculture, who was the head of the team.

These Germans were full of outspoken Christian indignation at what they were witnessing at close quarters. "Nobody could be more opposite than Germans and Vietnamese," said a Canadian Jesuit tolerantly; he had watched the German medical faculty in Hue trying to make some headway against dirt and local corruption. The Viet Cong, he said, would clean up that hospital in a day by simply shooting the chief grafters—a course that seemed to appeal to him as a man but not as a priest; as a priest, he counseled patience.

But the Knights of Malta were right to be scandalized. They had volunteered, it turned out, for a labor of Hercules and Sisyphus rolled into one. Yet at the same time, of all the Westerners I saw in Vietnam, only these German boys and girls (in particular, Wolfgang, the electrician) showed gentleness and compassion with the small, fragile Vietnamese, stroking a leper's shoulder, respectfully helping an old man scramble up to show the writing on a Buddhist altar. "You gimme cigarette!" a very small Vietnamese boy said to a young Knight, who refused and added in apology: "It is not good that they smoke."

The next camp they showed me was divided into three sections: Catholic, Buddhist, and Cao Dai—in all, about 4,500 people. It had been in existence over a year and was "better." That is, the huts had tin roofs and cement floors; the vegetable-growing was much more extensive, and the rows of seedlings—let-

tuces, cabbages, mustard greens, beans, onion sets, tomato plants
—better cared for and neater. Some camp leadership had developed. But again there was the water question. A well had finally
been dug. As we passed, the doctor bent down and sniffed it. He
made a face. "It's tainted?" He nodded. "Do they boil the water
for cooking?" "We have told them. Then we watch to see if they
will boil it. . . ." He raised his shoulders in a shrug.

This camp had a few more pigs, piglets, and chickens, a few
more ducklings; in the field behind, some water buffalo belonging to the refugees were grazing. But here again the garbage was
all-pervasive. There were no latrines, and again we saw skin
diseases, eye diseases, every kind of scurfy and scabious sore,
swollen stomachs, protruding bones, rickets. There was no school
and no work for the refugees, except in the tiny garden plots
between the serried huts. Some were growing flowers—marigolds. The doctor, a man in his fifties, seemed to think that the
Catholic section was in better order than the Buddhist section,
but I could not see any difference. All the children in this camp
were more disciplined than in the newer camp, where the doctor
had had to speak to them bluntly to keep them from hitting and
pushing me, not altogether in play—at any rate they had not
thrown stones at me, as they did in one "pacified" hamlet, when
the briefing officer was not looking.

We did not see the Cao Dai section because someone came to
tell the doctor that a plague case had been reported in a nearby
hamlet. He left. One of the German women stood sentinel while
I went to the toilet (which did not lock or have a light) in the
province headquarters; it was going to be a long drive in the
Red Cross station wagon back to the base at Da Nang. On the

way home, I remarked to the baron that, though conditions were appalling even in the "better" camp, I did not see that they were much worse than in the hamlets we were passing through and in others I had visited in Vietnam. Except for water. Water and work, he said. Otherwise there was not too much difference. The diseases in the camps were the same as the diseases in the hamlets; it was only that the crowding in the camps made epidemics more likely. And, having no work, the people had less to eat. Another bad feature of the situation was that the people in the hamlets looked down on the refugees—there were 150,000 in the province—and would not have anything to do with them.

In the hamlets, I had noticed, houses were sometimes quite clean on the inside, but outside there was the same filthy jetsam that you saw in the camps. I wondered if it had always been like this in Vietnam. The baron did not know. It seemed unlikely to me that the Vietnamese, who have the reputation of being an industrious people, could have lived in such conditions for centuries. One got the impression that a lapse into degradation had occurred in fairly recent times, just as there had been a lapse into illiteracy: before the French came, according to Donald Lancaster (*The Emancipation of French Indo-China*), the rural population had been literate; the French had wiped that out systematically in the nineteenth century.

At any rate, one thing was clear. Before the Americans came, there could have been no rusty Coca-Cola or beer cans or empty whiskey bottles. They had brought them. It was this indestructible mass-production garbage floating in swamps and creeks, lying about in fields and along the roadside that made the country, which must once have been beautiful, hideous. In the past, the "natural" garbage created by human beings and animals must have been reabsorbed by the landscape, like compost—fish bones, chicken bones, rice husks, dry bamboo, eggshells, vegetable peelings, excreta. The American way of life has donated this disfiguring industrial garbage to the Asian countryside, which is incapable of digesting it. And anyone who wishes to make a comparison, in Asian terms, has only to get a tourist visa for Cambodia, where the people are far less industrious and where even in the poorest sections of the capital and in remote hamlets everything is clean.*

Only in Hue, the old imperial capital of Annam, can you see what Vietnam must have looked like—dignified and melancholy —before the Americans came. There is scarcely any motor traffic; the Perfumed River is lined with dark sampans; the women, in traditional costume, carry the traditional twin baskets balanced on a pole. The reason is simple: Hue is off limits to U.S. troops, a pariah city. This is intended to be a punishment for the fighting and demonstrations during the Buddhist Struggle Movement in May-June 1966, when the USIS library was burned down by angry students. As a punishment, too, the corpse of the library has been allowed to stand near the center of the city, a You-Did-It-Yourself memorial. The few official Americans left in Hue— some OCO men, a JUSPAO man, a CIA man—with a small Vietnamese policeman on guard before each of their houses (there was no policeman to keep an eye on the lepers' pavilion), point out the blackened ruin with steely satisfaction: Hue is paying for its sins by being cut off from U.S. culture. You would think from their grim tone it was Auschwitz or Buchenwald, standing as a permanent lesson. Despite suggestions from the

---

* This, of course, was written before Nixon's Cambodian offensive, which started in spring, 1970.

University that it would be wiser to rebuild the library, the Americans, so far, have declined. Yet some U.S. culture, in the wider sense, can still be found in Hue. On a Sunday morning, I saw three middle-aged gun-toting civilians resembling Yukon prospectors alight from their car outside the sanctuary of the Emperors' Tombs, where Vietnamese were slowly walking under parasols around the lotus trees and pools filled with green plants and covered with a pale green scum. The three construction workers (I had seen them the day before in the hotel at Hue and was told they were engineers, probably, from the base at Phu Bai) advanced through the gates with a PX shopping bag full of beer cans. They were raising the first cans to their lips as they strode on toward the tombs and pagodas, which were guarded by gods and stone elephants. Where they tossed the empties, I cannot say.

Near any large American base in Vietnam, the countryside resembles nothing more than a dump or the lepers' pigyard, with backed-up cesspool, I would say, except that the lepers are too poor to afford Miller's High Life and too suspect politically to receive canned surplus products. Even the B-52's will not be able to "sterilize the area," since cans are not combustible. They can be flattened out, and a form of Pop Art is spreading in rural Vietnam; new house fronts (not just in refugee camps) are made of flattened-out cans, sometimes in bright patterns, as with beer, ginger ale, and Coca-Cola containers, and sometimes in plain old tin, as with corned beef hash and Campbell's soup. Yet even if every hut and hovel in Vietnam were faced with this new building material, it would hardly reduce the vast rubbish heap, the fecal matter of our civilization, we have left in the country. As our troops increase, there will be more and more.

Not to mention another kind of garbage. As we approached Da Nang, the baron pointed to some wreckage a few yards from the road. An American bomber had crashed there a few months ago, he said, killing eighty-one people. The crash was due to mechanical failure, which perhaps means that the eighty-one people should not be counted as war casualties but as simple victims of an accident, like the children burned by gasoline stoves (because of the kerosene shortage) or by the straw roofs and cardboard sidings catching fire in a crowded refugee camp, who must be carefully distinguished from children burned by napalm. The bomber wreck was lying with one wing atilt, its nose buried in a roof, amid the splinters of houses or buildings. Nobody had bothered to inter it. There was another one a few miles off, the baron said. He was not sure how many people it had killed.

Back in the Marine Press Base, there were Martinis-on-the-rocks, steaks, *vin rosé*, cognac. Behind the restaurant counter was a sign: "Have you taken your weekly malaria pill? Help yourself." And the Marines were all very nice, really nice, both officers and men; they asked what I had seen and was it interesting. Conditions were unspeakable, I said, mentioning the first camp's water supply. They nodded, hitched up chairs, as though they were glad to get the lowdown on those camps. And being Americans, they were disturbed to hear about the dirty water. As well as pleased to learn that the German team had paid them a compliment: the Marines, the baron told me, had been very helpful about getting them supplies and sometimes transport for the wounded.

The Marines' receptiveness was strikingly different from the behavior of civilian bureaucrats in Saigon, who, I discovered, did not want to hear about conditions in refugee camps; they stopped listening after the first words and picked up the telephone ("Excuse me a minute") or assumed an abstracted air, as though they were thinking of something more important—the Viet Cong weekly atrocity statistics perhaps. What was curious about the Marines' attitude was that they were interested, but in the way civilians back home might be interested—"You don't say!" Or as though they were leafing through a copy of the *National Geographic* and had hit on an item about a place they had been to on a world tour or a business trip. The same mild interest in "keeping up" that made them subscribe to news magazines and frown over photographs of the floods in Florence.

Whereas the civilian officials, on the whole, behaved like a team of promoters with a dubious "growth" stock they were brokering, many of the military, like these Marines, remained singularly detached, seeming to feel no need to justify the American presence or their own involvement, unconcerned with selling the war (for they in fact were not the salesmen but the product). The Marine colonel at his command post could say forthrightly, "We created the refugees"—something no civilian official would dare to admit, and quite rightly. They could tell stories out of school about Vietnamese corruption and thievery, which they regarded as almost universal, criticize the Chieu Hoi program, mock the ARVN, all this without noticing that if what they were saying was true the public rationale for American intervention disappeared. The Information officers behind them were more sensitive to the dangers of such free talk on the part of their superiors and tried, if possible, to forestall it. In a hamlet in the delta one morning, I asked some army officers what the local government had done about land reform; the briefing captain hurriedly opened his mouth and started to recite some figures, when the colonel cut in—*"Nothing."*

It may be that the Information officers, whose job is to give the reverse of information ("How many of the inhabitants have come back to Rach Kien?" Briefing captain: "About a thousand." Field major, half an hour later: "632"), are more honest, in a way, than the field officers who burst out with the truth. That is, the blunt colonels and sympathetic majors have not been able to realize that this is a war, unlike World War II or the Korean War, in which the truth must not be told, except when it cannot be hidden. Even then it must be turned upside down or restyled, *viz.*, "the problems of success," which also comprised inflation. Those who lie and cover up are implicitly acknowledging this, in some recess of their souls, while the outspoken field officer still lets himself think he is fighting the kind of war where an honest officer can gripe.

In reality, he gives away *less* than the double-talking U.S. bureaucrat in Saigon, who has the answers ready before you can ask the question, who can give you, straight as a die, the chemical formula for the defoliants, harmless to pets and humans, we have begun that day, he announces, to use in the DMZ (as though he had no inkling of the fact previously announced by him—has it slipped his mind?—that we have been bombing the Zone regularly for some time), who when asked if he can supply you with some figures on civilian casualties says no, unfortunately not, there are none, but offers you instead statistics on Viet Cong terror, who, like Johnson's emissary (now civilian head of "pacification");* can declare "simply" to the press, to back up an

---

* This was Robert Komer, later ambassador to Turkey, at present with the Rand Corporation.

optimistic estimate: "I feel a new sensa confidence in the air." A discovery I have made in Vietnam is that those who seek to project an "image" are unaware of how they look. The truth they are revealing has become invisible to them.

One example of this revealing blindness can illustrate. In the OCO offices in Saigon, I was offered a freshly typed list of Viet Cong acts of terror committed during the previous week; as the reader must have gathered, this material seems to be the favorite reading of our spokesmen. That and infiltration figures, to give the "background." As I looked down the list I noticed that it included an attack on a U.S. army post! "Is that terrorism?" I wondered, pointing. The official studied the item. "No. It doesn't belong there," he admitted, poring over the type-sheet with a mystified air, like one awakening from a dream. "We'll have to correct that," he added briskly. It was clear that he had offered me those figures in *good faith*, having seen nothing wrong with them; to him an attack on a U.S. army unit, even in wartime, was dastardly.

At present the terror statistics issued to the newspapers are blandly including kidnappings and "murders" of Rural Construction workers, which sounds very atrocious if you do not know (as everyone in Saigon does) that Rural Construction is the old name for Revolutionary Development—the "workers" are paramilitary elements trained and drilled in a special school and sent to "cleanse" (U.S. word) "pacified" hamlets; of each team of fifty-nine, thirty-four are armed for security purposes, *i.e.*, to repel a Viet Cong attack. The sudden switch to the old name is like an alert to the press to watch out for the oncoming lie. Why, you ask, are they cooking these particular statistics?

What is behind it? What are they up to now? Such transparent subterfuges awaken not just disgust but pity for a fast-talking nation that seems to think it is addressing itself to punchcards and mimeograph machines; even a computer, which has memory —if not reason—would jib.

Intellectuals

I*l faut une RÉVOLUTION!"* Major Be said, letting the *r* roll like a cannon ball in the school at Vung Tau. The Italian general listened with an air of dawning surprise. The short broad-faced Vietnamese major was not a military chieftain of the NLF, but the head of the government school for Revolutionary Development, training anti-Communist cadres. The former Italian Chief of Staff and I were being briefed in French by Major Be in a small classroom, while in the next room a group from NBC was being briefed in English by his assistant, Mr. Chau. Thin, slight Mr. Chau, dressed in flowing black calico trousers and a tight black tunic resembling an alb, had taken a degree in English literature at the Sorbonne—he had done his doctoral thesis on Virginia Woolf. Major Be, less at home in foreign languages, wore a black shirt open at the throat and black trousers cut like army fatigues. Their costumes were symbolic of the aims of the program. The 3,000 cadres now in the school (a cadre is one person), when they graduated, would start "constructing" hamlets in teams of fifty-nine, wearing the black-pajama garb of the Viet Cong, which itself had been copied from the dress of the poor peasants. Actually, the peasants today in government-controlled areas wear a medley of clothes, including baseball caps, shorts, and T-shirts; and the RD getup, I heard from a Vietnamese medical student, was regarded as ludicrous in the hamlets he had been visiting during Têt—"If they would only take off those silly pajamas, the people might not laugh at them."

119

"Vraiment une révolution," Major Be insisted. The Italian general cast an inquiring look at me. *"Qu'est-ce qu'il veut dire par ça?"* he murmured. I did not know what Major Be had in mind when he said that his country had to have a revolution, though I agreed with him, whatever he meant. It was monotonous to hear everywhere the same stories of graft and thieving at the expense of the poor; only yesterday an unusually frank OCO man had been telling about what had happened with a distribution of clothing donated through AID—the best clothes had been pilfered by the authorities and never reached the needy. To receive aid at all, he said sadly, poor families had to qualify as needy with the government. "You mean they had to pay to qualify as needy?" He looked at me in silence, by way of an answer.

Still, the briefing I had already had in Saigon on the RD program had hardly prepared me to meet a doctrinaire theoretician of the type of Major Be, who, warming to his subject, was now assuring us that Vietnamese society was *"complètement corrompue"*: the ruling classes, he said, as the general's eyes widened, had always used the laws to serve their own interests. Then, glancing at his watch, he switched to facts and figures.

The program had been started in December 1965. Twenty-eight thousand cadres were already in the field. The school training period lasted twelve weeks, during which each cadre accomplished eleven tasks and went through twelve stages. Upon graduation, each cadre team would work with a hamlet to establish or maintain eleven criteria; an additional nine criteria, achieved with cadre support, would turn a constructed or Old Life Hamlet into a New Life Hamlet. Good results had not yet been produced, but the program was on the way—*"dans la bonne direction."*

General Liuzzi was too new in the country to be up on some of the terminology. A "constructed" hamlet meant not a newly built one but a former Viet Cong hamlet that had been worked over politically to the point where it could now be considered pro-government. A "reconstructed" hamlet meant one that had been "constructed" and then backslid and had had to be "constructed" all over again, but this term, for some reason, had fallen into disfavor, and a "reconstructed" hamlet was now called a "consolidated" hamlet. Finally the goal of each was to become a "real New Life Hamlet."

A "constructed" hamlet backslid because a poor job had been done in rooting out the Viet Cong "infrastructure." Rooting out the "infrastructure," *i.e.*, conducting purges, was the most important task of Major Be's cadres. Major Be, to give him credit, did not use the expression, though the American briefers in Saigon had used it, repeatedly. That word, too freshly minted to be in my dictionary, is already a worn slug in American Vietnamese, tirelessly inserted into dinner-table conversations, briefings, newspaper and magazine articles. Its primary meaning is that the person using it (succinctly or sententiously, depending) has an up-to-date scientific grasp of the workings of underground Communism—a meaning that could not be conveyed by the word "organization" or even "cells." It is not restricted to the few— Harvard political science graduates or Princetonian school-of-government captains; it is as democratic as a subway token. One would not be surprised to hear it mumbled by some high-school dropout as he cleaned his weapon: "Got to get Charlie's infrastructure." To our propaganda men, who like to write of "the faceless Viet Cong" (sometimes appending their photographs), "infrastructure," aside from sounding knowledgeable and hard-headed, probably suggests infra-red—invisible rays just beyond red in the political spectrum.

Major Be and Mr. Chau are the Vietnamese counterparts of the American political scientists who have stamped their vocabulary and their habits of thought on this loony trial of strength in the Asian arena. Here for the first time, political science, as taught and studied in the big American universities, is being applied to war, where it often seems close to science fiction. Such a thing was scarcely dreamed of in World War II, despite the presence of a few professors and intellectuals in the OWI and OSS—no one thought of "studying" the Nazis and learning from them. Only the physical scientists became an auxiliary of the Defense Department.* The present phenomenon, more portentous for the future, if there is one, than Dr. Strangelove—conceivably you can outlaw the Bomb, but what about the Brain?—dates back to the Cold War, when the "science" of Kremlinology was discovered. The sinister Walt Rostow, said now to be closest to the cupped presidential ear, dates back also to that Age of Discovery. The behavior of the enemy was studied under university microscopes, with the aid of samples furnished by defectors to the Free World. Practical experiment, however, was not really feasible until the war in Vietnam provided a laboratory for testing the new weapon, an academic B-52 or Lazy Dog. Watching it operate in Vietnam, in conjunction with the sister "disciplines" of sociology and anthropology ("The Vietnamese don't know how to handle them," an Ameri-

---

* An exception, as we now learn, was the psychoanalyst commissioned by Colonel "Wild Bill" Donovan of the OSS to analyze the personality of Hitler.

can evangelical missionary kindly "filled in" a reporter, alluding to the Montagnard tribes the VC was winning over. "They have no anthropology to guide them"), you wonder whether this branch of knowledge can ever have been designed for anything but war. The notion of a "pure" political science here seems as remote from actuality as atoms-for-peace.

Right after the Geneva Accords, the paramilitary professors began moving into Vietnam, the first being Diem's inventor, Professor Wesley Fishel, of Michigan State. But as long as Eisenhower was in office, the academic expertise on Vietnam remained rather old-fogyish, like the prudent Eisenhower himself. Though the United States gave a large subsidy to Michigan State University to train a Vietnamese police force and to form Vietnamese adepts in Political Science and Public Administration, this, after all, was classic colonial practice. A new wrinkle —Civics 303?—was the addition of some undercover CIA men to the Michigan State faculty (they had academic rank but not tenure apparently), to start a Vietnamese Bureau of Investigation on the model of the FBI. But on the whole the MSU alumni and alumnae you still find in Vietnamese government nooks— nearly every Vietnamese who speaks English seems to have attended Michigan State and to be proud of it—have a certain démodé pathos, like the bangled, coquettish Dr. Hue, Professor of Public Administration at the National Institute of Administration in Saigon, who resembles a road-show revival of Madame Nhu. Professor Fishel's lasting contribution was not Nhu's CIA-trained Secret Police—where are they now?—but the introduction of the word "semantics" into official discourse about Vietnam. "We do ourselves and our Asian neighbors harm when we insist on stretching or shrinking them into our particular semantic bed," he wrote in *The New Leader*, arguing for a "new political vocabulary" in an article wonderfully entitled (Professor Fishel claims by the editors) "Vietnam's Democratic One-Man Rule"—the Procrustean subject was Diem. A democratic "dictator" or a "democratic" dictator? Words failed Professor Fishel. Diem has gone, but embarrassments of the kind he created have not. Almost daily in the press briefing, whenever a newsman raises his hand to ask for clarification of some mealymouthed statement: "I am not going to debate semantics with you," the spokesman replies. "Next?"

It took the New Frontier, though, to really update American "thinking" on Vietnam. A fresh look at the situation by the Kennedy men revealed the need for brand-new tactics with brand-new names: counter-insurgency, special warfare. The notion of counter-insurgency in reality was borrowed from elite French officers who used it in Algeria—with what results, we know. To implement the new approach, and with CIA support, the Army created its Special Forces—the Green Berets—whose task was to combine unconventional fighting (counter-guerrilla activity) with political savvy. The Vietnamese, separate but equal, got *their* Special Forces—the Red Berets—a counter-terror group wearing leopard-spotted uniforms with a tiger's head on the breast pocket; they are still in action, bringing the severed heads of guerrillas or putative guerrillas into a pacified hamlet to show the shocked American colonel. Concurrently, a new, less narrow-minded type of officer appeared in the field, with a traveling library; on the bookshelves in his mountain hideout were the works of Mao, Generals Giap and Grivas, Ho

Chi Minh—doubtless in paperback. Young West Pointers were turned into political strategists on the spot by crash courses in Communism and native psychology, and *Webster's Collegiate Dictionary* was placed on the desk of an old-style general, for convenient reference. The same year—1961—that the Special Forces were created, the Staley Plan was devised by a Stanford economist, Eugene Staley, whose name is now identified with Strategic Hamlets, though his Plan, in fact, was much more comprehensive and undertook a complete restyling of the Vietnamese economy, the political struggle, and the AID program.

No ordinary desk official in Washington could have imagined the Staley Plan. The idea of Strategic Hamlets was not new in itself; Diem and his brother Nhu had founded agrovilles—basically, fortified settlements, also on an Algerian model—which at one time bore the name of Camps of the Just Cause. But Staley *perfected* the agrovilles.* With a professor's fondness for the diagram, he divided the country into yellow zones, blue zones, red zones, the yellow zones being governmental (available for U.S. aid), the blue dubious, and the red VC. His plan was to transfer the population, wherever movable, into Prosperity Zones, which were to contain 15,000 model hamlets, for a starter, all heavily fortified and surrounded by barbed wire. With the enthusiastic co-operation of General Maxwell Taylor (who is still testifying before the Senate as an authority on Vietnam), about 2,500 Staleyized hamlets were actually built. Life in them was diagrammed down to the last detail. Everyone was obliged to purchase and wear a uniform—four different color

---

* I owe this description of Strategic Hamlets to Kuno Knoebel's interesting book, *Victor Charlie.* A very different account is given by Roger Hilsman in *To Move a Nation.*

combinations, according to age and sex—and to carry two identity cards, one for moving about in the hamlet and the other for
leaving it. The gates were closed by a guard every night at seven
o'clock and opened at six in the morning. Persons consenting to
be resettled in a strategic hamlet had their houses burned and
crops sprayed with poison chemicals, so as to leave a razed area
behind for the Viet Cong—this was the first widespread application of the science of chemistry to the political struggle. The
U.S. government paid compensation, of course.

Those who did not agree to relocation were removed forcibly
and their villages burned and sprayed anyway; some reluctant
peasants and village elders were executed, as examples, by the
Vietnamese army. Inside the hamlets, strict political control was
exercised; executions took place here, too. The settlers were
gouged for special taxes and other arbitrary impositions; the
compensation money was not turned over to them in many instances. They were ordered to get any relations they had in the
red zones to join them in the hamlet within three months; if
they failed to recruit them, they were punished. Professor Staley,
no doubt, was not responsible for the excesses of the program as
implemented; he had *only* drawn a totalitarian blueprint for
the Vietnamese and American advisers to follow, based on *his*
experience of the country.

The Staley Plan proved to be the greatest gift the U.S. gave
the Viet Cong. Naturally, revolts broke out in the strategic hamlets; sometimes the settlers put fire to them. When Diem fell, the
program was dropped, and Professor Staley apparently went to
Limbo, to join Professor Fishel. No one mentions them any
more. But in fact the Strategic Hamlet idea reappeared, in less

126

draconic form, in the Rural Construction program, which failed
and was replaced by the Revolutionary Development program.
Revolutionary Development adds the black pajamas, as a stiff-
ener, to Rural Construction. And the black-pajama uniform
proclaims a thing that was always implicit in such conceptions
as counter-insurgency and special warfare and in some features
of the Staley Plan—plagiarism of the enemy's techniques.

Indeed the "other" war dramatically declared by Johnson at
Honolulu is an idea rather tardily lifted from the Viet Cong.
Long before the Americans thought of it, the VC was building
schools for the peasantry, digging wells, teaching better methods of agriculture. But because the Viet Cong did not control
the mass media, the "secret" of its appeal remained a secret, at
least from the military, who are digging the wells, building the
schools, under the impression that this grass-roots courtship
originated in the big heart of America. It would not occur to a
general (unless he were Caesar) that he was plagiarizing from
the enemy; to a straight-shooting man of action, the thought is
distasteful.

And now here was Major Be, his slant eyes gleaming, talking
about a "revolution," stealing the NLF's thunder to pass on to
his cadres. Yet the NLF in its proclamations never speaks of
revolution, but, instead, of "raising the living standards of the
population," "economic progress without violent changes," a
"campaign for freedom against repression," "forming a broad
democratic base." That seems to have escaped Major Be's spon-
sors, who are sure they know what the NLF *really* intends—a
complete Communist take-over. Let us say they are right. What
follows is sheer comedy: the NLF aims at a social revolution,

127

while taking care not to pronounce the word, and the South Vietnamese junta launches a program styled "revolutionary," while failing to institute the mildest reforms. The attempt on the part of the Americans and their local star pupils to turn this into a war of ideas is something to make the angels, if there are any, dry their tears and laugh.

In the next room, NBC had finished its briefing session. But Major Be, carried away by the courteous old general's slightly puzzled interest, was quoting Mao: "The water protects the fish." The people, he elucidated, were the water in which the guerrilla swam like a fish while the alien enemy drowned. Revolutionary Development was adapting Mao's proverb to fight the VC. The school at Vung Tau was a hatchery to breed little fish—the cadres—to protect the water, which in turn would protect the big fish, that is, the government forces.

I decided to ask about land reform. Land reform, said the major, was useless without a "cultural base" to support it. Western ideas were necessary and Western technology. On the other hand, the Vietnamese people must not be turned into beggars. A tractor in each hamlet would be the most beautiful symbol of modern civilization. The tractor; not the airplane and the bomber. The general nodded thoughtfully. He was impressed by Major Be. He inquired where he had studied, meaning, no doubt, where on earth he had learned his ideology. *"Mon université est la campagne vietnamienne,"* replied the stocky major, who was not forthcoming about his past. Mr. Chau, who was, had been until recently a professor of French and English literature at Hue University. Probably he had left in disgust during the Struggle Movement of the previous year. He was against

TV, Hondas, transistors, and other corrupting influences on
Vietnamese youth.

We left the school buildings, which dated back to the French
and had a monastic atmosphere, like a Jesuit seminary, with
Major Be as the Father Superior, the organizing dynamo, and
Mr. Chau, more scholastic, in his black habit, as the Prefect of
studies. Major Be's predecessor as head of the Vung Tau school
had been a different type—the guitar-playing Major Mai, whom
the CIA was backing as a winner last year and who is now barely
recollected by the American officials who once vigorously en-
dorsed him. "What happened to Major Mai?" Gavin Young of
The Observer asked a leading figure in the Embassy. "*Who?* Oh
yes, him. Well, he didn't work out. Don't know where he is
now." "That's strange. You were so enthusiastic about him last
year." "Oh, I wouldn't say that, Gavin. You've got that wrong."
"But I have it in my notes." "He was *on probation*, Gavin," the
American said reproachfully. In the days of Major Mai, the
theme at Vung Tau had been pure Vietnamese nationalism; the
cadres got military training and close coaching in the story of
the Dragon King and the Lady of the Fairies—the legendary
parents of Vietnam—which was then the message designed to
win the hearts and minds of the Vietnamese people. In those
days the school had a corps of CIA advisers, dressed in black
pajamas and sandals, except for their chief, who, as pictured by
Young, was dressed and behaved like a deputy sheriff in Selma,
Alabama, with cigar between his teeth, and sport shirt hanging
out over his spilling belly. Now, however, there were no CIA
men around, unless deeply disguised (though invisible American "advisers" were mentioned as among the cadres' teachers,

and in fact the CIA is still backing the school), no Dragon King or Lady of the Fairies; there were only Major Be and "Virginia Woolf" and the teachings of Chairman Mao.

Out in the woods, we were taken to view the cadres. Here, said the major, indicating the sandy forest, theory was digested and turned into technique. Grouped on benches, in a large open hut, a class was receiving instruction from a native teacher and feeding it back in shouts, like a child's catechism: "Who made the world?" "God made the world." Or, as the brochures furnished to arriving journalists in their press kit present *our* sacred doctrine in easy question-and-answer form: "*Question:* Why is the United States waging war against North Vietnam? *Answer:* The U.S. is not doing that at all. We are helping the free government and people of the Republic of Vietnam defend their freedom and independence against aggression, directed and in part supplied from North Vietnam. . . . *Question:* How have the Viet Cong managed to gain and hold control over parts of South Vietnam? *Answer:* The Viet Cong rule by force and terror. Deliberate killings and kidnappings are instruments of their policy. . . . *Question:* Do the Viet Cong attack only South Vietnamese soldiers and civilian officials? *Answer:* By no means. The Viet Cong also attack teachers, agricultural technicians, anti-malaria teams—anybody, in fact, who is working to improve social and economic conditions in South Vietnam." Some Vietnamese version of this kind of thing was what the cadres in the forest were chanting. Major Be did not interpret. In Major Mai's time, the instruction went as follows: "*Question:* Are the Americans our friends if they defend the nation of the Great

King Hung Vuong, son of the Dragon? *Answer:* Yes. *Question:*
Are they our masters? *Answer:* Never."

Next, the cadres were lined up in military formation and
drilled. To each order, they responded with a terrifying howl.
As he surveyed the trainees, the Italian general's enthusiasm
cooled; very poor-grade military material, he observed. In Saigon, a Vietnamese girl had dismissed the whole outfit as "draft
dodgers"—a common view—but though some of these unpre-
possessing youths were evidently of military age, many would
have been dismissed as unfit for military service anywhere, and
as for the sad, somnolent, gray-haired grandfathers in the
ranks, whatever had caused them to enlist in this pathetic brigade of "revolutionary" youth, it cannot have been fear of the
draft.

We asked Major Be what qualifications a cadre had to have to
be admitted to the school. All had to be literate, he said, and
each new cadre had to be sponsored by two full-fledged member
cadres—a system patterned on that of the NLF and the People's
Revolutionary Party and suited to a clandestine organization or
secret fraternity. Evidently, an effort was being made to invest
the cadres with the aura of an initiate, through ritual and the
abracadabra of numbers. Each team, when it went into a hamlet
(where it would spend three to six months), would be given
ninety-eight "works" to accomplish; thirty-four cadres (this
figure is sometimes given as thirty-three) would be detailed to
security, nineteen to general staff, one to agriculture, one to
co-operatives, one to construction and public works, one to public health, one to education and culture, one to grievance and

public investigation. Given this division of labor, it was not surprising that I had never been able to see the RD cadres actually doing anything in a hamlet, except lounging around with a weapon or eating. Yet their training was evidently successful in instilling an elite spirit, to the extent that complaints of their "arrogance" and "insolence" are mentioned even in Vietnamese government reports.

As it is turning out, some of these "draft dodgers" would be safer in the ARVN: recent newspaper stories are full of the killings—always described as "murders"—of RD workers, who, despite their military training and the arms they carry, have been incapable of defending themselves in the hamlets they are assigned to against VC raids. Probably their overbearing ways make them popular targets.

The classes were breaking for lunch when a BBC cameraman arrived to film them. NBC was only taking notes. They reformed, to sing us a few stanzas of their school song; its theme was the eleven tasks, twelve stages. Most of the cadres in the forest were in Stage Two or Three. Twelve weeks, said the Italian general, regarding this performance, would not be enough. He eyed Major Be with misgiving. *"C'est un fanatique,"* he summed up, shaking his head. He would have liked to believe in Major Be. At lunch in the mess hall, talk turned to negotiations. Major Be's face darkened. *"La sale manoeuvre de la paix du pape,"* he said. The Pope's dirty peace trick. General Liuzzi refused the soup.

Across the table, Mr. Chau spoke contemptuously of South Vietnamese students in Paris who discussed and argued with North Vietnamese students. I defended them. *"La politique*

132

n'est pas un salon," he said in a venomous tone. To him, debate in politics, let alone compromise, was decadent, like formalism in art to an orthodox member of the Union of Soviet Writers. Here, as often in Vietnamese government circles, the mere word "*negotiations*" was enough to make a mask of cordiality drop.

Possibly "Virginia Woolf" and the major should be classed as fascists (as someone has put it, revolutionary slogans minus a revolution equals fascism), despite or even because of their likeness to doctrinaire Communists of the unreconstructed Stalinist type. Major Be's beautiful tractor advanced toward us out of the final sequence of an old Soviet movie, and "the Pope's dirty peace trick" could have been spat out equally well in Albania or possibly Peking. What had led this ascetic pair to work with the Americans was difficult to guess, especially in the case of the fastidious Mr. Chau, who clearly detested everything connected with the American way of life, everything soft, flabby, super-fatted, PX-distributed.

The Italian general elicited that Major Be had fought with the Viet Minh against the French, which meant he had served under Giap; he seemed to be a Northerner who had come south at some unstated time. The pure and unyielding principles of Hanoi exercise an attraction on the displaced intellectuals who fled the scene, including those who are most fanatically anti-Communist. The day after I visited Vung Tau, I met another "revolutionary," manifestly sincere, an army captain and acting district chief who in former life had been a private French teacher and a portrait photographer, like Ho, whose province he came from. He was eager for me to explain to the Americans, who might not understand, that it was "*le peuple, le bas peuple*" that mattered, not the government bureaucracy (of which he was an element) or the people on top. In the U.S. army command post, a salient in VC territory, he seized a ballpoint and drew diagrams. One, a pyramid with a demagogue on top and an unstable base, was "no good" (he illustrated how it could fall over); the other, a squat trapezoid, with a broad base, the people, on which a flat top rested, was good. The American junior officers listened indulgently; they had evidently heard all this before and considered him a visionary, though "a great guy." His views and didactic excitement reminded me of Major Be, and I asked him what he thought of Revolutionary Development. To my surprise, he disapproved. *"En toute franchise,"* he said, the school at Vung Tau was a perfect illustration of the "bad" pyramid. He also disapproved of the Constitutional Assembly: too much talk, he said, and too many competing blocs. Like Major Be, he spurned any thought of negotiations. He dreamed only of victory: "The march on Hanoi!" The Americans grinned and shook their heads; they had heard this before, too, and were not buying it. He looked hurt.

His case was typical. Many South Vietnamese have a double fear of the Americans: that, despite what they say, the Americans are there to take over their country, and that the Americans will betray them by making peace with Hanoi. That is, they are torn between the fear that the Americans will stay and the fear that they will go. It was the same with the French. Irredentists like the ex-photographer look back with trembling horror on *"le jour d'infâme"*—July 20, 1954, the infamous day of the Geneva Accords. Perhaps those who are working directly with the CIA, like Major Be and Mr. Chau, feel less distrust of their saviors than those who are obliged to work with the regular Army, which, in their eyes, is less reliable politically. And from their point of view they may be right. The Army, like all armies, basically wants to go home, while the CIA wants to stay, discreetly behind the scenes, furnishing money and encouragement to indigenous groups.

In any event, whatever sense of national emergency—or despair—had moved Major Be and Mr. Chau to work with the CIA, it was easy to see what had moved the CIA to work with *them*, even assuming that they, too, might be "on probation." The ties that have come to light between the CIA and the intellectual community in the United States have surprising parallels in Vietnam—surprising, at least, to anyone who has not observed the gradual and typically modern fusion of intelligence with "intelligence." The CIA has been a promoter of various unorthodox experiments in South Vietnam, supplying not just the funds and some of the personnel, but the spark, the touch of genius allied to lunacy. The Green Berets, for instance, are referred to as a Spook outfit by our own government people in Saigon—usually with a wink. It is impossible to say how many of the books, not all bad, published about Vietnam have been financed, with or without the author's knowledge, by the CIA. They are backing the Khmer-Serai (Free Khmer), a right-wing movement against Prince Sihanouk and using the Special Forces —the Ho Chi Minh readers—near the Cambodian border to train Khmer-Serai troops. They have their own airline, Air America.

As in the U.S., the CIA in Vietnam prides itself on being more catholic in its patronage than overt government agencies. Con-

135

gress, it is always argued in defense of secrecy, would be too stupid to vote appropriations for radical-sounding ventures, which is probably true. Congress might have bought Major Mai, strumming his guitar, but not Major Be. You would have to tone him down a bit for home consumption; what does he *mean*, Vietnamese society is completely corrupt? But beyond such practical considerations, the CIA has a real affinity with ex-leftists and pseudo-leftists of all stripes, as well as with the radical right. It *likes* intellectuals, which is natural, first because they are walking repositories of information, and second because the CIA sees itself as a lonely mastermind, the poet and unacknowledged legislator of the government. Finally, the CIA, collectively speaking, is an autodidact which never had time to get its Ph.D. and yearns to meet real, *motivated* political theorists and oddballs and have a *structured* conversation with them. The relentless resort to academic jargon about the war in Vietnam, on the part of half-educated spokesmen and commentators, doubtless reveals the CIA influence on people who may be unaware of it.

You never know whether someone you meet in Vietnam is a CIA agent or just a product of CIA thought. What about Sergeant Mulligan (not his real name), Boston College, B.A., Purdue University, M.A., did his Master's thesis on John C. Calhoun—"an original mind. The only original mind in American political thought. Jefferson stole everything from Locke and Adam Smith"? On the floor of his jeep is the *National Review* and *1964: The Fear Campaign Against Goldwater*. He despises the Arvin, who run instead of fighting (examples given); the only "friendly forces" he trusts in combat are the Khmer-Serai.

He is with "Special Services" but is on his way to dinner with the Green Berets (invitation extended): "the best talk in Saigon."

Or what about Colonel Corson (real name), a Marine tank commander in the hills above Da Nang, engaged in pacification? A graduate of the University of Chicago, studied with Korzybski, taught at a college in Florida, worked or served in China. Eleven thousand peasants are the material he has been given to mould. He defines the method he uses as Empirical Causality. He quotes Lenin: "Scratch a peasant, and you'll find a bourgeois." "Well, I'm scratching. And scratching." His young officers have made a painted scale model, like a crèche, in papier-mâché, of an ideal Vietnamese hamlet, which will probably really be built. Colonel Corson is ingenious. He has designed a large pigsty suited to local conditions and he is donating his Marine garbage to feed the peasants' pigs, solving two problems with one concise stroke. He has asked an engineer to design him a mill for the region, and the Marine engineer has designed the very latest thing. " 'Take it away,' I told him, 'and try to remember what a mill was like when you were a kid or when your father was a kid. Then build me that.' "

He is also cautious. He gave the peasants seeds and before going ahead with his hamlet program he waited to see whether they sold them on the black market. When they didn't, he proceeded. He is intelligent. He used Marine explosives to dynamite the fish in the river in order to show the peasants that there were bigger fish available than they were catching with their present nets. On the wall of his command post was a photograph of the dynamiting operation that seemed to be there mainly for his own pleasure. "I hope you're not planning to introduce fishing with dynamite to these people," I said. The answer was no. He had done it once, as a demonstration, and then given the fish to the peasants to sell on the market; with the profits, they were buying new and larger nets that would catch the bigger fish.

He is a cynic. To him, the profit motive is the sole incentive capable of spurring anybody to productive effort. "You wrote *The Group* to make money, didn't you?" When I answered no, the fact that it had made so much money had surprised me, he looked actually startled. "What do you write for, then?" In the center of the model hamlet, which his officers, like children at Christmas, had stayed up half the night to finish, was a large dollar sign, painted bronze. He gave a crooked smile. He was actually, or so he claimed, planning to erect it as a monument, seven feet high, in the hamlet. The young captain and the young lieutenant smiled. He was a man of whom it could be said, "He was worshipped by his officers." Partly because he amused them; he was witty and sardonic. And he had a sort of fantasy that did not chime badly with his brass tacks. In one corner of the model hamlet was a thatched apiary; one of the peasants was going to be transformed into a beekeeper. Bees and pigs and grains and big river fish—the colonel's georgic, though, had realism behind it. He was trying to wean the peasants away from the monoculture—rice—the French had saddled them with and which, with the rent system and government taxes, had turned them into paupers.

He did not want to be suspected of altruism. "I'm not doing any of this for the Vietnamese people. I'm doing it for *me*." He had challenged the Viet Cong to come into one of the hamlets, with a safe-conduct, at Christmas-time and debate him in the marketplace. They had refused the offer but then one night they had approached with loud-speakers, to broadcast against him to the people. " 'They just want you to make a buck,' the Viet Cong told them. And I said, 'Yeah. Yeah.' " There was a price, he was pleased to say, on the head of every one of his Civic Action people, which proved he was winning the argument. Empirical Causality was working. Or as he also called it, "the Charisma of Success."

He was not sparing of sarcasms for other American ideologists working in the field. He derided a study of a Vietnamese village made by an outfit of opinion-researchers that had worked for Kennedy in the 1960 election. "Two hundred thousand dollars was paid for that study, and they interviewed *six* Vietnamese." All the professorial research teams collecting and analyzing Vietnamese data—there are three, including RAND, on the scene—to the colonel, were softheaded or grafters or would-be thought-controllers or all three—a prejudiced opinion I shared, though I had not seen their studies, many of which are secret. I asked him what he thought of the Chieu Hoi program, to me one of the most odious features of the pacification drive. "We are just subsidizing traitors." The colonel agreed, though not for moral reasons. He thought it was stupid to try to make political converts of deserters. "Somebody dreamed that up in Arlington, Virginia. 'Open Arms!' If I want a man, I buy him." He did not seem to care for Johnson, whom he referred to as "Lyndon-Baby."

The thought that Colonel Corson was somewhat right-wing had been forcing itself into my mind, though I tried to shut the door on it. I drew a deep breath and asked him what he thought of Goldwater. The captain and the lieutenant at the neighboring desks stopped typing; they smiled quickly at each other. The colonel, musing, set down his beer glass. " 'In your heart you know he's stupid,' " he said with a grin. He had caught the direction of my question and told a story of throwing a one-armed (or one-legged) newspaperman down the stairs, back in Chicago. "He called me a Fascist and a Communist in the same breath." It was hard to find anybody on the American political horizon that Colonel Corson approved of, though he mentioned "a lady in Senator Jackson's office."

He believed in the $ as an instrument of Empirical Causality, but even in this profession of faith there was a note of saturnine self-mockery. The conversation became very confused when I remarked that most of his pacification ideas would work just as well in a socialist context. There was nothing specifically capitalist about feeding the Marines' garbage to the peasants' pigs. He tried to show me that the free market was crucial; Marx had not understood this. But I could not follow him because his language, suddenly, turned into an opaque forest of jargon substantives, and at that moment the unreality of the scene—the ironic colonel sitting like an unintelligible Socrates among his disciples with a model Vietnamese village on the table—struck me with wonder. He was good at gauging your thoughts. A few moments later, he said, as if idly, "There are no homosexuals in my battalion. If I find one, out he goes. The men that work for me have to like *girls*." And when I was complimenting him, mentally, on the peaceful idyl of his neat hut in the woods, he looked straight at me and said, as if to make sure there would be no misunderstanding: "I don't send anybody into Civic Action until they've been out and *killed*." Colonel Corson was playing God and the Devil up there in the hills behind Da Nang. Unlike less reflective and less capable officers, he held the little country of Vietnam—where the people wore conical hats and lived in bamboo thickets—like a toy in his hand.

At the other end of the verbal spectrum, this Marine officer is possibly more of a revolutionist than Major Be. He was certainly more forthright. But his tall bronze dollar sign is likely to remain his personal war monument—a symbol only, like Major Be's tractor. I doubted that Washington would ever let him build and unveil it. Despite his semantics, he is an *old-fashioned* free-enterpriser, being actually enterprising, for one thing, and out of sympathy with the principle of waste inherent in modern capitalism. And he exposed a little too frankly his contempt for the AID missionaries, for med-cap teams, and such sales gimmicks as the Chieu Hoi program, which other sources say is a brain child of the CIA. So that I would say no: the colonel, though sometimes scary and what he might call Machiavellian, is not a Spook.*

The Open Arms Program is a typical instance of counterinsurgency thinking and has the earmarks of a CIA project: the CIA has a special rapport with the traitor (who, if he is not bought, is usually an intellectual), like the symbiosis between the policeman and the criminal. Of course it is not new to use traitors in wartime, but in the past their function has been restricted to opening the city gates by stealth, spying, and smuggling out information, sowing discontent among the population, as was tried in World War II by the modern means of

---

* Colonel William Corson left the Marine Corps and wrote a highly critical book, *The Betrayal* (1968), about the war in Vietnam. What he opposed, though, was not the war but its *conduct*.

radio-beaming. It is true, too, that deserters have often helped swing the balance in war, even when they simply went home—as many of the ARVN do now—and took no further part in the fighting. But the experiences of the Cold War and, later, of Cuba opened the minds of the Americans to the uses of the "defector"—a traitor and a deserter combined in one *politically conscious* person. The difference between a refugee or an exile and a defector is that the refugee or exile does not take on his status as a profession.

The idea of the Chieu Hoi program is not just to cause wide-scale desertions from the Viet Cong by loud-speakers broadcasting from planes and helicopters and by pamphlet drops, with the usual promises of money and good treatment—a natural enough proceeding in a civil war—but to turn every deserter into a defector by "re-educating" him in a camp. The Chieu Hoi centers are even more depressing than the refugee camps, although they are much less crowded and do not lack water and elementary sanitation. A Hoi Chanh or "returnee," once he turns himself in, becomes a prisoner condemned to a forty-five-to-sixty-day stretch for having "chosen freedom." He is finger-printed, interrogated ("The informing they do is on a purely voluntary basis," the American adviser emphasizes), indoctrinated, and finally released into society with a set of identity papers. In the Chieu Hoi camps I saw, which resembled old-fashioned reform schools, the inmates were roaming dully about the yard or simply lying listless on their bunks; one or two were writing letters. In theory, each defector receives vocational training (indeed a job is promised him by the loud-speakers), but the only evidence of this that was visible in one camp was a

Hoi Chanh sitting in a barber's chair having his hair cut by another Hoi Chanh, while, across the small dirty room, two tailor's apprentices were cutting out a pajama; in the other camp, it was Têt, and no one was doing anything, but there was no sign of equipment or tools to work with.

The Americans agree that the vocational program is not "rolling"; one explanation given is that the defectors are coming in so fast that they are overtaxing the facilities—another of the "problems of success." And the job prospects of the Hoi Chanh, trained or not, are bad. He re-enters society with the stigma of having been a Viet Cong, to which is added the stigma of treachery. The Americans at one time hoped to organize an army of defectors (on the Bay of Pigs model, no doubt), with colonels, captains, and other ranks; this, it was argued, would give the defectors "status." But the thought did not appeal to the Vietnamese army.

The most active part of the day in the Chieu Hoi camps is spent in indoctrination classes, where the defectors are supposedly decontaminated of VC ideology. Yet it seems that quite often the first they learn of the Viet Cong program is in these sessions, and many find it attractive—which may account for the regular one per cent that defect back at the end of the training period.

To join an Armed Propaganda Squadron probably represents the best job future for a Hoi Chanh. These are defectors organized into armed groups of thirty-six who travel about the country, as proselytizers, with the ARVN and the U.S. armed forces; when a hamlet is captured, their job is to question suspects. "Mean little kid, that one," said an American civilian, of one he found torturing a villager. That is their reputation, and it may be that those volunteering show a special ability for the work.

In February, the Chieu Hoi statistics were rising like a barometer. The return of these prodigal sons caused more exultation among higher-up Americans than the destruction of a Viet Cong rice cache or a successful bomb strike on the North. A victory for their leaflets and loud-speakers had come to mean more to them than a victory in the field. (All the time, as we now know, the ranks of the Viet Cong were mysteriously swelling, while infiltration from the North had diminished.) The Vietnamese themselves are not especially interested in the Chieu Hoi —they might prefer simply to shoot them on arrival—and the ordinary American soldiers, according to reporters, view them with disfavor. This badly damaged human material is a strange and shifty base on which to build a society. If fear or near-starvation brought them in (tuberculosis is frequent among defectors, an American source says), their change of allegiance is pitiable. If the promise of a job and money brought them in, it is sad. If our propaganda appeals brought them in, it is farcical.

According to official figures, 20,242 Hoi Chanh came over in 1966. It is hoped, at the very least, to double that in 1967. The political scientists, the OCO men, the AID men are watching, as they say, to see. What they do not see is the implications. If the pressures on the Viet Cong and its dependents increase, this means that increasing numbers of peasant guerrillas and part-time guerrillas will desert the Viet Cong and their villages to become jobless defectors; the target, presumably, would be total defection. No other formula for "integrating" the Viet Cong into Vietnamese life has been suggested.

The Open Arms Program and Revolutionary Development
(which now, I notice, has quietly mutated into Rural Development—has Major Be been fired?)* are the core, it is said with
quiet satisfaction, of the U.S. and RVN pacification drive. The
best that can be said of them is that, though totalitarian in ambition—isolate population cells and "re-educate" them for democracy—they are very inefficient.

The Chieu Hoi program, of course, is not dependent for its
success on its absurd leaflets and broadcasts, but on military
pressure, especially bombing, defoliation, crop-spraying, destruction of rice supplies, and what is known as "Resources Control." The stated object is to deprive the Viet Cong of food and
other resources, including medical supplies and nurses: a native
nurse suspected of treating Viet Cong can be executed as an
enemy cadre, while an American nurse or an RVN nurse, if
kidnapped or killed by a Viet Cong terror group, is, naturally, a
civilian. What is not stated, though, is that the punitive measures
taken to starve and weaken the Viet Cong punish more cruelly
the non-combatants in VC territory, who, being non-combatants,
cannot even interest the CIA as defectors. It has been estimated
by a former Hoi Chanh who has made his way to Europe that a
quarter of the population—peasants—will be killed or die of
malnutrition or from lack of medical care.

To political scientists, however, the word "genocide" is quite
unsuitable to describe what is happening. Genocide is *deliberate*. It is the same with bombs and mortars. If the Viet Cong
plants a bomb in a theater, that is an atrocity, but if the Americans bomb a village that is "different." When you ask how it is
different, the answer is that the VC action was deliberate, while

---

* Major, now Colonel, Be is still (1973) head of the Vung Tan school, but there are
rumors that he will soon be replaced. Mr. Chau has been in jail since 1970 after a
military trial which was held to be unconstitutional by the Vietnamese Supreme
Court. He was charged with anti-government activities.

the U.S. action was accidental. But in what way accidental if the fliers saw the village and could assume there were people in it and knew from experience that the bombs would go off? Well, the fliers were really aiming at the Viet Cong; if they hit some civilians, that was unintentional—it just happened. But it happens all the time, doesn't it? Yes, but each time it is an accident. In the American view, no area bombing implies premeditation of the results that follow, while every grenade hurled by a Viet Cong is launched in conformance with a *theory* and therefore possesses will and consciousness.

It is peculiar that the academic experts who have been studying guerrilla techniques, Communism, "wars of liberation" for nearly two decades have been unable to face the question of intention in this kind of warfare, where combatants and non-combatants are all but inseparable, while U.S. means of killing and exterminating have been reaching a point close to perfection. Foreknowledge of the consequences of an action that is then performed generally argues the will to do it; if this occurs repeatedly, and the doer continues to protest that he did not will the consequences, that suggests an extreme and dangerous dissociation of the personality. Is that what is happening with the Americans in Vietnam, where words, as if "accidentally," have broken loose from their common meanings, where the Viet Cong guerrilla is pictured as a man utterly at one with his grenade, which fits him like an extension of his body, and the American, on the other hand, is pictured as completely sundered from his precision weaponry, as though he had no control over it, in the same way that Johnson, escalating, feigns to have no option in the war and to react, like an automat, to "moves" from Hanoi?

Solutions

W ell, what would you do?" Sooner or later, the critic of U.S. policy in Vietnam is faced with that question — a real crusher. Up to that point, he may have been winning the argument. His opponent may have conceded that it was a mistake to send American troops here in the first place, that there was no commitment under SEATO or any other "instrument" requiring it, that the war is horribly destructive, that pacification is not working, that Hanoi is not responding co-operatively to the bombing—in short, that everything that has been done up to the present instant has been wrong. But now resting comfortably on this mountain of errors, he looks down magnanimously on the critic and invites him to offer a solution. He is confident that the critic will be unable to come up with one. And in a sense he is right. If you say "Get Out"—the only sane answer—he pounces. "How?" And he sits back smiling. He has won. The tables are turned, and the critic is on the defensive. If he tries to outline a plan for rapid withdrawal, conscious that 464,000 troops, plus their civilian supporting services, cannot be pulled out overnight (and what about the "loyal" Vietnamese—should they be left behind or do we owe them an airlift to Taiwan?), the plan inevitably appears feeble and amateurish in comparison with the massed power and professionalism of the war actually being waged.

The fatal weakness in the thinking of most of Johnson's critics is not to perceive that that question is a booby trap. In general, the more eminent they are, the more alacrity they show in popping up with "positive recommendations for policy," "solutions," proposals for gradual and prudent disengagement, lest anybody think they are just carping and have no better alternatives of their own. Take the painful example of Arthur Schlesinger's *The Bitter Heritage*: "cogent, lucid, penetrating—tells us what really ought to be done about Vietnam" (John Gunther). It is cogent, lucid, penetrating *until* Schlesinger tells us what ought to be done in a wishful chapter entitled "The Middle Course," urging a political solution while insisting on the need to keep applying force (in moderation) to get it; the pursuit of negotiations while "tapering off" the bombing (no cease-fire on the ground, he warns—too dangerous); a promise to the Viet Cong of a "say" in the future of Vietnam but not, it is implied, too much of a say; reliance on Oriental "consensual procedures" or the precedent of Laos to solve any little difficulties in the way of a coalition government— a chapter that anyone who agrees with Schlesinger's negative arguments would like to snip out of the volume, working carefully with a razor blade so as to leave no traces before lending it to a less convinced friend. Presented with Schlesinger's formula for meeting the Communist "threat," the reader is likely to think that Johnson's formula is better.

The same sinking feeling was produced by Richard Goodwin in *The New Yorker*, by J. K. Galbraith's "moderate solution" (hailed by James Reston), by Senator Fulbright's eight-point program, and, sad to say, by the Fulbright hearings taken as a whole. What emerges, when all the talk is over, is that none of these people really opposes the war. Or not enough to stop thinking in terms of "solutions," all of which imply continuing the war by slightly different means until the Viet Cong or Hanoi (Schlesinger holds out the exciting possibility of an "exploitable split" between the Viet Cong and Hanoi) is ready to make peace.

Even a man like George Kennan, who evidently believes the war to be wrong and testified impressively against our policy before the Fulbright Committee, did not have an inner attorney to warn him to rest his case there. Instead, pressed by bullish senators to say what he would do in the President's place (never mind what he would have *done*), Kennan fell back on the enclave strategy, making an easy target for the military, who can demonstrate without trouble how enclaves failed the French in *their* war, how Tito's Partisans knew they had won when they finally maneuvered the Nazis into coastal enclaves, how in fact the last place you want to be when faced with guerrillas is holed up in an enclave. And Kennan himself must have known that he had lost a round in the fight for peace when he allowed himself to be cornered into offering inconsequent armchair recommendations, in the midst of the hostile terrain, bristling with alert TV aerials, of U.S. popular feeling.

These are the errors of an opposition that wants to be statesmanlike and responsible, in contrast to the "irresponsible" opposition that is burning its draft card or refusing to pay taxes. To make sure that it can be told apart from these undesirables, it behaves on occasion like a troop of Eagle Scouts. Think of the ludicrous message sent to North Vietnam by sixteen Congressional doves—an appeal to Ho to understand that they are

151

a) an unrepresentative minority and b) loyal Americans whose speeches were not meant to be overheard and "misinterpreted" by Hanoi.

Or it can assume the voice of Johnson. A recent New York *Post* editorial sternly criticized the Ky government's suspension of free speech (guaranteed by the new Constitution) and then continued: "We cannot heed the counsel of timid or misguided persons and withdraw. We dare not shrink from the duty democracy demands." The truth is, the *Post* is too cowardly to call for withdrawal. For the respectable opposition, unilateral withdrawal has become steadily more unthinkable as United States intervention has widened. It was perfectly thinkable before 1961. It was even thinkable for Bobby Kennedy as late as September 1963, at a meeting of the National Security Council, when he asked whether *now* might be the time to get out. It is still thinkable, though not by the Kennedy men, who, out of power, dare not reason as they might have in the privacy of a president's councils.

We could still, if we wished, take "French leave" of Vietnam, and *how* this should be done ought not to be the concern of those who oppose our presence there. When the French schoolteachers and intellectuals of the Committee of 121 insisted that France get out of Algeria, they did not supply De Gaulle with a ten-point program telling him how to do it. That was De Gaulle's business. He was responsible, not they. As intellectuals, they confronted their government with an unequivocal moral demand, and far from identifying themselves with that government and thinking helpfully on its behalf, they disassociated themselves from it totally so long as it continued to make war in Algeria. The administrative problems of winding up the war were left to those who had been waging it, just as the political problem of reconciling the French electorate to a defeat was left in the hands of De Gaulle, a politician by profession.

Our pamphleteers and polemicists, if they were resolute, would behave in the same way. Not: "We see your dilemma, Mr. President. It won't be easy to stop this war, but here are a few ideas." The country needs to understand that the war is wrong, and the sole job of the opposition should be to enforce that understanding and to turn it, whenever possible, into the language of action. It is clear that U.S. senators and former ambassadors are not going to sit in at the Pentagon or hurl themselves at troop trains; nobody expects that of them and nobody seriously expects elected or appointed officials to practice tax refusal. But one *could* expect practical support for the young people who are resisting the draft from a few courageous officeholders and from private figures with a genuine sense of public responsibility.

Instead of hoping to avoid identification with unruly picketers and other actionists, Americans who are serious in opposing the war should be refusing to identify themselves with the U.S. government, even a putative government that would change to a defensive "posture" and prepare, as they say, to sit the war out. The question is simple: Do I disapprove *more* of the sign that picket is carrying—and the beard he is wearing—or of the Vietnamese war? To judge by introspection, the answer is not pretty. For the middle-class, middle-aged "protestor," the war in Vietnam is easier to take—maybe because it is familiar—than a sign that says "JOHNSON MURDERER."

The war does not threaten our immediate well-being. It does not touch us in the consumer-habits that have given us literally our shape. Casualty figures, still low, seldom strike home outside rural and low-income groups—the silent part of society. The absence of sacrifices has had its effect on the opposition, which feels no need, on the whole, to turn away from its habitual standards and practices—what for? We have not withdrawn our sympathy from American power and from the way of life that is tied to it—a connection that is more evident to a low-grade G.I. in Vietnam than to most American intellectuals.

A sympathy, sneaking or otherwise, for American power is weakening the opposition's case against Johnson. He acts as if he had a mournful obligation to go on with the war unless and until somebody finds him an honorable exit from it. There is no honorable exit from a shameful course of action, though there may be a lucky escape. But the mirage of an honorable exit—a "middle road"—remains the deceptive premise of the liberal opposition, which urges the mistrustful President to attempt it on a pure trial-and-error basis; you never know, it may work.

For example, "Stop the bombing to get negotiations"—meaning the bombing of the North; strangely, nothing is said about the much worse bombing of the South. But in reality no one knows, unless it is Ho Chi Minh, whether a cessation of bombing would bring negotiations or not and, if it did, what the terms of Ho would be. Stop it for six months and see, suggests Bobby Kennedy. "Don't pin it down. Be vague," others say. But how does this differ, except in duration, from one of Johnson's famous bombing pauses, which failed, so he claimed, to produce any response? Moreover, if stopping the bombing is only a trick or maneuver to get negotiations (that is, to see the enemy's cards), then Rusk and Joseph Alsop have equal rights to argue that talk of negotiations, put about by the friends of Hanoi, is only a trick to stop the bombing and give the North a chance to rebuild. And what if the bombing stops and Hanoi does not come to the conference table or comes with intransigent terms? Then the opposition, it would seem, is bound to agree to more and perhaps bigger bombing. Advocates of a failed hypothesis in wartime can only fall silent and listen to Big Brother.

To demand a halt to the bombing unconditionally, without qualifications, is quite another matter. The citizen who makes that demand cannot be "proved" wrong by subsequent developments, *e.g.*, the obduracy of Hanoi or an increase in infiltration. Either it is *morally* wrong for the United States to bomb a small and virtually defenseless country or it is not, and a student picketing the Pentagon is just as great an expert in that realm, to say the least, as Dean Rusk or Joseph Alsop. Surely, in fact, the student who *demands* that the bombing stop speaks with a greater authority than the professor who *urges* it.

Not being a military specialist, I cannot plot the logistics of withdrawing 464,000 American boys from Vietnam, but I know that it can be done, if necessary, and Johnson knows it too. *Everybody* knows it. A defeat in battle on the order of Dien Bien Phu, if it happened, could provide Johnson's generals with the opportunity to plan and execute a retreat. That is their job, and Johnson might even snatch honor from it. Look at Churchill and the heroic exploit of Dunkirk, which did not depend on prior negotiations with Hitler. But we cannot wait for a major defeat in battle to cover Johnson's withdrawal with honor or even to save his face for him. Nor can we wait for a Soviet or a Chinese intervention, which might have the same effect (if not a quite different one) by precipitating a Cuban-style confrontation; the war could then terminate in a withdrawal of the big powers, leaving a wrecked Vietnam to the Vietnamese. That, no doubt, would be a "solution" acceptable to the men in power.

In politics, it seems, retreat is honorable if dictated by military considerations and shameful if even *suggested* for ethical reasons —as though, by some law of inertia, force could only yield to superior force or to some natural obstacle, such as unsuitable terrain or "General Winter," whom Napoleon met in Russia. Thus the immense American superiority of arms *in itself* becomes an argument for staying in Vietnam; indeed, at this point, the only argument. The more troops and matériel committed to Vietnam, the more retreat appears to be cut off—not by an enemy, but by our own numbers. To call for withdrawal in the face of that commitment (the only real one we have made to Vietnam) is to seem to argue not against a policy, but against *facts*, which by their very nature are unanswerable. In private, a U.S. spokesman may agree that the Americans cannot win in Vietnam. "But they can't lose either," he adds with a satisfied nod. Critics of U.S. policy, when they go to Vietnam, are expected to be convinced by the fact of 464,000 troops, once it sinks in; and indeed what can you say to it? Johnson's retort to his opponents has been to tersely add *more* facts, in the shape of men and arms. Their utility is not just to overwhelm the Viet Cong by sheer force of numbers, but to overwhelm domestic disbelief; if they cannot stop the VC, they can stop any talk of unilateral withdrawal. Under these circumstances, the idea that he subtract a few facts—de-escalation—is rejected by Johnson as illogical. The logic of numbers is the only one that convinces him of the rightness of the course he is bent on.

Meanwhile, the generals are sure they could win the war if they could only bomb the port of Haiphong and the Ho Chi Minh trail in Laos. They blame politics for their failure to win it, and by politics is meant the existence of counter-forces in the theater: China, Russia, the Pathet Lao, and simply people, civilians, a weak counter-force, but still an obstacle to total warfare under present conditions. It used to be said that the balance of terror would give rise to a series of limited wars. Up to now, this has been true, so far as geographical scale goes, but the abstention from the use of atomic arms, in Vietnam, has not exactly worked to moderate the war.

On the contrary, the military establishment, deprived for the time being of tactical atomic weapons (toys being kept in the closet) and held back from bombing the port of Haiphong and the Ho Chi Minh trail, has compensated for these limitations by developing other weapons and devices to the limit: antipersonnel bombs; a new, more adhesive napalm; a twenty-pound gadget, the E-63 manpack personnel detector, made by General Electric, replacing British-trained bloodhounds, to sniff out Viet Cong; a battery-powered blower that raises the temperature in a VC tunnel network to 1000 degrees Fahrenheit (loud-speakers, naturally, exhort the Viet Cong in the tunnels to surrender); improved tear gases; improved defoliants. The classic resistance offered by climate and terrain to armies of men, one of the ancient limitations on warfare, will doubtless be all but eliminated as new applications for patents pour into the U.S. Patent Office. The jungle will be leafless and creeperless, and the mangrove swamps dried out; the weather will be controlled, making bombing possible on a 365-day-a-year basis, exclusive of Buddha's birthday,

Christmas, and Têt. The diseases of the jungle and tropical climates are already pretty well confined to the native population, thanks to pills and immunization. In other words, for an advanced nation, practically no obstacles remain to the exercise of force except "politics."

U.S. technology is bent on leaving nothing to chance in the Vietnamese struggle, on taking the risk out of war (for ourselves, of course, while increasing the risk for the enemy). Whatever cannot be controlled scientifically—shifts of wind, rain—is bypassed by radar and electronics. Troop performance is fairly well guaranteed by the Selective Service system and by rotation; the "human element," represented by the Arvin, prone to desert or panic, is despised and feared. And if chance can be reduced to a minimum by the "miracle" of American technology, there is only one reality-check on American *hubris*: the danger of Chinese or Russian intervention, which computers in the Pentagon are steadily calculating, to take the risk out of *that*.

Yet the peculiar fact is that this has been a war of incredible blunders, on the American side; you never hear of blunders, though there must be some, on the part of the Viet Cong. Leaving aside the succession of political blunders, starting with the great Diem gamble and going right up to the Ky gamble (the current embarrassment of U.S. officials), there has been a startling number of military blunders: government villages bombed, Cambodian villages bombed, a Strategic Hamlet gunned by a U.S. helicopter on the day before the ambassador's scheduled visit, U.S. troops bombed and shelled by their own aircraft and artillery, "Friendlies" bombed and shelled, a Russian ship bombed in Haiphong harbor, overflights into China.

158

In the case of North Vietnam, blunder is surely a misnomer for what has been done with regularity to villages, churches, hospitals, a model leper colony, schools. American opinion refuses to hear of a "deliberate bombing pattern" in North Vietnam, though there is plenty of testimony and photographic evidence of the destruction of populated centers. The administration insists that we are bombing military targets only, though it has finally conceded, after too many had been found, that we were using antipersonnel bombs in the North, without specifying how these inventions, designed to fragment a soft human body, were effective against bridges, power plants, and railway yards. Yet even those who are unconvinced by the administration's regularly issued denials prefer to think that what is happening is the result of human or mechanical error—a possibility categorically excluded by the U.S. Navy.

On the nuclear carrier *Enterprise*, a squadron of Intruder pilots in their air-conditioned ready room assured journalists, myself included, that under no circumstances did they hit anything in the North but military targets. How did they know? Because they only bombed targets assigned to them, which had been carefully selected with the aid of computers working on aerial photographs. Besides, post-raid reconnaissance recorded on film the "impact" of every delivery; there was no chance of error. Did it never happen that, returning from a mission and having failed for some reason—flak or whatever—to reach their assigned targets, they jettisoned their bomb load on the countryside? Never. Always into the sea. What about those accounts of devastated villages and hamlets? Impossible. "Our aerial photographs would show it." You could not shake their placid, stolid, almost uninterested conviction. Yet somebody's cameras were lying. Those of the journalists and other witnesses who bring back ordinary photographs they have snapped in the North or the unmanned cameras of the U.S. Navy?

Their faith in technology had put these men, in their own eyes, above suspicion. They would as soon have suspected the totals of an adding machine. Was it conceivable that in flying they kept their attention glued to their instrument panels and their radar screen, watching out for MIGs and SAMs, no more interested in what was *below* them, in both senses, than they were in our questions?

The same faith in technology commands the administration to go on with the war, in defiance of any evidence of failure, bringing to bear American inventiveness, not only in the field of weaponry, but also in the field of propaganda—loud-speakers, broadcasts from the air, cunning messages inserted literally between the lines of ornamented New Year's calendars distributed free to the people—"We don't make it too obvious." The next step in this field would be subliminal suggestion, psychedelic bombardments in light and color to be pioneered by General Electric and offered to the population by the Special Forces, with CIA backing —the regular Army would disapprove.

"Politics" gets in the way of technology. If the world could be cleansed of politics, including South Vietnamese politicians, victory might be in sight. Politics, domestic and international, is evidently the only deterrent recognized by the Americans to an all-out onslaught on the Vietnamese nation; it is the replacement of the inner voice of conscience, which nobody but a few draft-resisters can hear. Johnson, who keeps acting as if he were

bowing to necessity, looks to "politics"—*i.e.*, Hanoi—to release
him, the prisoner of circumstance. He invites his enemy and his
critics to "show him the way out." At the same time he insists
that "the door is always open," which means, if anything, that
the portals of peace will swing wide at the bidding of Ho Chi
Minh but remain locked to *him*, beating and signaling from the
inside. What he appears to be saying is that Ho Chi Minh is free
whereas he and his advisers are not.

This hypocritical performance may, like most play-acting,
have a certain psychological truth. Johnson and his advisers, like
all Americans, are the conditioned subjects of the free-enterprise
system, which despite some controls and government manipulation, appears to function automatically, requiring no consent
on the part of those involved in it. A sense of compulsion, dictated by the laws of the market, permeates every nerve of the
national life. Industry, for example, has been "compelled" to
automate by the law of cost-cutting, which works in "free" capitalism with the same force as a theorem in geometry. And the
necessity to automate is accepted throughout society without any
question. The human damage involved, if seen close up, may
elicit a sigh, as when a co-operative apartment building fires its
old Negro elevator operators ("Been with us twenty years") to
put in self-service: "We had to, you see. It was cheaper." Or ask
a successful author why he has changed from his old publisher,
who was virtually his parent, to a new mass-market one. "I had
to," he explains, simply. "They offered me more money."

A feeling of having no choice is becoming more and more
widespread in American life, and particularly among successful
people, who supposedly are free beings. On a concrete plane, the

lack of choice is often a depressing reality. In national election years, you are free to choose between Johnson and Goldwater or Johnson and Romney or Reagan, which is the same as choosing between a Chevrolet and a Ford—there is a marginal difference in styling. Just as in American hotel rooms you can decide whether or not to turn on the air conditioner (that is *your* business), but you cannot open the window.

It is natural that in such a system the idea of freedom is associated with escape, whether through trips or "trips," rather than with the exercise of one's ordinary faculties. And at the same time one's feeling of imprisonment is joined to a conviction of innocence. Johnson, perhaps genuinely, would like to get out of his "commitment" to the war in Vietnam, and the more deeply he involves himself in it, the more abused and innocent he feels, and the less he is inclined to take any steps to release *himself*, for to do so would be to confess that he is culpable or—the same thing—that he has been free at any time to do what he would now be doing.

Those of Johnson's critics who, like Senator Fulbright, repudiate the thought of a "disorderly" retreat by implication favor an orderly retreat, with the panoply of negotiations, guarantees, and so on. *I.e.*, a retreat assisted and facilitated by Hanoi. But that choice, very likely, is no longer open, thanks to Johnson himself. He would be very lucky, at this point, to get negotiations at the mere cost to him of ending the bombing of the North—a cost that to Ho or any rational person seems derisory, since, as our military spokesmen have complained, there are no targets in North Vietnam left to destroy, except the port of Haiphong, which Johnson, for his own reasons and not to please Ho, has spared up to now. Indeed, to have something of value to offer short of troop withdrawal, Johnson's peculiar logic would lead him to *start* bombing the port of Haiphong in order to *stop* bombing it—exactly the chain of reasoning that sent our planes north back in February 1965, and has kept them pounding ever since.

The opposition's best hopes for an orderly retreat rest on the South Vietnamese, just as, probably, the administration's fears do. The notion that the elections this September *might* put in a government that could negotiate a separate peace with the NLF is once again reviving; some people are daring to bank on the return of General Minh as a coalition candidate. *If* he is permitted to return and if *he* is elected, with the support of the radical Buddhists and liberal groups in the Constitutional Assembly, that would allow the Americans to leave by invitation—a very attractive prospect. And were they to decline the invitation and try to depose him (as in effect they did once before, considering him too "leftish"), they might have a double civil war on their hands, a more serious repetition of what happened in the spring of 1966. In either case, the Vietnamese elections could be a turning point. Or, failing that, the American elections of 1968. The opposition prays for the nomination of a Romney or a Percy, who *might* beat Johnson and *might* end the war, as Eisenhower did in Korea. And it dreads the nomination of a Nixon or a Reagan, which would "compel" it to vote again for Johnson—a perfect illustration of American consumer choice.

These are all hopes for a Redeemer who will come from the *outside* to save us from our own actions: an Asian general, a Republican who does not fit into the party program or picture. In the same way, Johnson may be hoping for a Redeemer in the form of Kosygin to get him to the peace table. Or he may have a more far-reaching design: the eventual occupation of the North and the establishment of U.S. bases next to the Chinese border. Yet if such a design exists, it must be in the *back* of the administration's mind and be, itself, more a cunning hope than a businesslike calculation, a thought held in the pending file and marked "Cosmic."

Actually, so far as is known, Johnson has no program for ending the war in the South. Asked what *he* would do, he, too, no doubt would be reduced to head-scratching. He has given a promise to withdraw American troops as soon as hostilities are over, but can he seriously mean that? The consequences of bilateral withdrawal would be nearly as "disastrous" as the consequences of unilateral withdrawal: the return of the Viet Cong. The Vietnamese know this, which makes them uncertain what to fear most. A new man in the White House who might keep the presidential promise? Or permanent colonial status?

"The Vietnamese must choose for themselves," the Americans repeat, having done their best to deprive them of the power of choice during thirteen years of American military assistance that slowly turned into a full-scale American invasion—there is no other word for it. The Americans pretend that this was somehow forced on them; in reality, it was forced on the Vietnamese, as is clear from the low morale of their troops. "They just don't want to fight," American officers say with an air of puzzlement. If the Vietnamese want to be rid of the Americans, they must turn toward the NLF—a hard decision for some French-educated idealists, who, despite their experience with the American brand as an import product, still have hopes of democracy. Yet the brutality of the war is reconciling certain middle-class Saigon groups to making discreet overtures toward their class enemy; meanwhile, in the field, the Viet Cong forces have been increasing—which our spokesmen ascribe to "better recruiting methods." In their turn, Americans concerned for the future of the Republic, rather than for the future of American power, are reduced to hoping that the Viet Cong can hold out in the face of the overwhelming *facts* marshaled against it—as though its often primitive and homemade weapons possessed a ·moral force of resistance denied to members of the Great Society.

The uselessness of our free institutions, pleasurable in themselves, to interpose any check on a war of this character, opposed, though not enough, by most so-called thinking persons, suggests that freedom in the United States is no longer a political value and is seen simply as the right to self-expression, as in the dance, psychodrama, be-ins, kinky sex, or baking ceramics. The truth is, only a minority is *interested* in the war in Vietnam, and debate about the subject is treated as a minority pastime, looked on by the majority with more or less tolerance. "The country can afford it," is the attitude. Or: "It's a free country," which has come to mean "I've got mine, Jack. Everybody to his taste." A little less tolerance might harden the opposition. If the opposition wants to make itself felt politically, it ought to be acting so as to provoke intolerance. It is hurt because the administration ignores it. There are various ways of obliging the administration—and more importantly the country—to take notice: some extremely radical, like the bonze's way of self-immolation; some less so, ranging from tax refusal through the operation of underground railroads for protesting draftees, down to simple boycotts of key war industries; nobody who is against the war should be receiving dividends from the manufacture of napalm, for instance, which is calling to be outlawed.

Since the Revolution, this country has had no experience of foreign occupation and consequently of resistance movements; in that field, it lacks inspiration and inventiveness and is readily discouraged. But the professors and students who lost heart when the teach-ins failed to change U.S. policy might study the example of the Abolitionists—the nearest thing to a resistance movement the Republic has had. Obviously no single plan of action can stop the war in Vietnam, and maybe a hundred plans concerted could not stop it. But if it can be stopped, it will be through initiatives taken by persons or groups of persons (whether they be Johnson or Ho or a Republican president or Big Minh or the readers of this pamphlet) and not through cooked-up "solutions" handed to somebody else to act on, like inter-office memoranda. The "hard thinking" about this war needs to begin at home, with the critic asking himself what *he* can do against it, modestly or grandly, with friends or alone. From each according to his abilities, but to be in the town jail, as Thoreau knew, can relieve any sense of imaginary imprisonment.

HANOI

Foreword

As a preparatory exercise, the reader may be interested in the following controversy, which took place in the *New York Review of Books* a few months before my visit to Hanoi. The occasion was the magazine publication of "Solutions." Mrs. Trilling's letter to the editor, I felt, required reply in that it stated the arguments usually advanced for our staying in Vietnam. The fact that Mrs. Trilling, as the reader will see, does not advocate our staying in Vietnam reduces those arguments to the state of mere scruples or perplexities. Yet I am grateful to her for prompting me to deal with them and for her permission to reprint her letter.

M. McC.

On Withdrawing from Vietnam:
An Exchange

Diana Trilling:

Mary McCarthy's proposal in her recent article, "Vietnam: Solutions" (November 9), that we should stop worrying about means of terminating the war and concentrate our full energies on simply getting it brought to an end, is bound to be warmly welcomed by many opponents of the war. This is a weary time. It cannot but be a relief to be told that political effort, as it is demonstrated by the error and insufficiency of the present Administration both in foreign and domestic affairs, is unworthy of the intellectual life as that life is defined by its commitment to morality.

But unfortunately, in clearing the decks for an acceleration of protest unimpeded by practical political concerns, Miss McCarthy leaves one consideration out of account. She fails to mention, except in a contemptuous reference to airlifting "loyal" Vietnamese (the quotation marks are hers) to Taiwan, the problem which for some opponents of the war, myself included, makes the central issue of the Vietnam situation—what happens after America withdraws. Reading Miss McCarthy's piece one might suppose that "solution" of the war is just a matter of saving face for Johnson by finding a suitable device for negotiation of peace, and of evacuating half a million troops.

These problems Miss McCarthy assigns to the professional politicians and military tacticians—and who would not agree with her? A division of labor which spares intellectuals for thought, and leaves strategies and logistics to those who are trained in them, is eminently sensible. But the fact is that the question of how we should or should not go about negotiation of a peace settlement is not, as Miss McCarthy would have us think, "merely" political. It is a political problem which is also nothing if not a moral problem: it involves the fate of millions of human beings, at least as many as are involved by our presence in Vietnam. If South Vietnam falls to the Communists, who stifle opposition and kill their enemies, is this not of moral concern to intellectuals? Or is the disfavor in which we hold our present practice of democracy a sufficient warrant to regard Communism as the party of peace and freedom? Certainly Miss McCarthy's refusal to deal with a Communist victory in South Vietnam as any kind of threat to the values she would wish to see multiplied in the world characterizes the preference of American intellectuals for addressing but a single moral culprit, America. But this is a game we play. Most of us know better.

Miss McCarthy cites Kennan, Fulbright, Galbraith, Schlesinger, and Goodwin as instances of the way in which concern with political "solutions" can lead intellectuals to the betrayal of their sole moral duty, protest of the war. In these unhappy examples she would have us recognize an inevitable connection between engagement with the practical aspects of politics and a deteriorated moral sentiment—seemingly, when these men undertook to offer positive suggestions for how this country might proceed to end the war they were in objective effect conspiring with a government they were morally obligated to oppose and only oppose. Surely this carries us rather far in disgust with politics—if moral man is permitted only a negative relation to government, one wonders what keeps all of us who think of ourselves as moral persons from declaring ourselves Anarchists.

One also wonders whether Miss McCarthy, jealous as she is for the special domain of intellectuals, has let herself realize that by limiting the political role of intellectuals wholly to that of dissent she deprives them of an historical privilege they have claimed with some authority—the right to propose and even direct the positive operations of government. It is an honorable roster she now closes to us and it includes—need one remind her—not only liberals content to work within the given structure of the State but also radicals and even revolutionaries who wanted, and sometimes succeeded in achieving, actual governing power.

That old vexed question of the responsibility of intellectuals is, I know, not to be settled in debate with Miss McCarthy. And I am aware that the position she has taken in her article, that the single job of intellectuals and indeed of all decent people is to get us out of Vietnam, the sooner the better and who cares by what means or what follows on our withdrawal, is far too emotionally attractive to yield before a contrary view—namely, that no choice which is careless of its consequences is a moral choice. I think America was and is careless of certain deeply important consequences of going into Vietnam. I hardly think this justifies intellectuals in being similarly careless of the consequences of our getting out.

I too oppose this war and urge our withdrawal from Vietnam, on the well-explored ground that America cannot militarily win the third world from Communism without the gravest danger of thermonuclear war or, at the least, without conduct inconsistent with and damaging to the democratic principle and the principle of national sovereignty we would hope to protect and extend— the fact that in order to be even as little successful as we have so far been in resisting the Viet Cong America has in effect possessed the sovereign territory of South Vietnam dramatizes the threat to the autonomy of small nations inherent in such ill-considered procedures. But even as I take this stand I confront the grim reality that in withdrawing from Vietnam we consign untold numbers of Southeast Asian opponents of Communism to their death and countless more to the abrogation of the right of protest which we American intellectuals hold so dear. And if, unhappily, I have no answer to the torturing question of what can be done to save these distant lives, I don't regard this as proof of my moral purity or as an escape from what Miss McCarthy calls the "booby-trap" of "solutions." I hope that everyone, including intellectuals, will keep on trying to find the answer I lack. For without this effort the moral intransigence for which Miss McCarthy speaks is its own kind of callousness.

Mary McCarthy:

Mrs. Trilling has the gift of prophecy. I have not. I do not know what will happen to millions of human beings in Southeast Asia if the Americans pull out. Common sense suggests that the richer and more visible of the "loyal" South Vietnamese will follow their bank accounts to France and Switzerland. Quotation marks are called for since what these people are loyal to has not been determined. Their duly constituted government? Their country? Democratic principle? Their skins? When the Americans use the word, they mean loyal to *them:* "We can't let these guys down because they have stuck with us." Yet the depth of this sense of togetherness can be gauged by what happened to Diem, an outstanding "good Indian" who became a liability.

Let us drop the crocodile concern and talk about realities. It is perfectly true that many thousands of South Vietnamese have been compromised by working for the Americans, as interpreters, language teachers, nurses, drivers, construction workers, cleaning women, cooks, PX employees, and so on; there are at least 140,000 on the military payroll alone. No outsider can be long in Vietnam without feeling some misgivings as to what may happen to them "afterward." Their employers must occasionally ponder this, too. One can hope that an AID official, hurriedly packing to leave, will feel some qualms about Minh, who has been driving his car, that a few Marines will think twice about Kim, the girl who works in the canteen. But this is not politics but ordinary ethics: a responsibility felt for people whose lives have touched one's own and who therefore cannot be expected to vanish like stage scenery when the action shifts elsewhere.

In exceptional cases, something *will* be done, on a person-to-person basis, assuming Minh's and Kim's willingness: jobs and "sponsorship" will be found in the U.S.; voluntary agencies on the spot will help; neutral embassies will help. But the majority will be left to face the music; that is the tough luck of being a camp follower. The departure of an occupying force, the closing-down of an embassy or a mission means the curt abandonment of the local employees to the mercies of fortune and their compatriots. It happened in France last spring when the U.S. NATO forces were ordered out: what became of the 17,500 "faithful" French employees? It can be argued that that is De Gaulle's worry.

The work force of South Vietnamese who have "cast in their lot" with the Americans has drifted into politics through the accident or fatality of economics: they were looking for a job. Nobody could seriously place them among the "untold numbers of opponents of Communism," though in a literal sense that is what they are, and it is they, no doubt, who will have risked the most in the end if the sanguinary scenes imagined by Mrs. Trilling actually are enacted. In that event, one can hope for their sakes that they were secretly working for the Viet Cong (a suspicion that falls on them anyway), in short that they were political after all.

RVN government figures, who have contributed far less to the war effort, in fact who have positively hampered it through graft and other forms of crookedness, are more likely to benefit from a grateful U.S. The Seventh Fleet and the Air Force would probably stand ready to evacuate the various military men, province chiefs, district chiefs, ministers, and deputies who have been co-operating with us—whether they go to Thailand or are airlifted to Taiwan, the Philippines, Hawaii, or straight to the United States. In other words, the U.S. would look after those who are most able to look after themselves.

And what about the bourgeois intelligentsia, who are relatively few but who really are, for the most part, opponents of

Communism, though not necessarily in sympathy with the United States? Some of them, doubtless, will go into exile; others will prefer to stay and make terms with the NLF—signs of this are already evident, not only in the Saigon Assembly but among middle-of-the-road exile groups abroad. There are also the various sects and splinters of sects, Buddhists, Hoa Haos, Cao Daists, who are unlikely to choose exile in large numbers but who can be expected to survive as groups despite their religious commitments, just as Catholics and their priests have in the North.

This leaves the hamlet chiefs, village chiefs, schoolteachers, policemen who have collaborated with the Americans in pacified areas. Many of these people are in the same situation as the "little people" on the American payroll. That is, they have collaborated for non-political reasons, out of a natural wish to go on being schoolteachers, policemen, etc. But, having done so behind the American shield, they live in fear of the Viet Cong. Among the small local bureaucracy there are also convinced opponents of Communism and admirers of American power—of an eager-beaver type found all over the world. Most of these fully expect to be massacred if the Americans go and at the same time, masochistically, they place small reliance on American promises to stay. They see themselves being hacked to pieces, decapitated, along with the non-politicals, who are not quite so sure of their fate.

Indeed, a certainty as to what will happen in the event of a Viet Cong "take-over" is the principal article of faith in the anti-Communist credo. One is against Communism because one *knows* that Communists massacre whoever is against them. For example, a Jesuit father back from a long residence in Vietnam recently *guaranteed* me that two million people would be slaughtered if the NLF came to power—he did not say how he had arrived at this figure; his first estimate had been three million but he had knocked a third off as a concession to my disbelief. "You mean you *think* so, Father." "No, I *know* it," he replied with fervor. Only God knew the future, I reminded him, but he did not seem to agree.

To be fair, the missionary priest was reflecting, quite accurately, middle-class attitudes in Vietnam. The *fear* of the Viet Cong is a reality in the South. To an outsider, this graphic and detailed certainty appears phobic, the product of an overworked imagination. Eyewitness and secondhand accounts of Viet Cong terror are magnified and projected into the future, as though guerrilla warfare could be expected to *intensify* in the absence of an armed enemy. In Saigon one evening I talked to a group of twenty or so students who all seemed to be living in a fantasy, fed on atrocity stories, of what would happen to them if the Americans left. A New York *Times* reporter asked them what they were so afraid of: they were young, they were specialists; a Communist government would need their skills as engineers, teachers, doctors. . . . They were bewildered by what was plainly a totally new idea; it had not crossed their minds that their training could make them useful to their class enemy. They only thought of being shot, decapitated, etc. All these young people, with one exception, were Northerners, and it had not occurred to them either what this meant in terms of their persistent nightmare: contrary to their preconceptions, they were alive and whole, having been allowed to escape, with their parents, from the jaws of Communism back in 1954.

If it had been revealed to me in a vision that two million people would die as a consequence, I suppose I would not—lightheartedly, as Mrs. Trilling thinks—propose unilateral American withdrawal. The awful fact of having had the vision would lay their deaths squarely at my door. So I would try to hammer out some "solution," *e.g.*, a new partition of the already partitioned country—a notion already hinted at in J. K. Galbraith's *How to Get Out of Vietnam;* mindful of the loyal Vietnamese, he wonders whether Saigon could not be made a free city, on the model, presumably, of Danzig or Trieste, not good precedents when you come to think of it. But what about simple annexation of South Vietnam? This would require a million troops, the expedition of Free World colonists, private investment in factories and power plants, but it would have the advantage of *imposing* democratic institutions on the South Vietnamese; moreover, the war could be moderated in view of the fact that it would now be taking place on U.S. soil, destroying U.S. property and property-holders; if we concentrated on the task of development, we could seal the frontier, stop bombing North Vietnam—a waste of time—and even interdict napalm.

Short of annexation—a fifty-first state—no solution comes to mind that could give ironclad *permanent* protection to untold numbers of anti-Communists. All current proposals, starting with Johnson's at Manila, envision an eventual departure from the scene. If we do not want to extend the boundaries of the U.S., we are left with no alternative but to extend the war, *i.e.*, continue it along present lines, regularly escalating until all resistance has been eliminated or until our computers tell us that two million and one innocent persons have been killed—at that point the war would no longer be "worth it," and we could quit with a clear conscience.

Mrs. Trilling says that she opposes the war, but logically, in her own terms, she shouldn't unless she looks on the slaughter of millions of democrats as the lesser evil. She is also troubled by the threat to the right of protest that an American withdrawal would imply. No doubt it would, yet the lack of a right of protest in South Vietnam at this very minute is not a threat but a reality, as anybody should know from reading the papers. Americans are free to criticize the war in South Vietnam; the South Vietnamese are not. Admittedly, there is more diversity of opinion in the South on this subject than there is, probably, in the North, yet in neither place is there any real freedom of the press or of public debate.

For anybody but a pacifist, the balancing of means against ends in wartime is of course a problem, which can be real or false, depending on whether the end to be obtained is visible and concrete or merely conjectural. If it were known that Ho Chi Minh was sending millions of Catholics or members of ethnic minorities to gas chambers, there would be a real dilemma for intellectuals and non-intellectuals, too, as to how much force and what kind should be applied to stop him, whether napalm, phosphorus, magnesium and cluster bombs should be used against his population, whether his "sanctuaries" in Cambodia and China should be invaded. . . . But no one outside the Administration pretends that Ho is Hitler. Mrs. Trilling's tone suggests that she thinks he is Stalin, yet would she reproach U.S. intellectuals, herself included, for having failed to seek an "answer" to save the millions who perished in Stalin's prisons and slave-labor camps? Like the Bertrand Russell of the epoch, did she conscientiously *weigh* dropping an atom bomb?

There are no "answers" except in retrospect, when the right course to have followed seems magically clear to all. At present nobody can produce a policy for Vietnam that is warranted by its maker to be without defects. Quite aside from Communism, this is a civil war, and civil wars customarily end with a bloody settling of scores, because of the fratricidal passions involved and also for the obvious reason that the majority of the losers have nowhere to escape to; it is their country, too. But one can fear this for Vietnam whichever side wins. What safeguards exist for the Viet Cong and its millions of sympathizers and dependents if a victorious U.S. Army turns their disposal over to the ARVN—its cynical practice up to now? Does that not worry Mrs. Trilling? We *know* that the ARVN tortures its prisoners and executes civilians suspected of working with the VC. Despite the promises of the Open Arms program the VC, too, may anticipate a massacre if it definitively lays down its arms. Unlike the Jesuit missionary who "hadn't seen it in the paper," the VC must have heard about the recent anti-Communist coup in Indonesia, rejoiced over by American officials (who give our Vietnamese policy credit for it); it was followed by the *execution* of 500,000 Indonesians, and the unrecorded carnage is reckoned at two million.

Yet civil wars in modern history have not invariably ended with horrible mass reprisals, above all in Communist countries.

Take the Hungarian Revolution, which was a mixture of civil war and foreign occupation. To everyone's surprise, very few were killed in the aftermath, and an *increase* in general liberty followed. Or take the Communist seizure of Poland after World War II, when two Polish armies fought each other, one being backed by the Russians. It was not succeeded by a bloody purge; the virtue of Polish Communism, they say, is that *no one* was executed for political opposition even under Stalinism— Gomulka went to jail. Or take North Vietnam itself, after the French defeat; here, too, there was an element of civil war, since many Vietnamese fought on the side of and supported the French. Yet under the Geneva Accords, the North Vietnamese with minor exceptions did not interfere—sometimes even assisted—while 860,000 persons were evacuated (including 600,000 Catholics) by the French Army and the Seventh Fleet. It is true that the emigrants lost their property and that in the agrarian reform of 1955-56 numerous landowners, rich peasants, and others were executed—Bernard Fall quotes an estimate of 50,000. I do not have, for purposes of comparison, statistics on those who died in Diem's agricultural "experiment"—the Strategic Hamlets program—and if I had, it would not alter the ineluctable fact of 50,000 deaths. It is possible that this could repeat itself in South Vietnam, if collectivization is attempted. Against this is the fact that the mistake was recognized and amends made where still possible (The Rectification of Errors Campaign), and the point about an acknowledged mistake is not to repeat it.

The Hungarian and Polish examples suggest that if opposition is widespread in a Communist state a conciliatory policy is pursued; the turnabout in North Vietnam in 1956, when resistance to the land-reform purges led to open rebellion, further illustrates the point. If, on the other hand, opposition is confined to a minority, that minority is dealt with ruthlessly. Let us assume this principle applies: Mrs. Trilling should be reassured if she is confident that opponents of Communism in Southeast Asia can be counted in the millions. But if she overestimates their numbers, then indeed she has grounds for alarm. On the other hand, if they are relatively few—say, in the hundreds of thousands—evacuation ought not to present insuperable difficulties. As for their readjustment elsewhere, one cannot be sanguine. Nevertheless, here, too, there are precedents: the United States has been able, for instance, to absorb 300,000 escapees from Castro's Cuba—a statistic not usually remembered in this kind of discussion.

Of course this little principle, whatever comfort it may offer, is not a "law." Nor is evacuation of a whole minority of oppositionists imaginable except in a blueprint. Some would miss the boat. Let us suppose that whatever happens, a thousand will be left behind, to be tried and executed by People's Tribunals or cut to ribbons in their hamlets. Or a hundred. Or only one. It is the same. Mrs. Trilling would have his death on her conscience. She condemned him to die by her opposition to the war. She failed him. We all failed him. We ought to have thought harder—that is Mrs. Trilling's attitude. But we condemn thousands of people to death every day by not intervening when we could—read the Oxfam ads. Or the appeals in the morning mail; yesterday I condemned someone to die of muscular dystrophy. I judged some other cause "more important." Not to mention my own comforts and pleasures. I am calloused. Everyone today who is well off is calloused, some more, some less. This has always been the case, but modern means of communication have made it impossible not to know what one is *not* doing; charitable organizations are in business to tell us all about it. When Mrs. Trilling reproaches me as an intellectual for my lack of moral concern, she makes me think of the Polish proverb about the wolf who eats the lamb while choking with sobs and the wolf who just eats the lamb.

What Mrs. Trilling wants is a prize-winning recipe for stopping the war and stopping Communism at the same time; I cannot give it to her. Nor frankly do I think it admirable to try to stop Communism even by peaceful subversion. The alternatives to Communism offered by the Western countries are all ugly in their own ways and getting uglier. What I would hope for politically is an internal evolution in the Communist states toward greater freedom and plurality of choice. They have a better base, in my opinion, than we have to start from in dealing with such modern problems as automation, which in a socialist state could be simply a boon.

Certainly, town planning, city planning, conservation of natural and scenic resources are more in the spirit of socialism, even a despotic socialism, than in that of free enterprise. Today, in capitalist countries the only protection against the middle-aged spread of industrial society lies in such "socialistic" agencies as the Belle Arti and the Beaux-Arts, concerned with saving the countryside from the predations of speculators and competitive "developers," like real-estate developers. It seems possible, too, that Communism will be more able to decentralize industries through the exercise, paradoxically, of central control than the Welfare State has been. And variety of manufactures, encouragement of regional craft, ought to be easier for Communist planners whose enterprises are not obliged by the law of the market to show a profit or perish; there is no reason that "useless" and "wasteful" articles should be made only for the rich. In any case, external pressure is not going to liberalize Communist regimes; that seems to be fairly clear. It can only overthrow them or act to prevent them from taking power, with consequences that liberals, in view of Greece, Spain, Indonesia, might not be eager to "buy."

I should like to see what would happen if the pressure were taken off. What would Vietnam be like today if the United States had insisted on elections in '56 and the country had been unified by popular vote—which hindsight finally concedes might have been the best plan? Greatly daring, I should say that the best plan right now, eleven years later, might be to give the NLF a chance to enact its program. This calls for a National Assembly freely elected on the basis of universal suffrage, a coalition of classes for the reconstruction of the country, gradual and peaceful unification with the North, an independent and neutralist foreign policy. It guarantees the rights of private property and political, religious, and economic freedom. Whether this program, evidently designed to allay the alarms of the middle-class Vietnamese, is to be taken at face value, that is, whether the Front really means it, is something no one outside the Front's councils can know for certain. One can hope that it is so and fear that it is not. And even if the program, with its proffer of amnesty (and threat of punishment for those who persist in collaborating with the invader), is offered in good faith as a serious design for the future of the South, events may overtake it, *e.g.*, a right-wing rebellion, disastrous floods, a famine. . . . Yet for the Vietnamese this is the only "solution" at present available that gives any hope at all. Plans such as that of Philippe Devillers, proposing internationally supervised free elections to take place *first* in the Saigon-controlled zones (while the Americans retire to coastal enclaves) followed by *general* free elections in the whole of South Vietnam (after which the Americans would leave), amount in fact to showing a way in which the NLF program might be arrived at step by step with the co-operation of Saigon and of all interested parties.

Mrs. Trilling, doubtless, would think anybody a sucker who let himself be taken in by the promises of Communists, yet the promises of Communists sometimes correspond with their assessment of political realities: when Ho kept his word and let the emigrants go, he got rid of 860,000 opponents in one pacific stroke. Moreover, he had 860,000 fewer mouths to feed and a great deal of free land to distribute. The NLF would have the same motive to allow if not strongly to encourage the departure of oppositionists. Besides, if it is going to rebuild the country, the NLF will need co-operation from a variety of political and social groups, as well as credits, which might even come from the West, from General de Gaulle, for instance, from Sweden, Austria, Denmark, Canada.

The power of intellectuals, sadly limited, is to persuade, not to provide against all contingencies. They are not God, though Mrs. Trilling seems to feel that they have somehow replaced Him in taking on responsibility for every human event. This is a weird kind of *hubris*. In fact intellectuals and artists, as is well known, are not especially gifted for practical politics. Far from being statesmen with ubiquitous intelligence, they are usually not qualified to be mayor of a middle-sized city. What we *can* do, perhaps better than the next man, is smell a rat. That is what has occurred with the war in Vietnam, and our problem is to make others smell it, too. At the risk of being a nuisance, I reject Mrs. Trilling's call to order. The imminent danger for America is not of being "taken in" by Communism (which is what she is really accusing me of—that I have forgotten the old lessons, gone soft), but of being taken in by itself. If I can interfere with that process, I will. And if as a result of my ill-considered actions, world Communism comes to power, it will be too late then, I shall be told, to be sorry. Never mind. Some sort of life will continue, as Pasternak, Solzhenitsyn, Sinyavsky, Daniel have discovered, and I would rather be on their letterhead, if they would allow me, than on that of the American Committee for Cultural Freedom, which in its days of glory, as Mrs. Trilling will recall, was eager to exercise its right of protest by condemning the issue of a U.S. visa to Graham Greene and was actually divided within its ranks on the question of whether Senator Joseph McCarthy was a friend or enemy of domestic liberty.

Hanoi—March, 1968

*A*ttachez *vos ceintures, s'il vous plaît.*" "Fasten your seat belts." The hostess, plump, blonde, French, brown-eyed, in a light-blue smock, passed through, checking. It was funny to find a hostess on a military plane. Like the plane itself, loaded with mail, canned goods, cases of beer, she was a sort of last beep from the "other" world behind the mountains in Vientiane. Born in Hanoi, she had been making the run from Saigon with the I.C.C.—Poles, Indians, Canadians, of the inspection team—six times a month, weather permitting, for thirteen years, practically since the Geneva Accords.

As the I.C.C. plane, an obsolete non-pressurized Convair, circled in the dark above Hanoi, waiting to get the OK to land, out the window, by stretching against our seat belts, we could see tiny headlights of cars moving on the highways below and then the city all lit up like a big glowworm. In Phnom Penh, at the North Vietnamese Delegation, where they issued our visas, they had prepared us for this surprise, but it remained a surprise nonetheless. I thought of the Atlantic coast during World War II and the blackout curtains we had had to buy on the Cape —a Coast Guard order designed to foil enemy submarines. When the Convair taxied to a stop, it instantly doused its lights, though, and the hostess held a flashlight for the boarding officials to examine our papers. But then the airport, brilliant white and blazing with electricity. "You really don't have a blackout!" I exclaimed to the delegation from the Vietnamese Peace Committee who had come to meet us, with bouquets of snapdragons, pink sweet peas, pale-pink roses, larkspur, and little African daisies. A Japanese author and a journalist from a Tokyo paper were receiving bouquets, too. The Vietnamese did not know the word "blackout," and I tried *couvre-feu*. They dismissed the term "curfew" with laughter. "Passive defense!" In fact, there was no curfew of any sort in Hanoi—except the bell that rang at eleven o'clock nightly, closing the hotel bar—though there was one in Saigon. It was only when the sirens blew that the lights of the city went out and the cars and trucks halted and waited for the All Clear.

On the way from Gia Lam Airport into the city, we had our first alert—a pre-alert, really, given by loud-speakers; the pre-alert usually means the planes are sixty kilometers away; it is not till they are within thirty kilometers of the center that the sirens scream. Suddenly, still deep in the countryside, the driver braked the car; he had heard the pre-alert on his radio. He turned off the engine. I sat in the back seat, holding my bouquet in my lap and feeling quite apprehensive. On March 17, two days before, the much-feared swing-wing F-111A's had appeared in Thailand; there had been pictures of them in the Bangkok papers. The driver got out of the car. "He is looking for the shelter," one of my companions explained. "He has found the shelter," they announced a few minutes later, and we all climbed out of the car. In the moonlight, we could see the remains of a brick house, with its roof torn off; up the lane, there had been a hamlet, but now there were only indistinct masses of debris and, somewhere in the dark, the shelter, which

I never actually saw. It was enough to know that it was there.

Outside Hanoi, the driver's first job, I discovered, was to look for a shelter for the passengers whenever the alert or the pre-alert sounded. Every hamlet, sometimes every house, is equipped with a loud-speaker, and the alarm is rung out by the hamlet bell—the same bell that calls the peasants to work in the fields. When there is no hamlet nearby, a band of young soldiers, tramping along with a transistor radio, may warn you that the planes are coming. Once, in Hoa Binh Province, out in the west, I sat huddled in the car with the thin, large-eyed young woman interpreter while the driver conducted the search; he came back, and there was a quick conference in Vietnamese. "Here there is no shelter," she whispered, gravely touching my arm, as we listened to the bombs, fortunately some miles off. Though the shelter may be only a hole in the ground, the assurance that there is such a burrow handy gives a sort of animal comfort—possibly not unlike the ostrich's. Or maybe it is a grateful sense that somebody, an unknown friend, has thought about your safety; even if the uncovered earth shelter cannot protect you from a direct hit, the thought, as they say of small presents, is what counts.

In the city, there are individual cement cylinders, resembling manholes, every few feet, with round fitted covers of cement or of plaited reeds—good against fragmentation bombs. In a pinch, they will accommodate two small Vietnamese. But what happened, I wondered, if there were more people on a given street when the alarm sounded than there were shelters to hold them? As in a game of going to Jerusalem or musical chairs, who would be left outside? It is a schoolmen's problem, that of the outsider, which is posed in the scramble of extreme situations, and I was curious—anxious, even—about the socialist solution. But I never was able to observe for myself what did in fact occur: in my two and a half weeks in North Vietnam, it chanced that only once was I in the city streets during an alert and then only long enough to see the people scattering as our driver raced toward the hotel and its communal shelter. And I felt that it would be somehow impolite to express my curiosity in the form of a point-blank question; there are many questions one does not want to ask in Hanoi.

In any case, the target of the Hanoi government is one shelter per person within the city limits—I am not sure whether this ratio takes into account the communal shelters attached to institutions. During my stay, hundreds of brand-new cylinders were lying along the sidewalks, waiting for the pavement to be dug up and holes sunk to contain them, and every day trucks kept dumping more. Production and delivery were ahead of the picks and shovels. "Manufacturing shelters is one of our principal industries now," people remark, rather ruefully, watching the gray cylinders being put into place. What can be done with these grim manholes, war memorials, when and if peace comes? The only answer I could think of was to plant flowers in them.

Johnson's speech of March 31—and the subsequent eerie absence of alerts—did not cause even a momentary flagging in the shelter program. Yet, so far as I could tell, the shelters were more a symbol of determination than places to scuttle to when the planes approached. The city population had a certain disdain for using them. "There are toads in them," a pretty girl said, making a face. Like the white-gowned surgeon I met, a

Hero of Labor, who had calculated the statistical probabilities of being killed by a bomb in the night and decided that he preferred to stay in bed, to be fresh for operating the next morning, many people in Hanoi decline to leave their beds or their offices when the peremptory siren shrills; it is a matter of individual decision. Only foreign visitors are hustled to safety by their guides and interpreters and told to put on their steel helmets or their pellet-absorbent hats of woven reeds or straw. A pellet in the brain is the thing most dreaded by the Vietnamese—a dread that as a brain-worker I more than shared; unfortunately the hat they gave me was too small for my large Western head, and I had to trust to my helmet, hurriedly strapping it on as I trotted down the hotel stairs to the communal shelter and glad of the excuse of social duty to do what private fear was urging.

Your guides are held responsible by the authorities if anything happens to you while you are in their care. This applies particularly to guests invited by North Vietnamese organizations (which we were); accredited journalists are allowed more rein. I was asked not to go out into the street alone, even for a short walk, though the rule was relaxed when the bombing of Hanoi stopped on April 1—Hanoi time. This of course limited one's bodily freedom, but I accepted it, being a law-abiding person. Our hosts of the Peace Committee told us that they had been severely reprimanded because some frisky young South Americans had eluded their control last summer and roved unsupervised about the country; one got a pellet in the brain and had to be sent by plane to Moscow to be operated on; he lived. Whenever we traveled, one of the comrades of the Peace Committee made sure I had my helmet by personally carrying it for me. I was never alone, except in bed or writing in my room. In the provinces, when we stayed at a guesthouse or came to inspect a village, each time I went to the outlying toilet, the young woman interpreter went with me as far as the door, bearing my helmet, some sheets of tan toilet paper she had brought from Hanoi, and, at night, the trusty flashlight. She waited outside till I was through and then softly led me back.

That first night, driving in from the airport, everything was novel. The driver had left the radio turned on in the car when he switched off the lights. We could hear it talking, as if to itself, as we paced up and down, and I had the foolish notion that the planes, wherever they were, might hear it, too. Other shadowy sedans and passengers were grouped by the roadside; there had been a great influx at the airport that night because for over three weeks, four times running, the I.C.C. flight had not been able to make it down the narrow air corridor from Vientiane to Hanoi. On the road we had passed several cars with diplomatic license plates, one, surely, containing the Indonesian ambassador, who had boarded the plane with his golf clubs; he used them to exercise on his lawn. Now abruptly all the headlights went on again; motors started. "They are going away. They are going away," the radio voice had said in Vietnamese; the pre-alert was over.

Activity resumed. A chattering stream of people, mostly young, was flowing along the highway toward us from the city, walking or riding bicycles and motor bikes: boys in work clothes or uniforms, with camouflage leaves in their helmets, girls and women, some riding pillion, carrying baskets of salad greens; now and then a wrinkled old peasant, in black, with balance-pole on his shoulder or pushing a cart. A cow raised its head from a field. All that nocturnal movement and chatter gave an impression of revelry, as if a night ball game or a theater had just let out; probably a work shift had ended in the factories. Along the road's edge cases of supplies were stashed, covered with jute or tarpaulin. Jeeps and military trucks, some heavily camouflaged, were moving steadily in the opposite direction.

We were passing pretty rows of small, compact trees—perhaps pruned fruit trees; it was too dark to tell—a pre-alert to the fact that Hanoi is a shady, leafy city, like Minneapolis or Warsaw; like Minneapolis, too, it has lakes, treated as a municipal feature, with parks and promenades. The people are proud of the trees, particularly of the giant camphor, wreathed in a strange parasite with dangling coinlike leaves. Near the bombed brick house where we waited during the alert, there was a big bare blasted trunk, maybe an oak, which was putting out a few new leaves; my companions eagerly pointed them out, making sure I did not miss the symbol of resistance and rebirth. To the North Vietnamese, I soon became aware, everything is now a symbol, an ideogram, expressing the national resolve to overcome. All of Nature is with them, not just the "brother socialist countries." Nodding their heads in time with a vast patriotic orchestra, they are hearing tongues in trees, terrible sermons in stones and the twisted metal of downed aircraft. In Hung Yen Province, you eat a fresh-caught carp under a red-and-white-nylon canopy, like a billowing circus tent enclosing the whole room; it is the giant parachute of the pilotless reconnaissance plane they have shot down. Near Hanoi, in a village co-operative, raising model pigs and making handicrafts, they show you a small mute cluster bomb, olive drab, and, beside it, the mute rusty primitive soil-scratching implement the young peasant was using in the co-operative fields when pellets from the cluster bomb killed him. Visual education, they feel, for the people, and they are not afraid of hammering the lesson in. But it is Johnson, finally, they wish to give food for thought.

Growth statistics, offered everywhere, on bicycle ownership, irrigation, rice harvests, maternity clinics, literacy are the answer to "the war of destruction," which began February 7, 1965; a bombed oak putting out new leaves is a "reply" to the air pirates of the Air Force and the Seventh Fleet. All Communist countries are bent on furnishing growth statistics (it is their form of advertising), but with Hanoi this is something special, carrying a secondary meaning—defiance. On a big billboard in the city center, the number of U.S. planes shot down is revised forward almost daily in red paint—2,818, they claimed when I left, and the number keeps growing. In villages, the score is kept on a blackboard. Everything they build is dated, down to the family wells in a hamlet—a means of visibly recording progress, like penciling the heights of children, with the dates opposite, on a door. And each date has a clear significance in the story of resistance: 1965 or 1966, stamped on a well, proclaims that it was built *in spite of* the air pirates.

Hanoi, it is whispered, is going underground, digging shelters, factories, offices, operating theaters, preparing for "the worst," *i.e.*, for saturation bombing by the B-52's or even—draw a deep breath—for atom bombs, although if you mention

198

those to one of the leaders, he tersely answers that Johnson is
not crazy. This feverish digging, while dictated no doubt by a
very practical mistrust of the Pentagon, seems to have a secondary meaning, too—mythic, as though the city were an allegor-
ical character. Hanoi appears to be telling its people that it is
ready to go underground, harrow hell, to rise again like the rice
plants from the buried seed. To a Westerner, this sounds fantastic, so much so that I hesitate to bring it up; after all, you
can tell me, Hanoi's leaders are Marxists, and Marxists do not
believe in resurrection stories.

Yet the Vietnamese folk beliefs are highly animistic; they
venerate (or did) the souls of their ancestors, resting in the rice
fields, and the souls of rocks and trees. Their classic relief
sculpture surprises you with delicate, naturalistic representa-
tions of plants, birds, animals, and flowers—much more typical
of Vietnamese art than grotesque images of gods and the Buddha. The love of Nature is strong in their literature, too, and is
found even in the "captured enemy documents" the U.S. is fond
of distributing for publication. This helps explain their root-
attachment to the fatherland, as every observer has noticed,
going deeper than politics, into some sphere of immanence the
foreigner is almost embarrassed to name—"spiritual," "religious"? Much is made in the North of the fatherland's sacred,
indivisible unity, and, despite or because of a history of parti-
tions like Poland's, the sentiment of being one country seems
to be authentic and shared, incidentally, by the South Vietnamese firebrands who would like to "march on Hanoi." As a
symbol of that unity, the North has planted the coconut palm;

the visitor may be slow to grasp the significance of this. "Coconut trees." "Yes, I see them." "Before, here in the North, we did not have the coconut tree. It is a native of Saigon."

In Hanoi you find cabbages and tomato plants growing in the ornamental garden of a museum, in parks, around an anti-aircraft unit; the anti-aircraft battery has planted a large flower garden as well and it has chickens running around the gun-emplacements. Today the abundant use of camouflage—exuberant sprigs of plants, fronds, branches, leaves of coconut and banana on helmets, anti-aircraft, military vehicles, even tied to the backs of school children—cannot be meant entirely to fool the enemy overhead. For one thing, the foliage on the anti-aircraft artillery does not begin to conceal the guns' muzzles. This camouflage, snatched from Nature, must be partly a ritual decoration, a "palm" or "laurel" of prowess and connected with ancient notions of metamorphosis—pursued by a powerful enemy, you could "survive" in the verdant form of a tree. In Hanoi, the innocent protective mimicry of coconut leaves "disguising" military hardware always made me think of Palm Sunday in a Catholic country and the devout coming out of church with palm leaves or olive branches—a pre-Easter mood. In the country, a column of army trucks and half-tracks proceeding under its thatch of greenery made me feel that Birnam Wood was rolling on to Dunsinane: "Your leavy screens throw down,/ And show like those you are."

The determination of Hanoi appears at first incredible—legendary and bizarre; also disturbing. We came eventually to the pontoon bridge, floating on bamboo, the replacement, for automobiles, of the Paul Doumer Bridge that still hangs, half bombed, like a groping tentacle, over the Red River. On the bridge, the traffic goes single file, and you wait for the oncoming cars to finish their turn before a policeman gives you the signal to advance. This waiting in line by the river's edge is scary—there has been a lot of bombing in the area, as you can see by looking around—and it is even scarier when you start across the frail, wavy bridge; traffic moves very slowly, with many halts, and if the bombers should come while you are there, suspended over the water, there would be no escape; useless to look for shelters on the insubstantial bridge, obviously, and you could not jump into the dark, quite swift river. You just have to put your mind on something else, make conversation; I always dreaded this crossing, the sense of being imprisoned in a metal box, a helpless, all-but-motionless target, and I had the impression that the Vietnamese did not care for it either; each time, there was a general easing of tension when the bridge was finally negotiated.

In the hotel, to my stupefaction, there was hot water, plenty of it. During nearly a month spent in South Vietnam the year before, I had had *one* hot bath—on the U.S.S. *Enterprise.* In my room at the Continental in Saigon, there was only cold water, and when I was once offered a bath in the room of a New York *Times* correspondent,* the water ran dark red, too rusty to get into. In theory, they had hot water in the Marine Press Base at Da Nang, but in practice they didn't. Other luxuries I found at the Thong Nhat Hotel were sheets of toilet paper laid out on a box in a fan pattern (keys at the desk were laid out in a fan pattern, too), a thermos of hot water for making tea, a package of tea, a teapot, cups and saucers, candies, cigarettes, and a

---

* Jonathan Randal, now of the Washington *Post.*

mosquito net draped over the bed and tucked in; in Saigon, I had been tortured by mosquitoes.

It was obvious that the foreigners at the Thong Nhat lived better than the general population, but this could be said, too, of the foreigners at the Continental, who moreover had to pay for what they got, whereas in Hanoi a guest of a Vietnamese organization was not allowed to pay for anything—I never had to change so much as a dollar bill into dongs. The knowledge of living much better than others (the meals were very good) and at the expense of an impecunious government whose food-production areas were being pounded every day by my government produced a certain amount of uneasiness, which, however, wore off. There was nothing to be done about it anyway, and I soon was able to verify that outside no families were sleeping in the streets, as they had been in Saigon, nobody was begging or in rags, and the people appeared healthy, though tired in some cases, particularly those who were old and had doubtless been hungry a good part of their lives.

On opening the window, I found that there was an extraordinary amount of traffic, extremely noisy traffic, though nobody in Hanoi owns a private car—only bicycles and motor bikes. The honking of horns and screeching of brakes went on all night. To someone who lives in a European city where it is against the law to honk your horn, the constant deafening noise seems very old-fashioned. My ears had forgotten those sounds, as they had forgotten the clanging of streetcars and the crowing of cocks at 4:00 A.M. Hanoi still has both cocks and streetcars, and you can hear the whistle of trains, as well as the more up-to-date noise of MIGs overhead and the almost continuous voice of the loud-speakers, invariably feminine and soothing, sugared, in tone. Unless you know Vietnamese, you cannot guess whether they are announcing an air raid or telling you the planes have left or simply giving a news broadcast or a political diatribe.

There is a good deal in North Vietnam that unexpectedly recalls the past. Waiting to cross the Red River recalled my first trip to Italy, just after World War II, when most of the bridges were down ("Bombed by the Liberators," in Italian, was scrawled all over the devastated cities and towns) and our bus crossed the Po or the Adda on a tremulous pontoon bridge; the loud-speaker outside the hotel window ("Attention, citizens, attention") recalled the loud-speakers in Florence during a spring election campaign (*"Attenzione, cittadini, attenzione"*). Jouncing along a highway deeply pitted by pellets from cluster bombs made me think of my childhood: bumpy trips in northern Minnesota; Grandma in a motoring hat and duster; and how each time we struck a pothole her immense white head, preceded by the hat, would bounce up and hit the car's canvas top. North Vietnam is still pioneer country, where streams have to be forded; the ethnic minorities, Meos, Muongs, and Thais, in the mountains of the wild west, though they do not wear feathers, recall American Indians. The old-fashioned school desks and the geometry lesson on the blackboard in an evacuated school, the kerosene lamps in the villages, the basins of water filled from a well to use to wash up before meals on an open porch, the one- or two-seater toilets with a cow ruminating outside brought back buried fragments of my personal history. I was aware of a psychic upheaval, a sort of identity crisis, as when a bomb lays bare the medieval foundations of a house thought to be modern.

The daytime alerts in the hotel reminded me very much of fire drill in school. During my stay there was no bombing near the hotel, though the siren sometimes sent us to the shelter as often as six times in twenty-four hours. After a while you estimate the distance of the explosions you hear—six kilometers, ten, fifteen—and you think you can tell the dull, resounding noise a bomb makes from the crackle of ack-ack. In the hotel, I began to have a feeling of security, like the veteran correspondents who usually did not bother to get up during night raids or who, if they were up already, wandered out into the street to watch the anti-aircraft activity. In the daytime, it became a slightly tiresome routine to walk, not run, to the shelter, where a delegation of Chinese in gray uniforms—who never spoke to anyone—were always the first arrivals, and wait for the All Clear. And as in the case of fire drill, I began to half wish for some *real* excitement, for the bombs to come a bit nearer and make a louder bang. It got to be a disappointment if the alert was a false alarm, *i.e.*, when you simply sat in the shelter and heard no action at all. The other foreigners must have felt the same way, for when the explosions were noisy and the guns replied, the conversation in the shelter became much livelier, and there were giggles.

An alert was also a social event; you saw new faces and welcomed back old friends—that is, people you had known a few days—reappearing from a trip to Haiphong or Nam Dinh. One day in the shelter I met the Danish ambassador to Peking, and another time a whole diplomatic dinner party, men in dark suits, large, freshly waved ladies from the bloc countries in low-cut silks and satins, an Indian lady in a truly beautiful blue sari, joined us drab "regulars" on the underground benches, having left their double rows of wine glasses and their napkins on the table of the hotel's private dining room, reserved for parties— this eruption, as of a flight of butterflies, was a momentary wonder in our somewhat mothy, closet-like existence.

The late-night alerts were different. Though I had concluded that there was no real danger of bombing in the immediate neighborhood of the hotel—unless Johnson escalated again, with B-52's or "nukes," in which case my personal survival was not of any interest; I would not care to survive—at night, when the shrilling of the siren waked me, I forgot and would jerk up from the pillow with my heart pounding, grope my way out of the mosquito netting, find the flashlight in the dark, slippers, dressing gown, et cetera, and stumble, still unnerved, down the stairs and out through the hotel garden, pointing my flashlight down, searching for the entrance to the shelter. Those late-March night raids made everybody angry. According to the Vietnamese, who were experts on such matters, they consisted of one or two planes only, whereas before they had come in large purposeful waves; their object now must be psychological—without any military pretext—to harass the population at random, deprive it of sleep, while at the same time lessening the risk to themselves of being shot down, for it is harder to hit a single plane in the sky than to pick off one or two out of a serried dozen or twenty.

No planes, so far as I know, were shot down over Hanoi during my stay, though one, they said, an Intruder, had been shot down the day of our arrival. The foreign correspondents agreed that the bombing was slowing down, at least in the region of Hanoi, and they wondered whether the Americans could be short of planes, on account of the number destroyed or damaged in the late-January Têt offensive. The date of manufacture stamped on a shot-down plane was always of great interest; if a plane manufactured in July was shot down in August, this suggested that stocks were low.

In fact, though we did not know this in Hanoi, the "return" of the bombing, in dollars terms, had been added up early in the year by the accountants in Washington. The April number of *Foreign Affairs* was revealing that it had cost the U.S. six billion dollars to destroy an estimated 340 million dollars' worth of facilities: clearly a low-yield investment. The cost in lives of U.S. pilots in comparison with estimated North Vietnamese losses seems not to have been computed—where, on the balance sheet, would the lone target, working in a rice field, of an anti-personnel bomb figure? Left out of the calculations also— surely an oversight?—was the cost to the North Vietnamese government of the shelter program, not to mention the cost of the loud-speakers and the personnel to man them.

Only once in the city while I was there did a bomber "sneak through" the warning system. It happened once in the country, but there it was less spectacular to hear the thud of bombs be- fore, so to speak, listening to the overture of the sirens; in the country, as I said, there are no sirens anyway and surprises were to be expected. In Hanoi, it happened one evening at the

Museum of War Crimes, when we were sitting down to little cups of tea at a long table following a tour of the exhibits. Suddenly, there was a long-drawn-out, shrill, banshee-like, shrieking noise, succeeded by a shattering explosion. At the same time, out the window, we could see a plane streak across the sky. The museum director, an officer in uniform, rushed us out into the garden; guiding me by the arm, he was propelling me toward the shelter. Big red stars looking like skyrockets were bursting in the dark overhead. Then the siren must have blown, though I have no memory of hearing it. In the museum's shelter, we heard more bombs exploding. "The museum is near the bridge," the interpreter murmured, as if to excuse the fact that a raid had come so close. When the All Clear sounded, we went in and found the tea cold in our cups. Back at the hotel, during the next alert, one of the guests told us that there had been three bombs and a Shrike.

To return from a shelter to a disarrayed table where the tea has grown cold in the cups and resume a conversation at the precise point it had left off ("You were saying . . . ?") is a daily, sometimes an hourly, occurrence in the North—inevitably so, since tea is served visitors on every ceremonious occasion, and all occasions, however sickening or painful, are ceremonious. Hospitality requires that tea should be served at the beginning and end of any visit: tea, cigarettes, candies, and long slender little cakes that taste of bananas. The exceptions were the Journalists' Union and the War Crimes Commission, both of which served beer, and the prison where the captured pilots were held, which offered a choice of beer or a soft drink, plus bananas. I could never make out the reason behind these slight variations of an otherwise inflexible precept. It was easy to guess why beer was served to journalists (newsmen drink), while the Writers' and Artists' Union served tea, but why beer at the War Crimes *Commission* and tea at the War Crimes *Museum?* Maybe beer is more expensive, and Mr. Luu Quy Ky of the Journalists' Union and Colonel Ha Van Lau of the War Crimes Commission had bigger budgets than the others. In some instances, tea was followed by coffee.

Perhaps I should have asked, but the Vietnamese are sensitive, and to wonder aloud why beer was served instead of the customary tea might have been taken, I thought, as a criticism of the hospitality: "Why did they *not* serve tea?" In the same way, I was reluctant to ask why in some co-operatives, factories, and associations there were portraits of Marx, Engels, Lenin, Stalin, and Ho, while in others there was only Ho. Was it a matter of personal preference on the part of the administrator? That did not appear likely. Once, in a village co-operative I thought I saw Marx, Engels, Lenin, and Ho, and no Stalin— which made a joyful impression on me—but when I got up from my chair, I found that Stalin had been behind me all along, chuckling. The explanation may be that if the center you are visiting is a branch headquarters of the Lao Dong (Workers') Party, you get the whole pantheon; otherwise, only Ho. The absence of portraits of Mao and of the current Soviet leaders seemed self-explanatory ("Vietnam asserts its independence"), but it could not be remarked on, any more than you can remark to a host on the absence of certain persons who you might have thought would be invited to a party.

In the War Crimes Museum, that evening, among the exhibits they had showed us a Shrike, so that the sudden advent of the live missile had the air, to us, of a coincidence ("Speak of the devil . . ."), but of course, to the North Vietnamese, nearly all the exhibits in the museum "matched" what was befalling them regularly. The museum, unlike that at Auschwitz, is strictly contemporary. There were cluster bombs—guavas and pineapples—some of the delayed-action type, regarded as the most fiendish, ordinary placid TNT bombs of varying weights, ranging from babies of 200 to big daddies of 3,000 pounds, rockets, an assortment of missiles, crop-spraying powders (with the results in a bottle), tear gases, front and rear views of patients hit by a spray of pellets from the "mother" bomb, X rays of pellets in human skulls, photos of napalm and phosphorus victims (napalm has not been used in the vicinity of Hanoi and Haiphong, or, as the Vietnamese say, "not yet"), quite a collection of exhibits. And shuffling about among the displays was a small middle-aged Vietnamese woman in a bunched sweater, wide trousers, and sandals, who was staring, as if drawn by some morbid, fascinated curiosity, at the weapons and devices in the glass cases, at the big bombs arranged, like modern metal sculptures, on the floor; she bent to read the labels, sometimes furtively touched. They told us, lowering their voices, that she had been haunting the museum ever since she had lost her twenty-year-old son early in the year.

An American apologist might claim that she was an exhibit, too, a "plant" to invoke the sympathy of soft-headed pacifists and other bleeding hearts, but in fact the museum personnel seemed somewhat put out by her presence and by the occasional snuffling, sobbing noises she made, interrupting the scholarly presentation of the material. In short, they reacted like museum officials anywhere who were not lacking in heart but had their professional duties, which included discouraging nuts and people with "troubles" from intruding on official visits. It was true, she *was* causing our attention to stray. Then, as if guiltily conscious of being a disturbance, she would hastily quiet down and regain her composure, peering into the glass cases with an air of timid wonder, like a peasant viewing the tools of modern civilization and wondering what they were for. She seemed to be trying to put her lost son and these efficient implements together in some satisfactory manner, as though to make a connection and localize the source of her pain. Sometimes, appearing to find it for a moment, she actually smiled and nodded to herself.

She had gone, I guess, when the Shrike came. Perhaps one of the museum employees had persuaded her to go home finally or given her some tea in the kitchen. To tell the truth, when the Shrike came I forgot about her; I had got used to the fact that during an alert the ordinary Vietnamese—chambermaids, cooks, waiters, desk clerks, tea servers—vanished from sight, only to reappear when the alert was over. Either they proceeded to their own shelters, separate from those for foreign guests, or, like the chambermaids in the hotel who doubled as militia, they shouldered guns and went up to the roof, or they continued quietly with their jobs, like the cook I once glimpsed in the hotel sitting in his white apron and hat at the kitchen table when the All Clear blew. The siren was a Last Trump separating the sheep—us—from the nimble goats. At the

National Liberation Front Delegation, the distinction was marked by a heavy dark-brown curtain dividing the communal shelter between personnel, on one side, and, on the other, the Chief of Mission, his immediate staff, and his guests. To an American, such a frank distinction appears *ipso facto* undemocratic.

At the museum, in a parting ceremony, they presented us with rings made from downed U.S. aircraft. Like a wedding ring, mine is engraved August 1, 1966—the day the plane was shot down—and has the initials H. Y., which must stand for Hung Yen Province. They also gave me a woman's comb of the same material. Such souvenirs seem to be popular in Hanoi, but though, as they watched, I murmured *"Merci beaucoup"* and hurriedly, like one rapidly swallowing medicine, tried the blunt ring on my finger, I instantly slid it off and dropped it into my handbag; luckily, I had the excuse that it was a man's ring: too big. Back in the hotel, I shut it up in a drawer out of sight, but it kept troubling my mind, making me toss at night, like an unsettled score. For some reason, the comb, scalloped in the Vietnamese style, did not bother me.

Perhaps, if I had had the courage, I might have declined to take the ring, handed it back to the Vietnamese as soon as I realized what it was. As my grandmother tried to teach me, one need never be afraid to say no. But from their point of view, it was a symbol of friendship, a medal pinned on my chest. They were proud to bestow it. What was it that, deeper than politeness, which was urging me to do so, made it impossible for me to keep it on my finger, even for a few minutes—just not to give offense? Maybe the premonition that if I once put it on, I could never take it off; I could not sport it for the rest of my stay and then get rid of it as soon as I left the country—that would be base. Yet equally repugnant to my nature, to my identity, whatever that is, to the souls of my ancestors, would be to be wedded for life or at least for the duration of this detestable war to a piece of aluminum wreckage from a shot-down U.S. war plane. Or was it just the fact that it did not "go" with my other jewelry?

Nor could I drop it in the wastebasket of my hotel room. The chambermaids would find it and return it to me: *"Votre bague, madame."* Or, worse, they would feel that, to me, their friendship band was rubbish. But if respect for the feelings of others forbade my junking it in a wastebasket of the Thong Nhat Hotel, then there was no sea anywhere deep enough for me to drop it into. I had to keep it. The comb, presenting no problem, a simple keepsake and rather pretty, remained openly on my bureau in the Thong Nhat with my other toilet articles. Yet I now slowly realize that I never passed it through my hair. Mysterious. I cannot explain the physical aversion, evidently subliminal, to being touched by this metal. Quite a few of the questions one does not, as an American liberal, want to put in Hanoi are addressed to oneself.

The Party Car

In glaring contrast to Saigon, Hanoi is clean—much cleaner than New York, for example. The sidewalks are swept, there is no refuse piled up, and a matinal sprinkler truck comes through, washing down the streets. In the somewhat gloomy lobby of the hotel, where foreign correspondents sit conferring with their interpreters, like clients murmuring with their lawyers on the benches of a courtroom, a strong smell of furniture polish rises from the worn furniture. The abundant archaic towels in the bathroom are stiff from many launderings—in cold water, probably, and a harsh soap. Sanitation is almost a fetish, imbued with political fervor: *wiping the slate clean.* In Hanoi, there are no prostitutes on the streets (the claim is that they have all been reformed), no ragged children with sores. It is rare to see a child with a dirty face, though children themselves are fairly rare, most having been evacuated to the country, where their parents visit them on weekends.

The fiercer animals in the zoo—lions and tigers—have been evacuated, too, or, rather, turned loose in the mountain forests. According to a Western news agency, the severely rationed economy could not spare fresh meat to feed them—good news for the Pentagon, since, if true, it proved that the war was "hurting." Mr. Phan of the Peace Committee, who volunteered the story, told it differently. He said they sent the dangerous animals away in case an air strike should wreck their cages and let them escape into the streets. I prefer Mr. Phan's explanation, delivered with big grave eyes. It has its amusing side, like the thought, hilarious for children, of an elephant escaping from the circus. Yet of course the problem is serious and confronts any city under bombing, just as much as what to do with the pictures in the museums. In World War II, what happened to the animals in the London Zoo? Where did they put them?

Nor—excuse me—is it unthinkable that the U.S. Navy or the Air Force would consider bombing a zoo. The model leper colony of Quyn Lap was bombed not just once—which might have been an accident—but thirty-nine times; I have seen photographs of the pandemonic scenes as doctors and attendants sought to carry lepers to safety on their backs and on stretchers —limbs wasted to stumps, arms ending in knobs. One hundred and sixty secluded buildings, housing more than 2,000 lepers, were demolished (I apologize for using North Vietnamese statistics, but the Americans have not supplied any); the first raid netted 139 dead, some, it is said, machine-gunned as they scattered. "But what could be the motive?" Americans protest. "What is the *point* of bombing a model leper colony?" I do not know the motive but I know the result: the surviving lepers have been distributed to ordinary district and provincial hospitals, where they are, to put it mildly, a problem, a pathetic menace to public health. If you bomb lepers, why draw the line at captive lions and tigers, who could be quite a menace, too?

In any case, the Hanoi government has sent the four-footed carnivores back to the wild. They are the only instances of what the U.S. calls "refugees," *i.e.*, forcibly evacuated non-belligerents, the war has created in the North. The zoo, very spruce, with well-swept paths, now contains chiefly sage monkeys, intelligent chimpanzees, and, for disgust, some cruel vultures, whose cage, at feeding-time, is the star attraction; maybe for Communist citizens (I cannot forget the monstrous sated vultures of the zoo in Warsaw), they are a fascinating object lesson in insensate, ruthless greed.

Unlike the half-evacuated zoo devoted mainly to peaceful herbivores, the city of Hanoi, like a dragon, breathes fire at every corner. Besides the shelters, the anti-aircraft, the scoreboard of shot-down airplanes, the army trucks, the boys and girls in uniform, there are huge war posters everywhere, graphics of Liberation Front heroes, slogans; the current attraction at the movie houses is a story about the heroine of Ham Rong (Dragon's Jaw) Bridge, the beautiful leader of a militia unit in Thang Hoa Province, pictured on colossal billboards with helmet and rifle.

Some writers have pictured Hanoi, even before the air war, as drab, and this is true today, certainly, of the old mercantile streets, which nobody could think of as colorful. There is almost nothing to buy except, literally, hardware: *e.g.*, flashlights, thermoses, secondhand bicycles, and bicycle parts. Many shops are closed down. The principal private businesses seem to be barbershops and bicycle-repair shops. The very name Silk Street sends a pang through the luxury-loving passer-by. In Hung Yen Province, there are still mulberries and silkworms, but their product presumably goes for export. Cotton dress goods and woven table mats made by co-operatives are sold in the government department store. As in all Communist countries, books are cheap, but the shelves and counters of the Hanoi bookstores display, almost exclusively, textbooks of one sort or another: technical, scientific, political. Little fiction or poetry, and that mostly of an edifying or patriotic character; few translations of foreign classics, except Marx and Engels. The translation of modern European and American authors, a thriving industry in Poland, Czechoslovakia, Yugoslavia, is here still largely a dream for the future: "We have started to translate your progressive writers: Jack London and Mark Twain."

In the street, the population, riding its bicycles, is dressed in somber colors: black trousers, white shirt or blouse; khaki, gray, or navy blue zipper jackets. A few very old pedicabs or Cyclopousses, trembly relics of inequality, still circulate, usually as delivery carts, though occasionally you see a passenger aboard—a stout middle-aged woman with bundles. The alluring, transparent ao-dai, still the normal dress of women in the South, is worn here only by performers or by élite workers on occasions of welcome. It was startling to visit a generator factory and be received, with bouquets of gladiolas, by a bevy of young women dressed in bright ao-dais and with big red Cupid's bows, reminiscent of the twenties in America, painted on their lips. Assembled at the factory entrance, coloring shyly through the disks of rouge on their cheeks, they looked like bridesmaids emerging from a church. Ordinarily the women wear no make-up, and the only notes of color on the flying bicycles are supplied by girls' plastic rain capes, robin's-egg blue or pink. Despite the rainy winters, the umbrella, I was told, was discarded when the air war began. Mine attracted attention, and I began to be embarrassed by it, as though it had been a parasol. When not in work clothes, the men of Hanoi dressed neatly in Western suits, clean white shirt, and tie.

Hanoi is clean but defaced and stained, reminding one of a bathtub that has been scrubbed with an abrasive powder till the finish has worn off. Outside the old French residential quarter, which includes diplomats' houses, the presidential palace and gardens, and the colonnaded Ba Dinh Assembly, the buildings have not been "kept up" or renovated. Like the ancient elevator in the hotel, manufactured in Saigon in some other eon, and the sighing old French plumbing upstairs, shops, dwellings, and offices are survivors, veterans. The Catholic families who "followed the Holy Virgin south" after Geneva would not find many changes, except those wrought by time. A clubwoman I knew in Saigon, when she heard I might go to Hanoi, begged me to go and look at "her" drugstore, just as a dispossessed *ci-devant* baron might beg you to go look at "his" castle: "It is still there, my drugstore—on the Place du Marché." I undertook the pilgrimage, and the drugstore was there, all right, seemingly just as she had left it in 1954; only it needed new paint and shutters. The former U.S. consulate now flies the flag of the National Liberation Front Delegation; they have changed the official pictures in the reception room and built a shelter in the garden, but otherwise it still looks very much like any U.S. consulate in the South, minus the sandbags and the Marine guards.

The only important new building is the big empty Polytechnic University, finished just before the bombing started; classes had hardly begun when they had to be dispersed to the country, and this, no doubt, was taken as a sharp lesson. Hanoi, quite naturally, is closing down existing structures rather than adding to them. The central market is closed—too dangerous an assembly point—and peasant women sell flowers, fruit, and vegetables from little stands on the sidewalks. So far as I could see, repairing bomb damage was the only building activity going on in the city and its environs. If the damage is extensive, as in the case of blocks of workers' apartments badly hit (I saw them) in the suburbs, what is left of the buildings is simply condemned, for the time being, and nobody is supposed to live there, though in reality a few families do. If it is just a question of repairing a roof, this is done rapidly.

In the Two Sisters district, an outlying section of Hanoi, on the morning of March 28, I watched workmen repairing the roof of the Church of the Little Flower; it had been bombed on March 8, at 7:50 P.M. The congregation was at evening mass when the officiating priest heard the alert on the loud-speaker just outside the church; the bombers were forty kilometers off. He ordered the congregation to disperse, and nobody who had been in church was hurt except the statues on the altar and along the walls; St. John the Baptist, in a loincloth, with his rustic cross made of sticks, and a green polychromed angel were still recognizable, though headless; the Stations of the Cross were completely shattered. Near the Gothic-style church—stone, with many crockets—there were five big bomb craters, one filled with water, among the growing market crops. Eighteen bombs, the people said, had been dropped on this Catholic hamlet, remote from the main highway and from any discernible military target. Those who had gone to mass had been lucky. Eight people were killed, and eight wounded; fifteen houses had been razed. Yet already the rubble had been cleaned up—only a child's crib had been overlooked—and once the bomb craters were leveled off and replanted, a visitor would never guess what had happened unless he were shown photographs at the War Crimes Commission.

In the center of Hanoi, where raids took place in August and again in October last year on two thickly populated city blocks (the "industrial" targets being a small hardware store and a little bicycle-repair shop), you stand deep in rubble, amid twisted bedsprings; your guides point out where a partly destroyed house has been rebuilt, looking no newer—to your eyes —than the adjacent houses that escaped. Here there is no question of urban renewal. A patch of roof or wall is hastily applied to the old worn fabric of the city. Somehow, in Hanoi I missed seeing the bombed area visited by Harrison Salisbury and others, though from their description it must have been not far from the hotel. Maybe it has been rebuilt and blends, like camouflage materials, with the emaciated buildings around it. In Hanoi and its suburbs, I noticed, only relatively fresh bomb damage is called to the visitor's attention. The rest is documentation: museum material.

Despite the shade trees, lakes, and parks, Hanoi in peacetime could undoubtedly seem drab—a poor relation of the Western Communist capitals with their tourist attractions of rebuilt palaces, restored glittering churches, picturesque market places, pretty girls in miniskirts, shops full of "good design" handwoven rugs and embroidered place mats to take home. What makes the difference, now, is the militancy, the flame in the eyes, which sometimes darts out if you make an imprudent comparison. As a common purpose, repelling the invader is a more enlivening goal, it would appear, than building socialism, a sometimes zestless affair; here, building socialism is not just an end, which may seem to be perpetually receding, like a mirage, but a *means*; the reason for making sacrifices is clear and present to everyone. In Hanoi, you do not see the dispirited milling restless crowds of the cities of Eastern Europe; almost everybody here is in a hurry. Obviously there must be discontented people, grumblers, but where are they? There cannot be a government decree ordering them to stay in their houses. Yet wherever you go, you are met with smiles, cheers, hand clapping. Passers-by stop and wave to your car on the road. Once in a while, it is true, in a poor, historically "disadvantaged" province, you pass old black-clad peasants, with cross, obstinate faces, who do not raise their eyes—like people refusing to salute a flag—as you go by, smiling and raising dust. But this is almost reassuring; unanimity would be too abnormal.

In Hanoi, because of the war, the population goes to work at six in the morning. The stores open at five or even four. Few people eat at home any more or in restaurants. They take their meals in the government canteens, turning over their rationing tickets. An exception was Mr. Phan of the Peace Committee, a gourmet, who did his own cooking, his wife being either at work in a government office, in one of her two evening classes, or at committee meetings. He profited from trips to the country to shoot birds to bring home; so, in fact, did the driver.

It was plain that life in Hanoi was austere and strenuous,

though every effort was made to lessen this for the foreign visitor, who was regarded as a weaker vessel. The indulgences of the West were known to the North Vietnamese by repute, though their travel had usually been confined to attending congresses in Communist countries. They would apologize for the inconvenience caused by the alerts—an excess of courtesy when speaking to an American, I felt. They were solicitous about one's health, how one had slept, whether one was tired. Our tour of the recent bomb sites in the city required a 7:00 A.M. departure from the hotel, and they excused themselves for this. "We are sorry about it, but that way it is safer." The bombers, they told us, seldom arrived before 9:00 A.M. "You mean the pilots have to have a hot breakfast first," I said ironically. "We do not know the explanation," they replied. "But we have observed that this is the case." It did indeed appear to be so, as a general rule, in the countryside as well as in the city. In my notes I have marked down only one early-morning alert: at 5:45 A.M. on March 21.

For an overnight trip, you waited till late afternoon to start. Preparations were methodical. First, you were given time to rest in your room. Then a light supper was ordered in the dining room for precisely four-thirty. Your guides from the Peace Committee (it was never clear whether they themselves had eaten or whether they ever rested) were distressed, almost alarmed, if you protested at eating so early, having finished lunch at about two—luckily, I am docile about sitting down to table when told to. At the destination, you would be fed again— fed and fêted. Wherever you went, there would be basins of hot water and towels for you to wash up; I was never invited to

223

wash so often as in North Vietnam. And, when we stopped en route, young Mrs. Chi of the Peace Committee whispered: "Would you like to make water or shit?"

Each departure, smacking of danger, was an adventure. Shortly before six, the baggage waiting in the hotel lobby was carried out to the cars. In Vietnam, it gets dark about seven, all year round. By the time we went through the military checkpoint at the city limits (all automobiles entering or leaving the city are checked, but not bicycles or pedestrians), it was dusk, and trucks and military vehicles, which had been parked by the roadside, had begun moving, too, like sleepers awaking and stretching. This crepuscular stirring at nightfall, when good people should be preparing for bed, was full of excitement, half-childish, as though you were in a dense forest when the owls and other night creatures came into their own, and the effect was enhanced by the sibilant leaves of the camouflage. Gradually, headlights blinked on, the big trucks using only one, like the Cyclops. Lanterns hung over the tables of little country inns; a dim crowd of working people was waiting by the road's edge. "A bus stop." Under cover of darkness, the country was resupplying.

Respecting that cover, I never asked exactly what was in the trucks or where the convoys were going. I did not want to feel like a spy. Indeed, I had a strong desire not to observe any movement of men or vehicles that might have a military or political significance. I tried to restrict myself to innocent questions and speculations, such as "Was that thunder and lightning or a bomb?" This inhibition extended to observing my companions and attempting to study their attitudes and behavior, in the manner of a social scientist. A poor approach for a reporter, but I suspect it was rather general and dictated by courtesy to a people whose country was being invaded not only by fleets of bombers but also by reconnaissance planes, monitoring every pigsty and carp pond, while in the South, below the DMZ, North Vietnamese prisoners were being interrogated, their documents, little poems, and diaries read and studied by military intelligence and U.S. political scientists, hopeful of penetrating the medulla of North Vietnamese resistance to find evidence of homesickness, malnutrition, disillusion, war fatigue.

Nevertheless, I could not help noticing an awesome lot of military traffic, any more than I could help seeing that the car I was riding in was a Volga and that the car ahead, bearing another guest of the Peace Committee, was an old Peugeot, and the car ahead of that, bearing the doctor and the photographer (guests of the government, when traveling, must be accompanied by a doctor), a Warszawa.

Nor could I wholly disconnect the intelligence apparatus within my own head, which registered the evident fact that my companions were Communists, that they were sometimes guarded in their conversation and quick to correct a doctrinal error or slip on the part of a compatriot, as when, in the Museum of Art, the director, a gray-haired painter, while making some point about a fifteenth-century Vietnamese landscape with figures, had referred in a derogatory way to the Chinese, meaning plainly, I thought, "the cruel Mings," and the Peace Committee guide, with a sharp cough, interposed, "The Chinese feudal oppressors," lest we think we had heard a slur on the People's Republic of China. The embarrassing point of this little episode, in terms of political constraint, apparent to any Westerner, including a non-Party Russian, a Czech, or a Hungarian, was probably lost on our young guide, who must have felt simply that he had covered, with smiling rapidity, a tense moment, instead of, on the contrary, causing one.

He was a nice person, Mr. Van, modest, kind, amused at himself, with a startled harelike look, always dressed, when we went to the country, in a rather sporty cloth cap and scarf. I wished he had not had to do that or to nod to us with boyish satisfaction, like a senior approving a junior recitation, when the museum director promptly echoed, "Certainly; the Chinese feudal oppressors." But I did not blame him, really. I blamed the United States. If we had not been bombing his country, Mr. Van might be a free, or at least a freer, spirit, instead of an anxious chaperon fearful that his charges might draw an "improper" conclusion.

Often, when with our friends of the Peace Committee, I thought of other Communist countries I had been to, other and different conversations. In particular of Sarajevo in the winter of 1960. I had gone to Yugoslavia on a lecture tour for the State Department—itself an index of how time has flown, politically speaking, since. Between Sarajevo, the old Bosnian capital, and Hanoi there were quite a few points in common. The flowers on arrival. When I got off the train in Sarajevo, I was too green to know that this was a Communist custom—which must have derived, I think, from pre-Revolutionary Eastern Europe—and I was amazed and flattered to find some bundled-up officials from the Writers' Union waiting for me at the station in the snow with a large bouquet of red roses. They took me to a hotel with antique plumbing, quite a different milieu from the modern hotels of Belgrade and Zagreb; the Archduke Franz Ferdinand and his wife, Sophie, had stayed there on June 28, 1914, the day they were assassinated—their names must still be in the register. Around the corner there was a sort of Museum of the Revolution, which I was immediately taken to; it was devoted to fading photos and mementoes of Princip, the assassin, and the bridge nearby, over the Miljaka River, was named for him. Strange to find that here in Sarajevo this young man, who had caused World War I and, indirectly, all its sequelae, right down through Belsen and Auschwitz, was a Hero of the People. It gave you, as they say, a different perspective, like the ubiquitous likenesses of Stalin in North Vietnam.

In Sarajevo, I was warned ahead of time, the Party apparatus was tough and illiberal. The town was poor, shabby, provincial, half-Moslem, with a bazaar and minarets; the administration was under-favored by the Tito régime. I would be meeting old doctrinaire functionaries, reactionaries in the sense of being still unreconstructed from the Stalinist period. There would be no question of the audience's understanding English, as at Zagreb or Belgrade or Ljubljana; a translator would be supplied. My lecture was on the novel, and I tried to choose examples chiefly from Russian and classical French fiction that I thought the audience might know. At the end of the lecture, the bald-headed Party literary chief rose from his chair and demanded: "Why have you not mentioned your great writer Jack London?"

This question, really an accusation, had never been leveled at me elsewhere in Yugoslavia, still less in Poland, where I had been lecturing, too. It floored me, and I could only answer, mildly, that I had never read Jack London, except a book about a dog when I was a child. The answer made the literary chief angry (like any light dismissal of somebody else's taste), but it made me popular with the translators, of whom there turned out to be two, both very young. One had studied acting in summer school at Stratford-on-Avon and had played Hamlet in a student production; the other was the son of a professor. These young men, as I soon found out, were in very bad odor with the Writers' Union, but on the occasion of my visit they had become indispensable to it, since practically nobody else in the town knew English. Probably, as in Poland at the time and in North Vietnam today, English and French, the capitalist tongues, were discouraged in the local university, offered only as "second" or optional languages, while Russian was a "first" language and compulsory—in North Vietnam, if I understood right, there is a choice between Russian and Chinese as a "first" language.

In any case, the two young men, "Hamlet"—I could not master his last name—and his friend, were making the most of my presence, to tease and annoy the Party leadership. There was a whole group of contumacious young writers, it seemed, who met in a café and discussed Greek pre-Socratic philosophers and daring writers like Nietzsche. They invited me to the café (an honor, they told me, for I was the first person over thirty ever to be admitted to their table), and naturally I went.

It was in the café, I think, that the plot was hatched to get possession of the Party car, in order to take me to the mountains and go up on the ski lift. As in Hanoi, there were no private cars in Sarajevo—certainly none for young people to ride around in. The car belonging to the Writers' Union was very old, rusty, and battered—a real heap. But to "Hamlet" and his friends, it was a prize to be captured, with some co-operation from me. In the end, they got it—virtually hijacked it, I gathered —and somehow got the gasoline, too, and we all went off to the mountain lodge, a new socialist construction, which was empty, and rode back and forth on the ski lift over the fir-tree tops, even I, who am afraid of heights. They had struck a blow for freedom; that was how they saw this escapade.

What was interesting about this group was its seriousness. They were not literary Bohemians, but deeply interested in politics and philosophy. Moreover, they were committed to Marxism and hopeful of working out for themselves, in that backward Moslem town whose chief products were pure mountain air and "Turkish" carpets, some synthesis of Marxism with more libertarian philosophies. The neo-capitalist ideas coming out of Belgrade at the time did not attract them at all, but they were curious about that intransigent figure Simone Weil, and her little book on factory work. Nor had they been infected by the careerism typical of the young big-city intellectuals of Yugoslavia, who were mostly interested in making money, acquiring unspoiled seashore property at bargain prices for vacations and watching its value mount ("We bought it for 10,000 dinars and now it's worth ten times that"), getting showy apartments and studios from the government, and staying out of trouble politically. If the literary bureaucrats of Sarajevo were the most benighted and forbidding functionaries I met in Yugoslavia, "Hamlet" and his friends were the most advanced and freest—in the true sense—young beings. A sort of polarization had taken place.

Riding along in the Volga, I wondered what had happened to them. The worst (to my mind) would be if they themselves had slowly—or rapidly—climbed up the rungs of the Writers' Union and had reached the top. The best would be if they were teaching in the university. Perhaps "Hamlet" had become a player and was treading the boards in Belgrade. Comparison with the young translators of the Peace Committee was inevitable. Their situations were equivalent: as interpreters, they had become negotiators, in a sense, between their own society and friendly elements belonging (or half belonging) to ours. And humanly they were not unalike: idealistic, pensive, patriotic, proud of their native scenery and customs. Behind the Vietnamese, however, was a grimmer life experience; young as they were, they had fought with the Viet Minh against the French. And they were still obdurately fighting, though no longer with guns. In contrast to *their* seriousness, that of the young Bosnians appeared frivolous, irresponsible; at any rate, that was how young Mr. Hieu, small-featured, slender, delicate, hard-working (he had taught himself English by listening to the BBC and the Voice of America), and his wife, Mrs. Chi, would have regarded it. And it was true: it was easier to imagine "Hamlet" and his friends giving up the struggle finally, succumbing to the local temptations—slivovitz, sloth, neo-capitalist financial "incentives"—than to imagine Mr. Hieu, Mrs. Chi, or Mr. Van surrendering principle even for a half-hour.

In an ideal world, though, Mr. Van and Mr. Hieu—and why not shy Mrs. Chi?—would be free from the inner constraints that made them circumspect with the foreigners in their charge, from the self-imposed rationing system in the realm of ideas that limited their diet to what was strictly necessary to the national interest, free to speculate, to question authority; in fact, to hijack the old Peugeot up ahead and go off on a joy ride—in a Communist country, the Party car is Father's car. But until the Americans go home, Father's car or Uncle Ho's, garaged in North Vietnam, will be treated with deferential respect. No question of "borrowing" it for private, unlicensed enjoyment. The Americans have blocked such possibilities for the young Vietnamese, and for the old, too. They have frozen the country in a posture of wary vigilance, ears pricked up for the slightest violation of the defined intellectual and political boundaries, in the same way that in the Peugeot the driver's radio, though turned low, is alert to catch an announcement from the central network of a violation of the national air space. And until the Americans go home, translation probably will be arrested at the point of Mark Twain and Jack London.

But the ideal world I am speaking of is mine, not Mr. Van's and Mr. Hieu's. I had been able to share it, to my surprise and joy, with the young Bosnians, but the North Vietnamese would reprehend the thought of our having such a libertine world in common. An irony of the war is that so little can be shared, except opposition to the American participation, by the charming Vietnamese hosts and the Americans who come here as friends—pacifists, liberals, young members of the New Left, who share among themselves an attitude of incaution and resistance to any established authority.

Hence the parable of the Party car, though it kept recurring to me during those long night trips, had to remain unspoken; I felt slightly guilty, stealthy, in confiding it even to my notes.

To begin with, any comparison to revisionist Yugoslavia would have been, automatically, odious. As the Cyclopean trucks lumbered by, bound for some destination which I did not care to know—Laos? the Ho Chi Minh Trail?—the best course was to avoid reminiscence, black out large compromising areas of my past, and concentrate on the present. A flash in the sky ahead. "Lightning, do you think?" "Maybe." A double flash. "It *looks* like lightning." "No. Bombs."

North Vietnamese Bucolic

G o out into the field," American officials
last year, in blustery hectoring tones,
were telling newcomers to Saigon, meaning
get close to the fighting if you want to "connect" with the war.
In North Vietnam, officials do not stipulate a tour of the combat
zones as a condition for climbing aboard, "turning on," or, as
they would express it, "participating in the struggle of the Vietnamese people." Indeed, if I had wanted to be taken to the 17th
parallel, they would surely have said no: too long and dangerous
a trip for a fleeting guest of the Peace Committee. And too uncertain, given the uneven pace of travel by night, in convoy, to
plan ahead for suitable lodging, meals, entertainment. A reporter on the road can trust to potluck and his interpreter, but
for guests hospitality requires that everything be arranged in
advance, on the province and district, even the hamlet, level,
with the local delegates and representatives—stage-managed, a
hostile critic would say; though, if so, why the distinction between guests and correspondents? Anyway, that is how it is, and
I do not feel it as a deprivation that I failed to see the front
lines. The meaning of a war, if it has one, ought to be discernible in the rear, where the values being defended are situated;
at the front, war itself appears senseless, a confused butchery
that only the gods can understand; at least that is how Homer
and Tolstoy saw the picture, in close-up, though the North Vietnamese film studios certainly would not agree.

235

Nevertheless, it was a good idea—and encouraged by Hanoi officials—to get out of Hanoi and go, not into the field, but into the fields. In the countryside, you see the lyrical aspect of the struggle, *i.e.*, its revolutionary content. All revolutions have their lyrical phase (Castro with his men in an open boat embarking on the high seas), often confined to the overture, the first glorious days. This lyricism, which is pulsing in Paris today as I write, the red and black flags flying on the Sorbonne, where the revolting students have proclaimed a States General, is always tuned to a sudden hope of transformation—something everybody would like to do privately, be reborn, although most shrink from the baptism of fire entailed. Here in France the purifying revolution, which may be only a rebellion, is still in the stage of hymns to liberty, socialist oratory, mass chanting, while the majority looks on with a mixture of curiosity and tolerance. But in rural North Vietnam, under the stimulus of the U.S. bombing, a vast metamorphosis, or, as the French students would say, restructuring, is taking place, not as a figure of speech, but literally. Mountains, up to now, have not been moved, but deep caverns in them have been transformed into factories. Universities, schools, hospitals, whole towns have been picked up and transferred from their former sites, dispersed by stealth into the fields; streams have changed their courses. City children have turned into peasants. Nomad tribes—horse people —thanks to irrigation projects, have been settled as farmers and equipped with bicycles. Rice has been made to grow on dry land. However this revolution may be assessed finally in terms of economic cost and yield, whether it is temporary, a mere war epiphenomenon, or can continue as a permanent experiment, the fact of it is a plain wonder. No statistics recited in an office prepare the visitor for what is, to him, in part a delightful magic show, complete with movable scenery, changes of costumes, disguises.

The Vietnamese themselves, not loath to moralize, look on it more solemnly, in terms of strictly drawn contrasts. "In the past," they say, pointing to pale-green rice fields laid out geometrically in squares and rectangles, "those fields made a crazy pattern." "Yes," I say, "like a crazy quilt," regretting, in my heart, the classic pattern of individual small-scale ownership. Mr. Phan, who likes words (he is a veteran war correspondent), nods to himself, filing the phrase away, smiles broadly. "I myself," he declares, "hate anything artificial, but I make an exception of the rice fields." We are in Hung Yen Province, flat, watery, famous for mulberries and for bees attracted by the very sweet fruit of the dragon's eye tree—the longan, which grows rank here. He excepts too, though more doubtfully, the ugly prefabricated honeycombs, made of paraffin and beeswax, they are showing us in a movie. "In the past," he says, translating the sound track, "honey production in the province was a fifth of what it is at present." "In the past" or "formerly" introduces every third sentence once you leave Hanoi. In the past, they say, this province had one small hospital; now, besides the province hospital, there is a dispensary in every village, and each district has a hospital of its own. "Formerly there was no second-level school in the entire province; now each village has a second-level school."

"In the past" and "formerly" = under the French or, in some contexts, under the old native landowners, "the cruel *langs*."

But it is not necessary to have known the "Before" to appreciate the "After." South Vietnam, under the Americans, is a present and terrible "Before." Last year I saw the filthy hamlets there and the refugee camps. Here everything I am shown is clean. It is true that I am on an official visit, but in the South, outside of Saigon, wherever I went, I was conducted by an AID man or a U.S. or Friendly Forces officer—the exception being a tour of some refugee camps counted as "middling" by the shocked German social workers who were showing them. In the South, they cannot hide the dirt, disease, and misery. They would not know where to begin. It is true that in the North there is no fighting; a U.S. invasion might help equalize things, spreading hunger and squalor.

At any rate, in the North I saw no children with sores and scalp diseases, no trachoma (it has been almost wiped out, according to the Ministry of Health), no rotten teeth or wasted consumptive-looking frames. You do not need plague shots to visit the North, or cholera shots, for that matter. They say there is still some malaria in the northwestern mountains. In the countryside, children and young people were radiant with health; as far as I could judge, everybody under forty was in peak physical condition. Peasants and agricultural workers are favored by the rationing system and they are allowed a small percentage of land for their privately owned garden crops and animals; the difference is apparent, but not glaring—seeing them side by side with the desk workers of Hanoi, you might put it down to the difference between the country and the city, outdoors and indoors.

It was clear that in the hamlets the people had few posses-

sions: some cooking utensils, plates and cups, bedding, a Buddhist altar with a few ornaments, one change of clothes, the
small children's usually being patched and faded. The clothes
in the South, chiefly army castoffs and charitable donations, were
better on the whole. In the house of a peasant family in the
North, you wonder at the absence of bureaus, chests, trunks,
until it comes to you that they have so little to store. On the
other hand, they had new-driven wells and clean outhouse toilets,
sometimes one to a family, sometimes public. There was no
garbage around the houses or floating in the streams. There were
no smells. Pretty new brick walks led into the hamlets we visited,
and a central square was often paved with brick. I remember
the little *place* of the Dai Ta co-operative, under the shade of
four interlacing secular banyan trees on top of which, like a tree
house, a lookout tower was perched with a boy from the militia
on duty; nearby was the old hamlet bell. In this particular hamlet, an old man, speaking French, dressed in faded army khakis,
evidently a gentle *lang,* was grafting new varieties onto lemon
trees, which wore cloth bandages where the insertions had been
made. He had come out of retirement, he said, to give his aged
skills to his country: under his guidance, young papaya and
grapefruit trees had been planted along the walks; he indicated
a Rhode Island Red rooster, scratching in the dirt, that he was
trying to cross with the small local chickens to get a bigger
breed.

Each hamlet and co-operative we visited boasted—and that is
the word—a robust girl midwife, barely nubile herself. In the
schools, we saw boys and girls with glasses, which gave them a
surprisingly "Western" industrious look; I could not recall see-

ing a single child wearing glasses in the South. Formerly, our guides say, the peasantry was illiterate; now everyone can read and write. In fact, the Ministry of Education speaks of pockets of illiteracy remaining in the north, near the Chinese border, but the people themselves believe that they have made education universal, the young teaching the old, if necessary, husbands teaching wives. Outside the schoolhouses, though, I did not see any books in the rural areas, and indeed, as in many farm communities, reading did not seem to be practicable, on account of the early risings and bedtimes and the poor lighting—it was impossible to read a line by the tiny kerosene lamp in a province guesthouse. "Where do the people read?" I asked a woman district representative in an "ethnic" village, and the answer was: "In their offices. But mostly just newspapers. They do not have the time." She was speaking of people like herself. The peasants listen to the radio. Yet here, as in most Communist countries, there is a great hunger for books, it is said—a hunger arising partly from a former scarcity and the novelty of print.

During our travels, the one lack I felt, in comparison with the South, was the sparkle and mischief of the little boys. In the North, the children were friendly but timid, unlike the infant black marketers and bold suppliants of the South. I cannot say I *missed* having stones thrown at me or being pummeled for a cigarette, but I might have been glad to see a troop of naughty, fearless children tagging along behind us as we walked along the neat brick walks of a village co-operative, pausing to inspect a loom or a model pigsty. Here the children, even the rare show-offs, are models of conduct. A little girl, not much bigger than a doll, urged forward, entrusts her hand to mine: "Hello,

Auntie." "Auntie," for the Vietnamese, is a term of respect, like "Uncle" (hence Uncle Ho; in the Vietnamese family, the senior uncle, not the father, is the source of authority), and to call an American woman "Aunt" is an act, for a child, of extraordinary docile faith. These country people, who have never before seen an American, unless possibly a shot-down pilot, seem to accept without question the notion that there are "good" Americans—something that, in their place, lacking further evidence, I might be disinclined to believe. Never in the North did I find a woman watching me with eyes full of hatred, though this happened often in the South. Here there was only curiosity and often a desire to touch, as with a new object. Young girls would press close to me, entwine hands or arms with me, particularly when we were lined up for a photograph or to listen to a speech of welcome. The absence of a common language created a "little" language of soft gazes, smiles, caresses. Good-byes were like those at a school graduation, with parents (in this case our guides) waiting to perform the surgery of separation.

It was useful to have been in South Vietnam, to make comparisons. Yet one could have dropped from the moon into Hung Yen or Hoa Binh Province and known at once that something marvelous, in the old sense, was astir. Schools in the fields, for instance, dispersed over miles of flat landscape, hidden under thatched roofs of coconut palm or straw, so that they are almost invisible from the air. No doubt there must be historical parallels for this; I know that according to family legend, my great-great-grandfather and his brothers, denied formal education by the English, were taught their lessons by priests in the Irish wheat fields, hidden from the oppressor's view by tall rows of grain. The Irish and the Vietnamese have a bond of patriotic struggle, I was told one night at the Writers' Union by a plump, middle-aged Vietnamese poet, a troubadour or wandering minstrel, he called himself, because he had been reciting poems to the troops along the DMZ, accompanying himself on an instrument (his debased equivalent, I suppose, would be the belly dancers who minister to the Marines); when he was young, under the French colonialists, he had been in love with Irish history, he said—"C'était ma passion"—we talked about Parnell. But the Irish story, if true, is only a fairly tall tale, while the North Vietnamese dispersal of pupils and teachers into bamboo groves and rice fields is a living saga. The magnitude of the phenomenon, the sheer geographic spread, suggests the early Christian hermits dotted about on the Libyan Desert and in the caverns of the Red Sea.

In Hung Yen Province, you leave your cars by the roadside and walk across the dikes. A group of young teachers accompanies you; one, they say with pride, is from the South. In the North you are introduced to quite a few young people who were born on the other side of the parallel; they are the children of Viet Minh fighters who regrouped to the North in 1954 and '55. To have one of these Southerners—duskier, often, if they come from the Mekong Delta, and with round snub features, broad faces, and slightly frizzy, ashier hair—in your school or cooperative is considered a distinction: "She is from Bien Hoa Province, near Saigon."

Leading the way, the literature teacher, male, says politely that he gives his pupils extracts from American writers to read. "My pupils prefer Burchett, of all your authors." "But Wilfred

Burchett is an Australian. I have met him in Hanoi." Burchett is a Communist journalist who carries a North Vietnamese passport. "They like very much also *Ten Days That Shook the World.*" "Yes. He was an American." Here in the Red River Delta, it has been raining heavily. Beside the flooded fields, old peasants are scooping up water, using an implement resembling a lacrosse cradle. The school huts are new, brick, with palm roofs, and set among banana trees. In the teachers' common room, there is a bust of Beethoven, awarded every year for excellence in literature. You enter a classroom, where the teacher, a thin, serious young man, is at the blackboard. The pupils rise from the desks and clap. Clapping is a mode of welcome, and the guest (if I was not mistaken) is meant to clap, too. They are having a history lesson.

Chalked on the blackboard is a map of what is evidently a military action—a battle fought against the French in 1950, Mrs. Chi whispers. This comes as a slight shock, for I do not think of that as "history" yet, *i.e.,* as classroom material. Each pupil has a textbook with photographic illustrations. Glancing over the shoulder of the young girl next to me on the school bench, I guess that it is a history of the French resistance struggle; by the end of the term, they will get to Dien Bien Phu. Today's subject, though, is not exactly history; it is a lesson in military tactics. Tapping his pointer on the map, the teacher is explaining how the Viet Minh achieved its purpose, which was to lure the French out of a fort into the forest. He illustrates his theme with anecdotes. Called on to recite, a pupil tells a funny story about the cook who got some hungry French to surrender by offering them a little rice in a saucepan. Everyone laughs.

It is a good class, attentive and lively. The girls are well dressed in long brown fitted corduroy jackets. The class age must be fifteen or sixteen; this is a second-level school, equivalent, probably, to middle high school in America. The atmosphere is reminiscent of schoolrooms in my childhood. You would not find such a well-disciplined class in America today. Yet in my school days, after World War I, we would never have been studying the tactics of Soissons or Château-Thierry. American history was the Civil War and "Remember the Maine" and the War of Independence. Maybe we "had" Gettysburg or Antietam or Chancellorsville, but I cannot remember being drilled in the tactics of those battles. The only tactics we learned, if memory serves, were Caesar's: how he built that bridge over the Rhine and caught the boats of the Veneti in his fleet's long grappling hooks. And something about Waterloo and the British square. To my mind, formed in those habits, that is still the way history *should* be taught: firmly set in the past, beyond partisan passions, and yet capable of exciting the imagination. Children in my day took sides and had heroes; you quarreled with your friends over who was superior, Napoleon or Wellington, Marlborough or Prince Eugene, Hector or Achilles. Confederate generals offered a wide range of preference: Beauregard, Stonewall Jackson, Morgan the Raider. But your heroes were not the official heroes of the nation, often the opposite; you could "like" spies and traitors: Major André and Benedict Arnold, rather than Paul Revere. Like most spirited young people, I was generally on the side of the losers. History taught, or, rather, learned, in that fashion is close to art; it is a "story."

It was too early to hope, obviously, that these embattled, endangered children could find a soft spot in their hearts for De Lattre de Tassigny, still less for the inept General Navarre. History, as taught by the French to the Vietnamese, was bound to incite a spirit of revenge on the old French Empire textbooks. Mr. Phan was fond of quoting, with a short acerbic laugh, from the first words of the history he had had to memorize as a boy: *"Nos ancêtres, les Gaulois . . ."* In literature, Mr. Phan and I had had the same textbooks—Crouzet, Desgranges—but being an American I had no scars to show from the experience; it had not hurt my national pride.

Still, I was sorry to find that map on the blackboard. Beyond my personal disarray and regret at what appeared to me a kind of indigence (history was richer than those children knew), I was sensitive to the fact that at home this lesson would be regarded as sheer propaganda: "They indoctrinate the school children." Yet it was not ideological instruction they were receiving here, except for one set phrase, run together like a printer's slug—"The French colonialists aided by the American aggressors"—which had the merit of being factually true: Indochina in 1950 was a French colony, which was getting large quantities of military aid from the Americans, whose intentions were certainly not defensive so far as the Vietnamese were concerned. Rather, what the children were studying in the textbook and following on the map was a practical guide to action. This was a class in Preparedness. It would have been foolish, I guess, to expect to find them studying the Mongol invasions of the thirteenth century. They had probably had that in grade school, along with the history of the Two Sisters, Vietnamese Boadiceas, who had repelled the Chinese invader in the first century A.D. and ruled as queens until, defeated at the head of their army, they drowned themselves together in a river from grief.

In the next classroom we visited, they were having a lesson in solid geometry. The class rising from its desks was a trifle older, about seventeen, and there was only one girl member, somewhat plain. The boys were good-looking, some beautiful, even, with lustrous hair, shining eyes, soft clear skin—no acne in North Vietnam. The teacher at the blackboard, not much older than they, was very handsome himself, gay, laughing, kind. Most of these students, Mr. Phan thought, were the children of peasants; the teachers, who came from "away," lived in with the peasant families, as used to happen fifty or sixty years ago in rural America, when the schoolteacher boarded with farmers. Middle-class specialists from Hanoi were also housed with the local peasants, teaching them new farming methods: this province, formerly, had been backward. "Our experts have learned much from the people, too," Mrs. Chi, conscientious, appended. "It is a new experience for them." The need for learning from the people is often emphasized in the North; we have heard about that before, in the Soviet Union, where erring writers are sent to "learn from the people," as young delinquents in the capitalist world are sent to reform school. But on Mrs. Chi's lips the expression has a tender, Tolstoyan sound, a mild, soft, reverent note I have heard in the South, too, but there turning bitter or melancholy: the South Vietnamese on the U.S. side who care for the poor and the peasants—and there *were* some of these last year—despair of the American advisers' learning anything about the people, let alone from them.

In this classroom, I felt more comfortable. The conic sections on the blackboard were eternal, universal, democratic, the same in Hung Yen Province as in Tacoma, Washington. Here the class, when called on, unlike the history pupils, did not get the answer right on the first try; the problem was harder, requiring thought, not just memory of what was in the textbook. The teacher gently prompted and, seeing that his students were abashed before the visitors, quickly wrote the solution himself on the blackboard. I was invited to make a speech to the class. At the conclusion of a visit or tour, the guest is likely to be called on to sum up. "Now give us, please, your impressions of our factory/co-operative/school/dispensary." I was never any good at this and usually left it gratefully to my companion, but today I felt more confident. Having had that restorative impression of geometry as a binding universal, I wanted, in turn, to impress it on *them*. But either something went wrong with the translation or my thought, which was really propaganda for a disinterested world of pure forms, was too crazily tangential to their own interests or to what they were expecting to hear—anyway, whatever the reason, it fell flat. When the translator finished, the whole class looked bewildered, as if the words that had reached them had been an empty envelope that had traveled all the way from the U.S., airmail, special delivery, with no message inside.

Back at the province guesthouse, we ate a second meal under the parachute of the Drone they had shot down. At one end of the room was the wreckage of a bomber plane, which had lettered on it what appeared to be part of a name: "Lt. Ed. Van Or . . ." The Vice-President of the province (in the South he would be called the deputy province chief) was a former Viet Minh fighter: around his neck, he wore another trophy—a French jungle camouflage scarf. The cook, an old army cook resembling a sailor, had prepared a splendid carp—fished that afternoon from a pond nearby—with dill, tomatoes, rounds of carrots. The Vice-President poured little glassfuls of mandarin wine, a pink alcohol, very good, though sweetish, and many toasts were exchanged. As he drank the mandarin wine, under the leaking tent of the striped parachute (it was raining hard), his somewhat splayed features grew darker, his gold tooth glinted, and he made me think of that tough character Stenka Razin, the anarchist hero and brigand leader of the Russian marshes, who planted an egalitarian Cossack Republic along the whole length of the Volga in the time of Alexius—seventeenth century. (Does the reader feel that some of these comparisons are farfetched? They mostly come from my notebook and were taken down on the spot, hurriedly, lest I forget; for example, while Mrs. Chi, opposite, at our bedroom table in the guesthouse sat poring over the *Report of the Third Party Congress on Agricultural Matters.* A curious and maybe important thing about North Vietnam is just this historical resonance. Whatever seems strange and new there at the same time has an insistent familiarity: "Who or what does this suddenly remind me of?" Farfetched may be the right word.)

It was too muddy for the tour of a co-operative that had been scheduled. Instead, they showed us movies, and the Vice-President gave us many statistics about the province. He talked about the bombing, but there was not a great deal to tell; Hung Yen Province has not been heavily bombed—that was why it had been chosen for our visit. Only Xuan Duc, completely destroyed by 300 ordinary bombs; Minh Hai, badly damaged by phosphorus bombs; Lai Vu. He said American planes had dropped butterflies on the crops, which seemed strange: in the car, going home, Mr. Phan, for once erroneously, explained that he had meant insects—actually there is a bomb known as the butterfly. I asked if we could visit the province capital, which was only a mile or so off, but no, there was nothing to see there any more, they replied apologetically—just shut-up buildings; it had been totally evacuated.

Along the main roads of the North the visitor finds these ghost towns, ghost factories, ghost hospitals, suggestive of Death Valley, like the big still University of Hanoi. In Hoa Binh Province, the following week, we came one morning to a very large yellow modern building, with a number of outlying buildings behind it: Hoa Binh Hospital. It had been bombed on August 20, 1966. The roof of the main building—on which, our guides said, a red cross had been painted—was smashed in, and in the tall grass and weeds there were huge bomb craters. In the wilderness behind, the maternity pavilion was relatively undamaged; inside, patients' records were blowing about or lying scattered on the floor. We picked some of them up and examined them: mother, pyelitis; child, diarrhea, and so on. Along the main walk, ornamental plants were still growing, though choked by weeds. This desolate picture made one fear to ask the question "How many were killed?" "Nobody," our guides said, smiling. "But how is that possible?" "We had evacuated the hospital before the bombers came." They stood nodding. This was quite a usual thing. It had happened, for example, with the Thai Nguyen steel factory, the pride of the North. When the bombers came pounding, it was empty. Nobody home. Americans who dismiss talk of war crimes as "propaganda" would no doubt argue, if confronted with photographs, that the Hoa Binh Hospital might have been evacuated to serve as an arms depot. Possibly. Yet there were no signs of this, no evidence that the hospital had ever been occupied by anybody except medical staff and patients. The hospital looked as if it had been left in a hurry and as if nobody had come back since except bemused, head-shaking visitors like ourselves.

Such derelict structures would be pathetic, like forsaken hopes (the province hospital had been a new socialist achievement), if the story ended there. But, fantastically, a new crop of hospitals has replaced them, springing up in the fields and woods, sometimes under the protection of an overhanging cliff. A surgery is improvised in a grotto or in a thatched hut, with a generator run by kerosene and a tiny old frigidaire, kerosene-powered, too, stocked with serums and vaccines. The result of this migration of doctors and equipment may have been an actual improvement in public health: for instance, a highly trained young doctor from Hanoi has been "dispersed" to a traditional Thai community living in wooden houses on stilts. Clustering together in a valley, they look from a distance like natural elements of the wild landscape—a species of bird colony or apiary. We were received in one of those remote communities, still in some ways barbaric in its customs or savage in the old sense of the word. You take off your shoes before climbing up into the family dwelling; inside, there are two big central fireplaces, recalling the discovery of fire, one for the men to sit by, talking, the other for the women to cook over. There are mats and homespun coverlets on the floor for sleeping, the men at one end of the room, the women at the other. The women are chattering and heating food in iron pots under a smoke-blackened shelf where edible roots and ears of corn are drying; I am given a piece of fresh-roasted manioc—tapioca. Around the necks of the baby boys are silver collars or necklaces; the women wear earrings, and the young girls' breasts are bound, for reasons of modesty, in a tight, flattening bodice of hand-woven cotton. Yet thanks to the proximity of the evacuated hospital across a teetering log bridge, these primitive families have quickly learned hygiene: boiling their water, washing, making use of the new cement latrines. Their pigs, which used to live in refuse under the high-perched houses, are now installed in clean pigsties; these people are fond of pork. And the rapid evolution in folkways has been effected (credit must be given) by the "Johnsons" flying overhead and strewing a few bombs casually on another slumbrous Thai hamlet down the road a few miles, missing the hospital, if that was what they were looking for—there are no other "military" targets—in its shelter under a beetling crag.

"Out of this nettle danger we pick this flower safety" (Hotspur) could serve as Hanoi's motto in contemptuous answer to the Pentagon. Contempt for the adversary and for material obstacles and difficulties is the mood of the provinces, which now harbor most of the country's resources, like hidden talents:

dispersed industries, laboratories, medical staff, the young. Ho Chi Minh himself, according to rumor, is in a safe place in the country; that is why he has not been available to recent visitors to Hanoi. Imagination situates him in a cavern, like Frederick Barbarossa, waiting for his country's need to summon him back. In fact, on his return to what was then Indochina, in 1940, and again at the end of World War II, he *was* living in a cave beside a mountain brook, at Pac Bo, near the Chinese border. In the Museum of the Revolution, you are shown photographs of the cave, and his few simple possessions, relics of the hegira, are on exhibit, the most touching being his "suitcase," a small flat reed basket; he traveled light. With his many changes of name, which seem to signify so many protean incarnations, he is a legendary figure, a flitting place spirit or *genius loci*. The whole saga now being enacted of the dispersal bears his imprint: *mobility, simplicity, privation, resourcefulness*. The Vietnamese revolution has recovered its lyricism by returning to its primal myth of Ho's cave; the bombers furnished the inspiration.

Hoa Binh Province, to the west of Hanoi, is mountainous country, full of natural wonders and fantasies: caves, natural bridges, sugar-loaf peaks, weird stone formations resembling upright tombstones. The Black River winds through it, and it is not far from the Dien Bien Phu region, which, they say, has a similar geology and vegetation: the *ban* tree, linked with the memory of the Dien Bien Phu campaign, as much as the poppies of Flanders with World War I, grows in abundance on the mountain slopes. The first evidences of a Vietnamese culture of the Neolithic Age, about 5000 B.C., were discovered in the caves and grottoes of this province, when human remains known as

Hoa Binh Man were brought to light. Later remains, Bac Son Man, were found near Hanoi. Archaeological digs have not been halted by the war; in fact, they are part of the war effort, for the most recent Bronze Age finds are proving, at least to Vietnamese satisfaction, that already in the Bronze Age there existed a specific Vietnamese civilization having nothing to do with the contemporaneous Chinese civilization of the Han period —in short, that Vietnam, as an indissoluble entity, has always been and always will be.

A local official, introduced as the Permanent Member of the Administrative Committee, had come to meet us in the dark when our cars crossed the province border; he was an old resistance fighter from Quang Ngai Province, south of the parallel, plainly of peasant origin, with a kind, lined face and large genial-looking teeth. Through the woods, on foot, by the beam of a flashlight, he led us to an evacuated factory, which consisted of a series of workshops cleverly built under a cliff, a natural bombproof shelter. This was remarkable enough, but he was saving a surprise for us: a chamber or "room" in the mountain, closed on four sides except for a man-made portal; here Hoa Binh Man's descendants were manufacturing farm machinery. Some boys had found the cavern, lowering themselves into it from a small aperture in the top, through which now you could see a few stars; the people had blasted an entrance with dynamite, and an electric cable had been run in from the generator below. The night shift was at work (the factory ran continuously, on three eight-hour shifts), almost all of them young people, including some Muong girls from another "ethnic" tribe of these mountains wearing their tribal earrings and bracelets and shy as birds of strangers. In the glow of a forge, under the natural vaulting, it was an operatic scene, which Verdi might have scored, with a chorus of revolutionary patriots; I thought of *Ernani*. As in the factory in Hanoi, where the young girls had been making generators by hand, the work in this secret chamber was *artisanal*, handicraft applied to turning out labor-saving machinery, *e.g.*, a power tea-roller for extracting the juice from the leaves.

In the woods, not far from the workshops, was the wreckage of a U.S. plane; they took us to see this artifact of an Aluminum Age civilization, directing shafts of light on it from their screened flashlights to find its number and make: somewhere nearby was the pilot's grave. Again I thought of *Ernani* and the night scene at the tomb of Charles V. Verdi's *risorgimento* music, his love of storms, night, patriots, freedom fighters, is well suited to the North Vietnamese theme of struggle. On our return to Hanoi, two nights later, we passed a crowd assembling at the entrance to a large grotto in the mountainside; it was Saturday night, and the country people were going to the movies in an "evacuated" movie house.

Hoa Binh Province, though considered relatively safe, had been bombed more often than Hung Yen Province. There was some bombing while we were there, and one morning we saw a flight of Air Force planes pass over on the way from Thailand, but they did not bother with our little procession of cars. The bomb damage in this region disclosed no pattern of attack: here the hospital, there some houses for workers from a sugar plantation, here a small repair shop for farm trucks, there huts and fields, here an agricultural school (March 4, 1966, forty rockets, twenty fragmentation bombs; one worker killed in the school laboratory, laboratory destroyed, three teachers injured). Out the car window I glimpsed a stone bridge collapsed over a stream. "Air Force?" Mr. Phan, with a big smile, shook his head. "*We* did it. In our war against the French." I would never have known the difference, of course, but Mr. Phan was a proud stickler for accuracy; he did not want any mistakes in my notebook. Along a short stretch of the road on which we were driving, Route 6, 4,000 CBU (anti-personnel) bombs had been dropped last year.

The danger was made vivid by the miles of trenches surrounding the reconstructed agricultural school, now spread out over a wide area in camouflaged huts in which were installed classrooms, dormitories, a refectory. You had to wade through a stream to reach the school or approach it more adventurously from another direction by motorboat or sampan—they would not let me do this. The narrow straw-lined tunnel trenches, like mole runs, with points of entry every few feet, were supposed to be particularly effective against CBUs. This underground network extended for three and a half miles. Every morning boys and girls coming to school across the fields toted their bundles of possessions with them and deposited them in neat piles at the tunnel outlet nearest their classroom: homespun coverlets, sleeping mats, zipper bags—everything they owned. This was in case their strawy dormitories caught fire from a raid in their absence. Yet despite the danger and the hardship, perhaps even because of it, spirits in the school were high. Classes were being held outdoors, under the trees, in a pre-holiday atmosphere resembling that of a small American college in June, when seminars are gathered under an oak or an elm. On a table moved out into the sunlight, a makeshift chemistry laboratory was set up for an experiment; the students, who were going to be agricultural technicians, were getting a foundation in the sciences. A school chorus entertained us with songs. Our pictures were taken. But their lunch was waiting on the refectory tables: rice, a hot stew, vegetables. We left.

Some of the teachers walked with us as far as the stream we had to ford. I remarked on the evident, glowing health of the students. A woman teacher agreed. "The life outdoors is good for them." She sighed a little, shaking her head. I do not know what shadow was crossing her mind. Possibly she was reflecting on the mystery of good coming out of evil or—a related thought —on what would happen afterward, when the bombers went away once and for all. Would this pastoral scene be dismantled, as helmets were put away, camouflage leaves brushed off, city children returned to their parents? I frequently wondered, myself, especially in such idyllic circumstances, how the population would react when the spur of the bombing was removed. There would be no further need for factories hidden in the mountains, disguised schoolhouses strung along the fields and woods, tunnel networks. Could all that art and artifice be institutionalized— photographed and stored in museums?

But possibly the teacher was thinking of something quite different: the front. While we stood by the stream exchanging formal good-byes, at Khe Sanh the Americans would be totting up the morning's North Vietnamese body count. That subject is never mentioned in the North, at least not when company is present. Being human, they must talk about it among themselves.

Yet hearing no allusion to battle casualties (though they do not deny, except officially, having troops fighting in the South), you actually forget that the sons, husbands, fiancés, brothers, cousins of the cordial people you meet are being killed in a certain proportion every day. It was only when I left North Vietnam and opened a capitalist newspaper that I was reminded, with a start, of the North Vietnamese dead. I asked myself how for two and a half weeks, with young soldiers everywhere, training or marching, I could have let that slip my mind. The power of persuasion, no doubt. The North Vietnamese, confident of the immortality of their nation, of its powers of dispersal and subterfuge, had infected me with their sense of superiority to the daily facts of death.

A subsidiary explanation might be that there were no reminders present—no wounded limping or being lifted, white and bloody, into a helicopter, such as I had seen in the South, no field hospitals, no corpses packed up for shipping as at the airport at Phu Bai. The North Vietnamese soldiery was dying elsewhere. Out of sight, out of mind, then? Yet quite often in the North, I remembered our Marines at Khe Sanh, and only the night before, in the hostel where we were staying, the Permanent Member, a good man, I thought, had been talking of that hell with pity and horror for the young Americans trapped in it; the older North Vietnamese, especially men who had been in combat themselves during the earlier war, would sometimes reveal an earnest, unfeigned sympathy for the American ground soldier—a sympathy they did not extend to the pilots taking off from their comfortable, secure bases in Thailand or from the carriers of the Seventh Fleet to release their bomb loads on the population and return home for supper. So what was happening just south of the parallel must have been in the minds of all.

When the North Vietnamese maintain silence about their losses —to the wonderment of the foreign press, no over-all statistics are furnished even on the domestic casualties inflicted by the U.S. bombers and the guns of the fleet—it cannot be that there is an official conspiracy to conceal the truth from the population. The Voice of America and the BBC are not jammed, and, so far as I know, there is no ban on listening to them. The official silence must rest on a general consent: "We do not discuss our losses." No wonder the foreign guest does not seek to know, does not let his mind stray in that direction. I asked what was the name of the little stream we were about to wade through. The school principal scratched his head; he interrogated the teachers. "It seems it does not have a name," Mrs. Chi translated. "There are so many streams here; they cannot give names to them all." Everybody burst out laughing, as though the idea of fixing a name, like a ticket, to a minor natural occurrence resembling countless others was a bizarre American notion. And they were laughing, too, surely, at the prompt resourcefulness of their answer: how a seeming poverty—lack of a name— was turned into a proof of inexhaustible wealth—streams so abundant that speech could not find words for them.

Language

C ommunication was no problem with the North Vietnamese. Though only a few interpreters spoke English, some officials read it, and everybody I met of middle-class origin over the age of forty—ministers, poets, critics, museum workers, doctors, specialists in information, the head of the Supreme Court— spoke French fluently. Even those who had no second language, a factory manager, for instance, were remarkably well informed about the United States. Coming from the West, eagerly bearing news of American political developments, we found they knew it all already: the New Hampshire primary, the dollar crisis, the latest editorial in the *Wall Street Journal*. Nor were they dependent on "peace" sources; I kept seeing old copies of *U. S. News & World Report*. They were familiar with the voting records of Congressmen whose names I had barely heard of. The head of the Writers' Union referred to Noam Chomsky's work in linguistics and helped me out while I was groping for the author of *"Nihil humanum mihi alienum puto"*—Terence. You did not have to explain to them what a primary election was, a just-about-hopeless job with French political intellectuals, or sit squirming as I had done recently at a Paris press con- ference on the draft-resistance movement while speakers invoked "Samuel Bellow" and "William Thoreau." The events that happened during my stay in Hanoi—the reassignment of West- moreland and Admiral Sharp, Johnson's March 31 speech, the

Wisconsin primary, the murder of Martin Luther King—were instantly known in the Thong Nhat Hotel; I heard Johnson, live, on the Voice of America, and our friends from the Peace Committee came to tell us, with a delicate sympathy—"Perhaps it may not be true"—of the death of King. As I established when I got home (my husband had saved the French and American and English papers), no important happening in the West had missed us in Hanoi or been distorted in the reporting. The only gap was in news from the East: Poland and Czechoslovakia.

Yet there *was* a difficulty in the sphere of communication—a sort of speech impediment. Though we talked of the same things, we did not always use the same language. Take "Viet Cong." This name, which started out as a derogatory, derisive label, like "Commie" a few years ago in the United States, has passed into popular currency in the Western world, becoming the normal straightforward term for the insurgent forces in the South. If the term were taken away, nobody in Saigon could write a newspaper dispatch. In the South last year it had no pejorative sound, any more than "Gothic," originally injurious, for a cathedral. The derogatory word was "Charlie": "We caught Charlie with his pants down," "Charlie is hurting bad." By contrast, the abbreviation "VC" was a half-affectionate diminutive, like "G.I." But in the North, as I quickly perceived, the term "Viet Cong" was impermissible, since "Cong" was short for Communist, which was what they insistently denied about the leadership and inspiration of the movement. The right expression was "the People's Liberation Army."

I could not use it. For one thing, it was too long. For another, it was too heavily sloganized, like our "Free World Forces" to describe the Australians and Koreans in the South, which I could never use either, not if they gave me the water torture while a U.S. soldier watched. Maybe it is a literary prejudice to dislike such words as "free" and "people" when what they refer to is uncertain. When Johnson talks about "the American people," he means the supporters of his war policy, and when the North Vietnamese talk about "the American people," as against "the Johnson clique," they mean the opposite. Are the American people the majority or the workers or the peace movement or who? Perhaps they are a Platonic Idea.

On the other hand, I found it perfectly natural to say "the Front" or "the NLF," meaning the political entity. The National Liberation Front was its name, and one does not argue about the names of political parties and organizations. Such names, by common consent, have turned into simple signs, and only a sinister demagogue like Senator Joe McCarthy, who made a point of talking about "the Democrat party," instead of the Democratic party, will try to smudge them. But a political entity is abstract, unlike guerrilla fighters in Ho Chi Minh sandals and black pajamas. For me, "the VC" is the human and evocative term. Finally, on my tongue "the People's Liberation Army" would have been horribly hypocritical, considering how often last year on the other side of the parallel I had been saying "Viet Cong" and "VC." One cannot use language as a sort of reversible raincoat, wearing the side out that is best suited to the political climate where one happens to be at the time.

This "block" gave rise to problems, which in retrospect have their amusing aspect, I being the embarrassed comedian doing the splits. In the North, people were curious to hear about my

experiences in the South, particularly those who were Southerners. Some, trustful of the Geneva Accords, had left their
families behind in 1954, like Mr. Ngo Dien, of the Foreign
Ministry, whose seventy-six-year-old mother was living in a
village somewhere south of Saigon—he still hoped to see her
before she died. The separation of families, assumed at the time
to be temporary, is one source of the bitter sense of betrayal felt
in the North and directed toward Diem and his memory as
well as toward the Americans. When the men of the Viet Minh
went north, they counted on the elections, promised for 1956,
to reunify the country; they also counted on postal service
between the two halves, which Diem abolished. The theme of
separation plays a great part in the war literature of the North,
and two little volumes, *Letters from South Vietnam*, have been
translated into English: these letters, mostly from women—
wife writes to husband, sister to sister, daughter to mother—
reached their addressees, the reader is told, by undisclosed
routes. And even if they may have been considerably edited to
suit the popular taste ("My darling, Today is the happiest day in
my life. That is why I must write to you. I have just been appointed to the leading committee of self-defense groups in our
village!"), the popular taste is there, and reading them, as the
Preface explains, will give comfort to the many families without
news. Of course I had no news of a family kind to tell, or of
guerrilla defense units either, but I could name off the towns
and villages I had visited, and even those former Southerners
who had left no close relations behind wanted to hear about their
native places. "What is it really like in Saigon now?" "When
you were in Hue, did you go to see the Emperors' Tombs?"

The last question, simple enough to answer, you would think, led immediately into difficult terrain. "I saw one." "Only one?" "Yes. Americans were told not to go there. They said the tombs were full of Viet Cong. But a young German took me one Sunday in a Red Cross station wagon to visit Tu Duc's tomb; it was very peaceful actually. Only ordinary people from Hue walking around the little lake with parasols. It was sad; the little pools on the terraces were covered with green scum. But we didn't try to go to the more remote ones, which I guess really were in VC territory." Such sentences, I found, were possible because very light, almost invisible quotation marks were placed, as if by agreement, around the words "Viet Cong" and "VC." Implied was a faint dramatic irony, which permitted the listeners to smile indulgently, as though hearing a disembodied voice coming from AID or JUSPAO. Similarly with "What is the attitude of the students in Saigon University?" "They don't like the Americans but, being middle-class, they're terrified of the Viet Cong. As your President Ho Chi Minh said once, speaking of students and intellectuals, it is a confused milieu." Laughter. Or "In Saigon, everyone is nervous, looking over his shoulder. They say, for instance, that all the pedicab drivers are VC." No doubt the North Vietnamese, who are intelligent, perceived my discomfort. Perhaps they would have found it ludicrous to hear: "The tombs are full of People's Liberation Army cadres." Or "The pedicab drivers are all militants of the People's Liberation Army." Or perhaps not.

Those hovering quotation marks were a convenient traffic device for circumventing obstacles, and I sometimes had the impression that the Vietnamese with whom I was talking, especially when they were men of my own age or older, rather enjoyed the rapid navigation around enemy words and expressions. And it is not clear to me, looking back, whether the quotation marks were put there weakly by me or whether they sprang up all by themselves. Sometimes a sudden hesitation or gulp, as when, not looking where I was going, I arrived at "Viet Cong" big as life in a sentence and could find no way around it, produced that effect of framing or distancing—an alienation effect.

A worse problem was "the war of destruction," for here there was no question of light humor. But I was averse to using those words to describe the thing; to my ears they sounded like one agglutinated word, stuck together once and for all so that you could not unstick it. If emotive phrases are wanted, I prefer to put them together myself—bourgeois individualism. Yet to avoid the expression involved painful circumlocution when the simple word "bombing" would not fit the case; I would have to falter out something like "The bombing and shelling of your country which began in February 1965 and is still going on," as we chatted in the shelter waiting for the All Clear. Still less could I say "the U.S. imperialists," "the U.S. imperialist aggressors," or "the neo-colonialists." My word was "We."

Quite early, and with violence, I resolved that never, no matter what, would I hear myself reciting "the puppet government," "the puppet troops" when called on to speak of the Thieu-Ky government and the Arvin. It was no better in French. *"Le gouvernement fantoche." "Les fantoches."* Nor could I explain why that word led all the rest on my aversion list, especially in the mouth of a Westerner; I did not mind it so much when the Vietnamese said it, except that it made reply awkward. When somebody has been talking steadily about "the puppet government," you cannot chime in with "the South Vietnamese government," since their point is that Thieu and Ky are not a legitimate government, but American tools. The same with the army. My solution was to talk of "the Saigon government" and "the Arvin." Yet why all the inward fuss about that word? It could not be mere American touchiness. I do not care for the word "satellite" when applied to the Eastern countries of the Soviet bloc. Perhaps it is because men, even if they do not fight very well and are corrupt and steal chickens, are not puppets; a puppet is made of cloth. It is quite possible to say or write "The Saigon government is a puppet of the United States." Agreed. But to reiterate the notion every hour on the hour, far from making it truer, awakens the critical spirit: for a puppet, Ky, for instance, has been quite a handful. A figure of speech, overworked, takes its revenge by coming to life, and you wonder who is the puppet, the Arvin soldier or the orator who does not tire of calling him that, mechanically, like a recording.

Yet the North Vietnamese attach great importance to this formula. You can read in the daily English news bulletin published in Hanoi a dispatch from Reuters or UP: "The South Vietnamese [puppet, Ed.] government met this afternoon to discuss a draft of eighteen-year-olds." Conversely, when a U.S. agency quotes Radio Hanoi, you read: "The puppet [South Vietnamese government, Ed.] forces suffered heavy losses today at Bien Hoa." At that point, it becomes a war of words on both sides, a fight between blue pencils conducting search-and-destroy operations on a daily basis.

One awkwardness for a Western writer in a Communist country is that he is committed to a convention of freshness, of making it new. In antiquity, originality was not so highly valued, and it has occurred to me that the set phrases of North Vietnamese diction are really Homeric epithets. Compare "the insolent wooers," "the long-haired Achaeans," "cloud-gathering Zeus," "the hateful Furies" with "the American aggressors," "the American imperialists," "the war of destruction," "the air pirates." And no doubt, too, they are Oriental ideograms; some, like the "just cause," are the same in the South as in the North, though with different referents, of course. There is also a prescribed, quite angry Marxist language in the Eastern European countries, but behind the Iron Curtain, as opposed to the Bamboo, it is not a *spoken* language; the *Izvestia* correspondent in the Thong Nhat Hotel used the ordinary vernacular when he drew up a chair to our table, like party members in Warsaw, Cracow, Budapest, but probably when he wrote for his paper he used the official language, just as a man in the Middle Ages wrote in Latin and spoke in the vulgar tongue.

Anyway, it has to be acknowledged that in capitalist society, with its herds of hippies, originality has become a sort of fringe benefit, a *mere* convention, with accepted obsolescence, the Beatnik model being turned in for the Hippie model, as though strangely obedient to capitalist laws of marketing. Not only that; the writer's "craft" is more machine-tooled today than the poor scribe likes to think. How could he compose without his apparatus of dictionaries, thesauruses of synonyms and antonyms, atlases, glossaries, Fowler, Follett, to direct him to the right word? In prose our industrial revolution dates back to the Flaubert process, invented about 1850, which can be roughly defined as the avoidance of verbal repetition: except for emphasis, do not use a word (excluding prepositions, pronouns, articles, and connectives) that you have already used a few pages back; find another, *i.e.*, a synonym. Application of this unnatural process is now all but automatic with us—second nature. This may be because we keep on describing the same old things—that is, bourgeois society—and some stylistic variation is needed or everyone would die of boredom. A magazine like *The New Yorker* is especially nervous about the repetition of words and phrases; underscoring and marginal question marks call the contributor's attention to the fact that an adjective he has used ("employed"??) on galley 3 reappears on galley 8. Similarly, a phobic dread of clichés is manifest in the jittery styling of *Time*, whose whole editorial policy is to reduce people and events to filler and boiler plate.*

Nevertheless, an American is what he is, and a writer perhaps more than most, in that he has to stick close to his language, listening to what it will let him say, and it will not let him talk in ready-made phrases except in jest or mockery—mockery of authority and the sacrosanct. The American language is self-conscious, like a young person. Hence the cat sometimes got my tongue during long car rides with my friends of the Peace Committee, and when we conversed I tried to bypass subjects that

* *Time* has improved since 1968.

would oblige me to say "the Americans" or "We" while they were saying "the neo-colonialists" or "the Johnson-McNamara clique."

Instead, I asked them about the flora and fauna of the regions through which we were driving. In that way, I learned something about the native trees, flowers, birds, folk remedies, how the rice seedlings were transplanted, the difference between Vietnamese tea and Chinese tea. Like the geometry lesson on the blackboard in the school in Hung Yen Province, botany and zoology reassured me with the promise that they would be there when the war was over and the last "Johnson" had been shot down from the skies. My companions probably thought me quite a strange person—superficial—and indeed I felt myself that to be so concerned about the names of flowers and trees (the dragon's eye—*Nephelium longanum;* the early-flowering bridal *ban* tree, slightly reminiscent of the New England shadbush; the red-flowered kapok, the abrasin—an oleaginous tree whose product is used to polish airplane parts and gun bores) was a luxury typical of a capitalist author, who could afford the pedantry of nomenclature, just as if North Vietnam were still Tonkin (another unmentionable word, of colonialist memory, like Annam, which made it tricky to discuss the Tonkin Bay incident), and Frenchmen in tropical helmets were still exploring the upper reaches of the Mekong, looking for the shortest route to China, while Englishmen were writing in the Britannica (eleventh edition): "In the wooded regions of the mountains, the tiger, elephant, and panther are found, and wild buffalo, deer and monkeys are common. The delta is the home of ducks and other aquatic birds. Tea, cardamon and mulberry grow

wild. . . . The natives are skilled at enamelling and the chasing
and ornamentation of gold and other metals." If only that were
all, but the unnamed ethnographer had more to contribute: "The
Annamese (see ANNAM) is of somewhat better physique than
those of the rest of Indo-China. . . . (ANNAM) . . . The Annamese
is the worst-built and ugliest of all the Indo-Chinese who belong
to the Mongolian race. He is scarcely of middle height and is
shorter and less vigorous than his neighbors . . . his hair is
black, coarse, and long; his skin is thick, his forehead low. . . .
Though fond of ease the Annamese are more industrious than
the neighboring peoples. They show much outward respect for
superiors and parents, but they are insincere and incapable of
deep emotion." The old Britannica would not be spared if we
white people began our cultural revolution; that doubtless
whiskery Edwardian who looked on the "natives" as zoological
specimens was a cultured ancestor of the G.I.'s who cut
"Charlie's" ears off as souvenirs—it was just a fad, they say.
But the tea, the cardamon, and the mulberry? Must the mind
be forbidden to collect them in its neo-colonialist trunk?

Luckily Mr. Phan shared my (let me still hope) harmless
interest in the names and properties of things in Nature, and
he was always happy to acquire an English word, "seedling,"
for instance, in exchange for a Vietnamese word, and to chide
me when I kept saying "betel," when I ought to be saying
"areca." "The *betel leaf*," he wrote firmly in my notebook, and
"the *areca nut*." The point is that the betel leaf, which comes
from a pepper plant, is chewed together with the areca nut,
which comes from a palm. Or *used* to be chewed. In the North
that bad habit (betel acts like a drug or intoxicant) has prac-

tically disappeared; to my surprise, only once or twice did I
see the blackened teeth and gums so familiar in the South. Mr.
Phan confirmed my observation. Small, sturdy, dark-skinned,
with a wide, confiding grin ("They say I am a Stokely Car-
michael"), chain-smoking, in a brown leather jacket, he was
something of an explorer himself. We compared travel notes.
He knew China, Russia, Poland, Cuba, where he had stayed at
the Havana Hilton. He showed me a short piece he had written
in English about a trip he had taken last summer through his
own country in which he had carefully set down the good points
and the bad of what he had seen. He gave me "the Vietnamese
man-of-letters recipe for making tea": the pot must be scalded,
and the water be just below the boiling point—first the bubbles
coming to the surface will be the size of a crab's eye; wait till
they are the size of a fish's eye, then pour over the tea leaves.
Mr. Phan was a harbinger and a bustler and often prepared our
"visits." His great ambition was to visit France.*

Clearly in these conversations, while searching for common
ground, I was trying to hold onto my identity—a matter of
loyalty, refusing to betray oneself. But this could be read two
ways. In that very refusal was I not betraying myself in the unpleasant sense of showing my true colors? Having been an anti-
Stalinist ever since the Moscow Trials, I had remained, I
thought, a socialist of a utopian kind. In North Vietnam, the
vocabulary repelled me precisely by its familiarity. I had heard
that jargon before, and too many lies had been told in it: "the
people's democracies." Yet *were* they all lies? I suddenly recalled the comfortable American joshing of U.S. officials in
Europe a few years back: "You old capitalist warmonger, you!"

---

* He realized that ambition in 1972, when he joined the North Vietnamese delegation
to the talks, and he has since made many trips around Europe.

Ha ha. But if not true at the time, let us say up to 1960, it was already in the process of becoming true, prophetically, as those decent, amiable men were confidently laughing it off. The Bay of Pigs was waiting in the wings. And from the Vietnamese point of view—a point of view which I must say I gave little thought to until it was too late, *i.e.*, until 1964—the United States had been capitalist-warmongering at the side of the French practically since the death of Roosevelt and right up through Dien Bien Phu. And the current term "the American imperialist aggressors," like it or not, expressed the current truth. Whatever the motives, originally, behind the U.S. intervention in Vietnam, at present there was no doubt that it had turned, as if by itself, perhaps with nobody in particular propelling it, into a war of aggression, and capital investments were waiting to follow the flag, personified at a low level by the would-be real-estate developers piloting airplanes I had met in the South and at a high level by Mr. Lilienthal and his Mekong Valley development project.

As for the air war against the North, it was certainly a war of destruction and not of interdiction, which was at first pretended, unless the two terms are synonymous; you could "interdict" the flow of men and supplies to the South by destroying all life in the North, a program, I hear, that is within the technical capacity of the U.S. but is not contemplated because of the damage foreseen to the American "image."

What the United States calls propaganda is in fact reiteration. Our officials, like our writers, want to "make it new." Give us a little variety, the U.S. delegates at the Paris conference and their echoes, American newsmen, moan after the North Vietnamese

273

delegates have said, once again, that all acts of war against the Democratic Republic of Vietnam must cease. Meanwhile, U.S. policy, unvarying in content, has been clothed in seasonal changes of words as the years have rolled by. Johnson "limits" the bombing by announcement March 31 while actually intensifying it in terms of missions flown; his speech writers design new wardrobes for the steely corpus of his Baltimore address, which reappears in Manila, San Antonio, Washington, thickly disguised in woolly presidential "offers," intended surely for the American electorate, since the Vietnamese have no difficulty seeing through to the old naked proposition: reciprocity.

It is reiteration that even sympathetic Americans find wearisome in the North. "Are they still harping on that leper colony?" an American said to me when I mentioned the subject in the Thong Nhat Hotel; he had heard all about it last year, on an earlier visit, and his attitude was that they ought to change the phonograph record. "Well, actually I *asked* them about it," I replied, defensive. "I'm interested in lepers because of the ones I saw in the South." He accepted the excuse, but there was no doubt that he felt that the North Vietnamese were over-exposing their cause. As though they could use some lessons in public relations, the soft sell.

Yet, to be fair, it was natural to get bored and impatient sometimes when obliged to listen to what you already knew—otherwise, why would you be here? Tangible facts never bored me, facts of destruction and counterfacts of growth, nor did real exchanges of ideas or snatches of autobiography, but it was different with formal speeches, feature films, documentaries, plays, playlets, songs, poems, lithographs, oil paintings, which were all implacably about war and defiance. The documentaries were fairly interesting in themselves, educational (though at home a little of that marital bee culture might have gone a long way), and the feature film they showed us was superior to most Hollywood war movies, yet it was understandable for a Westerner (especially one who is not very fond of movies) to suffer a loss of affect after three or four private screenings and then immediately feel ashamed. Once I looked around restlessly in a projection room during a sentimental sequence—the heroine was leaving her father to risk her life standing guard over a delayed-action bomb —and found a Vietnamese girl silently weeping in the next seat.

They are moved by their films, by their graphics, by the endless photographs and mementos in the Museum of the Revolution. They delight in the animated relief model of Dien Bien Phu displayed in another museum whose name I forget—a panorama of the battle with little trucks and foot soldiers deploying, cannon firing, lights winking on and off, which in fact was delightful and extremely ingenious, like the electronic *crèche* I had seen in Sicily last winter with the Magi arriving on camels and shepherds grazing their sheep around the Eiffel Tower, the Colosseum, the Taj Mahal, and the Empire State Building. Pop devotional art, combining the reverent and the playful; people's art for once in the real sense.

Some of the weariness I felt was unselfish. If I longed for a change of theme, that was partly for my companions' sake, for the whole Vietnamese population. But the North Vietnamese cannot get enough of this material, which to them is, quite simply, true to life. If a magic carpet were to transport them to a performance of *Don Giovanni,* they might find it false and tedious. The girl who was crying at the movie had been prompted by the pellet bombs we had seen in the War Crimes Museum to tell me, softly, about one of her friends, a schoolteacher, who had been walking along a country road with a pupil when the planes came; she flattened herself out to cover the child and was lucky —she got the pellets only in her back. Next year that story, sufficiently commonplace in the North to command universal belief, might be turned into a movie using newsreel shots of real bomber planes. As they explained to us matter-of-factly in the Hanoi feature-film studio, they had plenty of footage of bombers; such shots did not have to be faked. In the U.S., scenes of the "air pirates" attacking schoolteachers and children would be dismissed as crude "propaganda." "I'm allergic to propaganda," an American newscaster said to me, later, in Paris, as we left a showing of some North Vietnamese documentaries. He made this avowal with a sort of modest national pride. Did he mean he liked his news "hard" without any tincture of feeling? In the war art of all kinds I saw in North Vietnam there was nothing that to *me* was recognizable as untrue.

One-sided, you might argue, except that in my opinion the Americans do not *have* a side in this war, that is, do not have an excuse, surely not that of ignorance. This war is no *Antigone,* where both Antigone and her uncle Creon are right according to their lights. No *Iliad* either. Furthermore, the Americans as shown in North Vietnamese feature films and animated cartoons are not so much villains as merry caricatures; they are meant to be laughed at, like the French colonialists, who, in their day, were satirized in witty colored prints. Nor are they only targets for humor. At the Writers' Union, a young writer described the plan of his new novel: to present in alternate chapters two points of view, that of a simple G.I. and that of a North Vietnamese soldier—both would be sympathetic. No doubt somewhat wooden also, but that is not the point. At the War Crimes Commission, Colonel Ha Van Lau, a delicate-featured, slender, refined officer from Hue, of mandarin ancestry (he reminded me of Prince Andrei in *War and Peace*), talked in an objective way about the problem of conscience for the U.S. pilots; some, he thought, were aware of what they were doing and some were naïve or deceived. The pilots in North Vietnamese hands are brought to repent (if in reality they genuinely do) not by being fed lies nor, in my judgment, mysterious drugs, but by a simpler method: shortly after their capture, or as soon as they are able, they are taken to see some bomb sites—the first step, it is hoped, in their reformation.

What you see on the stage, in films, and in street posters is not untrue or viciously biased, unless you think that rubble of a school, church, hospital, TB sanatorium is biased. On the screen and in graphics, you are shown heroes and heroines, but the Pentagon itself would not deny that the North Vietnamese people are heroic, though "tough" would be the word preferred. Even if they exaggerated the number of planes shot down (and I have no way of testing this), their defense of their land has the quality of an epic, *i.e.*, of a work of art surpassing the dimensions of realism. Seen in movie terms, it is a thriller, a cowboys-and-Indians story, in which the Indians, for once, are repelling the cowboys, instead of the other way around. No normal person, set down in a North Vietnamese rice field beside an anti-aircraft unit manned by excited boys and girls, could help being thrilled, whereas in the South, beside an artillery battery, surrounded by sandbags, you share the sullen gloom of the population and the sardonic resentment of the soldiers.

Nevertheless, the Westerner in North Vietnam, stirred and convinced by the real thing, finally resists its aggressions in art and falls back on some Wordsworthian preference for emotion recollected in tranquillity. Besides, hortatory art has the troubling property of resembling all other hortatory art, which makes it difficult to distinguish, for instance, fascist architecture from Stalinist architecture or socialist realist painting from Roman Catholic oleographs. In the visual field, North Vietnam is no exception to this rule; the declamatory painting and sculpture seem to be reliving, phylogenetically, the history not just of socialist realism but of allied species including U.S. post-office murals and paintings of Pope John. A war monument in Hanoi is interchangeable stylistically with the war monument in Saigon, and neither has any relation to Vietnamese tradition, which in the North survives only in folk art—charming decalcomania-like designs of fish, birds, roosters, who by a blessed exception have not been recruited to the war effort.

Obviously, in a short official stay in North Vietnam, I was not in a position to meet dissenters, if they existed. But I was able to use my eyes and when feeling bored during long speeches in Vietnamese, film showings, protracted visits, I could look around me, seeking a fellow-sufferer. Boredom is one of the hardest of human emotions to conceal, and the Vietnamese are the reverse of inscrutable (though they sometimes leave you to guess the cause of the lively emotions that are passing across their faces), yet it only happened twice that I noticed a sign of flagging interest except in myself. Every member of the audience was following what was said or shown with evident absorption and approval.

The exceptions stand out. One was in the Hanoi feature-film studio, where a young director was openly, obdurately bored while his chief was talking. Artistic "temperament"? Hostility to U.S. intellectuals, regarded scornfully as tourists? The other was during a visit to a Hanoi anti-aircraft unit when the blushing young political commissar of the battery read aloud an especially long speech of welcome he had evidently written out that morning, with great pains, in a round schoolboyish script. It was the day the bombing stopped north of the 20th parallel—April 1, Hanoi time. Glancing over the boy's shoulder, the lieutenant of the outfit, a somewhat older man, ascertained after fifteen minutes or so that the orator still had two closely spaced pages to go (a point I had been checking on myself from the other side of the table) and kindly but firmly indicated that the speech should draw to a close. "That's enough," is what he said, in Vietnamese. Everybody smiled broadly, with grateful relief, and perhaps especially the boy, as he folded up the sheets of paper and tucked them back in his pocket.

Not only were there no signs of disaffection; the announcement, on March 21, of a decree against "counter-revolutionary crimes" took even long-resident foreign journalists by surprise. Nobody could understand what or whom was aimed at. The list of fifteen counter-revolutionary crimes punishable by jail or death comprised treason, espionage, plotting, armed rebellion, sabotage, defecting to the enemy, disrupting public order, making propaganda, intruding into the territory of the DRVN. The last perhaps offered a clue. These activities, after all, must already have been highly illegal, as most of them would be in any country, but just then the possibility of a U.S. invasion was being discussed in the American press, which of course was read in Hanoi. Was the Hanoi government issuing a warning to future collaborators of the punishment that would certainly follow? But who *were* those future collaborators, unheard and unseen until this moment and now produced like a photo negative by the law formulated *against* them?

Perhaps they were a mere apprehension in the mind of Hanoi. What was striking here in comparison to other Communist states was the utter, total absence in conversation, movies, plays, pictures, short stories, of the theme of treason. Not a word about backsliding, incorrigible elements, "former" people. The figure of the "wrecker" or evil counselor never cast his shadow. There was no question of any villain or faint heart opposing the war; at most, there could be a problem of priorities, whether, as in a play they took us to, it was more important for a young medical student to continue his studies at the university or go to the front. Mr. Phan decided that two acts of the play were enough, so we never saw the end, but it was clear that the hesitant student would choose whichever action was shown to be more "productive," regardless of his personal tastes.

"Former" people must exist in North Vietnamese society but the only evidence of this I had came from Saigon ("My uncle in Hanoi," said a lady, "used to own eighty houses; now he has only one"). In Hanoi I did not hear of that uncle or anyone like him. "What has happened to the landowners?" I asked once. "The ones who didn't go south?" "If they agree to work with us, we accept them," was the reply. "We do not hold their past against them." The subject did not seem to be of much interest. If an ex-landowner were to appear in a film script, he would be already reformed. No, there is another possibility: he might undergo a conversion from "former" to present, bad to good, as he saw the bombs falling on the irrigation project, the dikes, the sweet-potato field—a perfectly plausible story which no doubt could be documented by many real-life examples.

Conversion, from bad to good, or vice versa, which was the great theme of Western nineteenth-century fiction and of early movies, is never represented in Western novels these days and seldom on the screen. It is as though the West had agreed that people were incapable of change. You do not see Bonnie and Clyde *decide* to become mass murderers; no choice seems to be offered them. In the Free World, to judge by its artifacts, nobody is free to make a decision to be different from what he is. But in the un-Free World, the opposite is assumed, and one indication of revisionist tendencies in a Communist country is the gradual disappearance of regenerative themes in popular art. By this criterion, Hanoi, unlike Belgrade, Prague, Budapest, even Moscow, is a bastion of anti-revisionism.

Nor is this found only in movies and plays. While Novotny,* say, in Czechoslovakia has been given up as a bad job, the North Vietnamese still have hopes of converting even their worst enemies. The idea of forgiveness and rehabilitation is underlined by North Vietnamese and NLF officials in discussing the government functionaries of the South. "Anyone who wishes to come over to us is welcome." Once, in a conversation with Ngo

---

* Now Dubcek.

Dien, the small, gentle, slightly mournful Press Chief of the Foreign Ministry (the one whose mother is in the South), the topic came up, and I, half teasing, tried to test him, choosing the most horrendous example: "What about Ky?" "Even Nguyen Cao Ky," he said, gravely nodding his head up and down while at the same time smiling at the enormity of the thought.

Whether Nguyen Cao Ky would have to do penance—and how much—is another matter. What I am trying to describe is a state of mind I found in the North, at once categorical and in a strange way indulgent. People say of Communists that they see everything in black and white, which is certainly true of the North Vietnamese rhetoric: "bandits" engage in "dark maneuvers" with the aid of "pen hirelings." But beneath the forbidding rhetoric there is something else. Unlike Western liberals, they do not accept difference, but they accept change axiomatically as a revolutionary possibility in human conduct—which Western liberals do not; that is why liberals have to be tolerant of difference, resigned to it.

The North Vietnamese reiteration of their "correct position" implies the conviction that their enemies, if they hear it stated often enough, will understand; it is so *clear*, they seem to be saying. "Johnson," officials repeated, "can call off the bombing *in five minutes* and have talks. Why not, then?" This was said with genuine mystification, in the plaintive hope of getting an answer to a puzzle. Johnson was pursuing a mistaken policy; even the stock market was telling him so. Why *not* correct it? Far more than his American critics, the North Vietnamese officials put themselves in the President's place. They spoke of offering him "an honorable exit," an idea repugnant to *me*. Their questions, in short, rested on the proposition that Johnson was free, like any other human being, to change his course. The opposite is pretended and possibly believed by Johnson, who acts like the honest prisoner of circumstances, locked into a bombing policy that now bears the name of "a first step in unilateral de-escalation." In the Stalinist days, we used to detest a vocabulary that had to be read in terms of antonyms—"volunteers," denoting conscripts, "democracy," tyranny, and so on. Insensibly, in Vietnam, starting with the little word "advisers," we have adopted this slippery Aesopian language ourselves, whereas the North Vietnamese, in their stiff phraseology, persist in speaking quite plainly; the term "regroupees" (infiltrators, Ed.), mainly accurate at the outset to describe North Vietnamese forces fighting in the South, has quietly been withdrawn from the dialogue. Although we complain of the monotony, the truth, renamed by us "propaganda," has shifted to the other side.

First Principles

O ne morning early in our stay, they took us to visit the Hanoi University Surgical Hospital—pale-yellow pavilions in the French colonial style set around an older central building in land-scaped grounds. It was known as the German-Vietnamese Friend-ship Hospital because funds to rebuild and enlarge it had been given by the East German government. In the South, the Medi-cal School at Hue University had been set up by the Adenauer government, with a staff of West German doctors: challenge and response. In the Hanoi hospital, there were no German doctors. The staff was Vietnamese. The chief surgeon and head of the hospital had been trained in Hanoi under the French; he had formed his first surgical team in the forest during the Re-sistance War, operating sometimes forty-eight hours at a stretch. Twenty years later, Professor Ton That Tung was still forming surgical teams, but his work schedule had dropped to eight hours a day; he had younger doctors under him, qualified nurses, laboratories, asepsis.

When they had dressed us in sterile gowns, we were admitted into the operating rooms, which contained the latest thing in equipment and instruments, gauges of all kinds, sterilizers, tanks, looking very much like home, despite the fact that some of it was of Chinese and Soviet make; the pride of the hospital, though, seemed to be equipment from England. They had no emergency cases that morning; the doctors had long finished operating, and there was the usual mid-morning lull of a big well-run hospital.

The wards were clean and tranquil, though the walls could have stood some paint and the sheets were grayish, possibly from the lack of a "magic ingredient" in the washing powders used; I thought of those old ads showing a shamefaced housewife and her Monday wash on the line and the words "tattletale gray." They said they had found that sheets lasted longer than the traditional mats. The white iron beds were adjustable, and each had a mosquito net and pillow. The floors were swept; patients in fresh hospital jackets were reading quietly; some had vases of flowers. Many were receiving intravenous drip injections. Charts were clipped at the foot of each bed. It was the "slow season" for bomb victims, they told us, because of the monsoon; most of the patients were ordinary surgical cases. No surgical hospital can be anything but grim, but conditions here, including the state of the bedding, compared favorably with what I had seen in the surgery ward of a big Parisian public hospital.

They showed us photographs of the old hospital, as it had been in the French times: half-naked patients two or three to a bed (in one ward some were lying, semi-animate, on the floor), no mosquito nets, no bedding, general misery and squalor. "But that's exactly what I saw last year in the South!" I said excitedly, and Dr. Ton That Tung, plump, pink, pleasant, with horn-rimmed glasses and white hair in a kind of bob, fell back a pace, his jaw dropping. "No!" "There were no patients on the floors," I emended. "But two to a bed, yes. And people said there were often three."

288

He shook his head several times, incredulous. He came from Hue, of royal stock, he had just been telling us, and like many Southerners I met in the North had an automatic reaction of disbelief when "filled in" by a foreigner about his native place. Perhaps he had been assuming that the NLF stories he had heard were propaganda. In the North, I found, they cannot really imagine the South as it is today, above all the refugee camps; they have no experience to match it. And contrary to what their enemies might think, the men of Hanoi do not enjoy hearing about disease, suffering, degradation, in the U.S.-held areas of the South. Like Dr. Ton That Tung, they change the subject.

With American intellectuals, far from the scene, it is different; they are shocked but content to be shocked, in that it proves their point: they are *right* to oppose the war. What all this shows, no doubt, is that Americans need reassurance in their opposition to Johnson's Vietnam policy, while the Vietnamese don't. For the Americans over forty, a doubt persists, as it did for veteran Marxists at the time of the Moscow Trials; a Trotskyite friend once confided that he used to wake up at night sweating: "What if Stalin is right?" Thus the terrible news of the slave-labor camps was welcomed by us, as confirmation, while the news of the Nazi death camps was received at first with stunned disbelief, the distinction being that we were certain Hitler was evil and shrank, quite humanly, from further proof of it—the correctness of our judgment was not in question. Not that the fear of being wrong politically is an undesirable quality per se; only, when it starts feeding on human suffering to fortify an *argument*, it is time to watch out. This happens on

289

both sides of the Great Debate on Vietnam. Nobody could pretend that the U.S. negotiators in Paris were *sorry* about Viet Cong rocket attacks on Saigon. If Tocqueville was right, and we are a nation of lawyers, it would explain a good deal.

Leading us rapidly through the hospital garden, with a glance at the slightly overcast sky (there was no alert that morning), Dr. Tung showed us the underground operating room. If necessary, he operated in the shelter, but he did not like to do so, because of the damp and the mold. Pointing at a fungus stain on the ceiling, he made an angry grimace. In his office, he discussed the extraction of bomb pellets from the brain, passing around photographs and X rays of a woman teacher and a young boy. Often the best course was to leave the pellet and remove the splinters, which cause abscessing. He indicated the tiny entry hole in the woman's thick hair; without an X ray machine available, it was sometimes impossible to find where the little steel balls had penetrated the skull; in such cases, the patient usually died. He showed us X rays of patients with pellets in the chest, to illustrate the zigzagging path the pellet described, in contrast to the ordinary gunshot. As he held the X rays up to the light, in his short-sleeved white gown with vigorous forearms bared, he seemed a "pure" professor of surgery lecturing on the interesting problems presented by these novel projectiles. All the cases he was describing had recovered; he brought out another series of photographs showing them walking in the hospital grounds. "I took a special interest in that boy," he interjected, pointing to a youth of about fifteen—a complicated chest case with multiple wounds.

Extraordinary that so many recovered, someone said. Dr.

Tung nodded. Most bombing victims—from cluster bombs or
normal explosive bombs—could be saved if they were operated
on promptly, within six hours at most. Speed, they had discovered, was of the greatest importance. In the case of multiple
wounds, he would have three teams operating simultaneously
on the patient. And he applied oxygen inhalers throughout the
operation—a new technique they had learned in the war. I
asked him about anesthetics. Most socialist countries, he said,
used local anesthetics, but he preferred Sodium Pentothal. But
the kind of anesthetic was secondary. The main thing was to
make sure that the bomb victim was given injections of plasma
or a saline solution—against shock—as soon as he reached a
doctor or a medical technician. Plasma was not always available, and his surgical teams had found, to their surprise, that
it did not matter greatly what you injected; the point was to in-
ject it. Even water would do. I thought I had not heard right.
He smiled. Yes. Plain water. The question of finding a cure for
the coma induced by pellet bombs was of great popular interest,
I learned later. In the play they took us to see, a young doctor,
the wavering hero's mentor and influence for the good, has gone
to the front—*i.e.*, South Vietnam—to work on such a cure in the
laboratory of the battlefield.

It was typical of the North Vietnamese to hit on a curative
element, water, so basic that medical research had overlooked
it up till now. Like the purloined letter hiding where everybody
could see it. A return to first principles (which signifies to *the
people*) gives them much delight, especially when it can also
demonstrate the exercise of ingenuity. Such a first principle is
bamboo. I had the impression that the North Vietnamese were

almost pleased when a metal bridge was bombed, so that they could get together and make a pontoon bridge, lashed into place with bamboo; still more, one of those folding bamboo bridges, taken up in the morning and hidden all day from the straining "round" eyes overhead, to be swiftly replaced at nightfall, when the supply trucks start to roll. The resources of bamboo make it a folk-tale trickster. "Look!" said Mr. Phan, pointing to the electric-power poles strung along the highway in Hung Yen Province. "Yes. Rural electrification," I said, missing the point. "Bamboo!" he exclaimed, laughing. "In this province there is not much wood!"

For fractures, Hanoi-trained surgeons have been trying a system of bamboo splints used in folk medicine. The aerial war and the dispersion have given an impetus to the scientific study of folk or, as they call it, traditional medicine, side by side with advanced Western techniques—an idea long favored by the Minister of Health, Dr. Thach, French-trained, and of royal blood also, a cousin of the deposed Bao Dai.* In his mountain dispensary, a young surgeon, Dr. Tung's pupil, has a frigidaire stocked with serums for operations and a cupboard stocked with jars of traditional remedies for snake bite, rheumatism, and other local ills. It is reasonable that tribesmen living for centuries in a snake-infested region should have found successful antidotes, but what about a plant juice that experiment has shown to be astonishingly effective when injected against bomb coma? And according to Mr. Phan, an old wives' poultice made of a live young chicken pounded into a paste, laughed at for generations by city people, has proved to be a remarkable healing agent for war wounds.

* Dr. Thach died in the fall of 1968 of an infection contracted at the "front," in the jungle, where he had gone to study war-generated diseases on the spot.

292

In his office, Dr. Tung talked of folk medicine. As a Vietnamese he was excited by the idea of progress through deliberate and controlled regression, *i.e.*, by rediscovery. On his desk was a Champa head of a woman (ninth to eleventh century, southern Annam), of a style rather similar to the Khmer style; reproductions of this head are quite common—she is the North Vietnamese Nefertiti. Like French doctors with a good practice, he was interested in art and archaeology. As a present, he gave me a pretty bronze arrowhead of the Chou dynasty (classical Bronze Age), and a volume of Vietnamese poetry rendered into French; some of the translations were by him. In return, I sent him Konrad Lorenz's *On Aggression*, which I had been reading; he was aware of Lorenz's scientific work.

On the floor were a number of large cartons containing surgical and medical supplies waiting to be opened; they had arrived that morning from a London committee for medical aid to North Vietnam. He took us to the hospital library, which had shelves lined with medical classics in a variety of languages, mainly Western, and stacks of recent publications from France, England, Germany, America. He kept up with professional developments in the United States. He remembered American surgeons he had met at conventions and found their names and addresses in his notebook. "Before the war of destruction," he said, his field had been liver transplants, which he had successfully performed on animals; he was following with interest American results with human beings.

He showed us the laboratories, with a slight air of apology. After the war, they would build a new hospital, maybe, with more modern facilities and better experimental equipment. Now the medical school, hospitals, and laboratories were nearly all dispersed to the provinces. Most bomb victims were treated at the district level; only the more complicated cases were sent to Hanoi. It was not possible, in any event, to expand a research center when a bomb could destroy it tomorrow. American doctors, I remarked, to cheer him up, were too dependent on the laboratory. They were losing the gift of diagnosis. Soon they would not be able to spot a case of measles without the help of a computer. He nodded. The present sickness of the world, in his view, was the result of a lag in adjustment to technology. It was odd that the same thought had been expressed to me long ago on a beach on Cape Cod by a Hungarian psychoanalyst, who estimated that it would take mankind two centuries to recover from the effects of the Industrial Revolution. Dr. Tung sighed. "Neolithic man with a bomb in his hand." Here in Vietnam the problem was not acute, fortunately. "I operate with my ten fingers." He held out his "surgeon's hands"—with the characteristic broad palm and long slender fingers—and looked at them, smiling, as at a set of favorite tools. Surgery, ultimately, was a tactile matter. Touch—the second sense. "Of course sometimes I use instruments," he added. "But they are not essential. In the forest we did not always have instruments."

Last year at Saigon University, I told him, there had been much agitation for giving medical instruction in Vietnamese; I had heard a lot of debate about it. Here there was no debate, he said. Instruction was given in Vietnamese. But what about the vocabulary, I asked. To me, it had seemed a clumsy and (though I did not say so) chauvinistic proceeding to create a medical terminology in a minority language that did not have

294

the words for it, especially when a majority language—French
—was already implanted in the country. What would happen
to a young doctor with a strictly Vietnamese medical vocabulary
who was invited to attend a congress in Bordeaux, for instance?
And how could he keep up with the medical literature?

Dr. Tung recognized the objections. *"Oui, madame."* But
the decision to teach in Vietnamese had not been a matter of
choice. Language, after all, was the key to medical understanding, and the new state had needed to form a corps of doctors
fast, drawing on the peasantry as well as on what remained of
the former privileged classes. It would have taken too long to
train medical students if you had had to teach them French
first. Of course, they had been right, I had to admit, and righter
than they could have known at the time: when the Air Force
came, a medical corps was waiting for it.

The practical wisdom of the decision, if it required demonstration, was evident when you thought of the South (750 doctors
last year for a population of sixteen million and most of those
serving in the Army), where civilian casualties were infinitely
more numerous and where the presence of foreign medical
teams, a drop in the bucket in any case, aggravated xenophobia
in the native medical personnel, leading to petty feuds, theft of
AID supplies, and actual obstruction. In the North, a single
province, Hung Yen, now has fifty doctors and 800 assistant
doctors for a population of 670,000 (one doctor and four nurses
in 1954). The North, moreover, has kept its independence from
its allies, in medicine as in the military sphere. No foreign doctors are serving in the country (no Russians, no Chinese);
though aid is accepted, it remains in Vietnamese hands. Even in

pharmaceuticals, they have aimed, when possible, at self-suffi-
ciency. Against tuberculosis, they have found a vaccine that
differs from the Western type in that it uses dead bacilli instead
of live ones. For the Sabin vaccine against polio, which requires
refrigeration and hence is unsuited to local conditions, they have
substituted a similar vaccine of their own invention that will
keep for a month at normal temperatures.

It had not been too difficult, Dr. Tung said, to create a Viet-
namese medical vocabulary. They had based themselves on the
Chinese, which had all the terms they needed. Here his own
French training was a handicap; he was still learning the new
Vietnamese words. Inwardly I blushed. I had forgotten about
Chinese medicine. It was perhaps not such a deprivation that
Dr. Tung's pupils would be unable to make themselves understood at medical congresses in Bordeaux or Montpellier. Or
even New York. What would send them there? They would be
meeting colleagues in Moscow or Peking, which should not be
a reason for grief. Just the same, I found it slightly disquieting
to see that the professor's young white-gowned, white-capped
associates, though they nodded and beamed, could not follow
a word we were saying. It was like that with the young people
everywhere in the North: doctors, factory engineers, army men,
film-makers, the whole new intelligentsia, a few literary men
excepted. I felt sorry for the French language, which was dying
out in a country where it had lived so long—extinct or extir-
pated, like the passenger pigeon. My conservationist instincts
protested. In another twenty years, who would be able to read
the medical texts in the hospital library?

To regret the passing of French was to regret the passing of the cosmopolitan old order, "the language of diplomacy," and so on. But it was also to regret those fluent old revolutionaries pentecostally blessed, like the Apostles, with the gift of tongues —Lenin, Trotsky, Ho Chi Minh, and behind them Rosa Luxemburg, Marx, Bakunin, and our own Benjamin Franklin, who sits like a funny antique in the garden of the American Embassy in Paris. Among the young, all over the world, the coming Western language is English, and North Vietnam is not an exception, though held back by a shortage of teachers. English has a demonstrable utility, which gives both a socialist incentive and an excuse for learning it, just as being an interpreter or a professional translator excuses an American or a Russian for having a second language in the eyes of his monolingual compatriots—it is OK if he has to do it for a living. But this narrow view of my own language distressed me, liking frills and "useless" knowledge for myself and everyone else. I was sorry to see young people in North Vietnam discard French, when they had it, in order to push forward with English. On the other hand, the eagerness to learn and practice English showed an amazing lack of chauvinism. Young militants from the peace movement arriving in the North had even created a preference for *American* English over the language of the BBC—an entering wedge perhaps for a whole range of U.S. folkways, appetites, and habits. Or would Americanization, a creeping disease, stop with Joan Baez, Bob Dylan, and protest songs?

Visitors from the peace movement were not the only teachers. When I was allowed to see two captured pilots in the living room of a Hanoi villa (I am not sure whether this was their actual place of confinement), it was clear that the North Vietnamese officer present was following the general drift of the conversation, not having to wait for the interpreter to determine if I was transgressing the boundaries of the questions I had been asked to submit in advance. In fact, I did transgress them in the nervous give-and-take of the talk (we quickly exhausted "Health," "Family," "Treatment," "Current View of the War"), but the officer indicated that it was all right to go ahead eliciting such facts as that a pilot was raising carp in a pond and learning to play chess with his fellow-prisoners, that he would have voted for Goldwater if he had been registered in 1964 ("because the Army was for Goldwater"), that when peace came he would like to get out of the Army and teach math and coach athletics in a high school. Before the interview, I had been told not to mention Johnson's speech, which we heard that morning (April 1, Hanoi time) but which the North Vietnamese people had not yet been informed of. I did not mention it, but one of the pilots did: "I know Johnson has said that he isn't going to run again." "Where did you hear that?" I exclaimed, startled. "I read it in a UP report." I glanced at the Vietnamese officer, but he merely smiled and let the conversation continue. "I see you know English," I said to him at one point. He shrugged. "A little." But the guards, who were younger, were not shy of showing off the words and expressions they had been picking up from their prisoners. A strange sort of cultural exchange, largely one-way, for though one pilot told me he had read "a lot" of Vietnamese history in jail, he seemed wholly unmodified by his experience, and the sole question he put me was "Can you tell me how the Chicago Cubs are doing?" The second prisoner, an older man, had not changed his cultural spots either, except in one respect: he claimed to like Vietnamese candy.

The Vietnamese, one hears, have been taken aback by the low mental attainments of the pilots, who have officer rank (the gaunt, squirrel-faced older man led in to see me was a lieutenant colonel)*and usually college degrees, which must be leading their captors to wonder about American university education. I was taken aback myself by a stiffness of phraseology and naïve rote-thinking, childish, like the handwriting on the envelopes the Vietnamese officer emptied from a sack for me to mail on my return for other captive pilots (the regular mail from North Vietnam is slow), printed or in round laboriously joined cursive letters. If these men had been robotized, I felt, it had been an insensible process starting in grade school and finished off by the Army, which had passed them for duty as high-precision instruments, equipped with survival kits and the rudiments of reading and writing. Far from being an élite or members of an "establishment," they were somewhat pathetic cases of mental malnutrition. Quite a few American visitors shrink from interviewing the pilots, and before I went, acquaintances in the hotel (including our guides) expressed sympathy: it would be painful to meet one's own countrymen in such circumstances. Avoid questions of guilt and conscience was the general advice. It *was* painful, because of the distance between being free and being under duress, between leaning forward on a comfortable sofa and sitting upright on a stool, but also because of another, unexpected distance—not a moral one, for I did not feel morally superior to those American strangers in prison pajamas, if anything the reverse, since they were "paying" and I wasn't,

---

* This was Robinson ("Robbie") Risner, today a widely admired hardliner and Nixon zealot. From my notes: "tight lined face, wilted eyes, somewhat squirrely. Fawns on Vietnamese officers. Servile. Zealot. Has seen error of ways. Looks at Bananas. Grateful: 'Oh, gee, bananas too?' Speaks of his 'sweet tooth.' Loves the Vietnamese candy. Effusive about it. Perhaps ostracized by his fellow prisoners. Speaks English slowly, like a Vietnamese practicing the language. Stereotyped language . . ."

but a cultural distance so wide that I could see myself reflected in their puzzled, somewhat frightened eyes as a foreigner. As between co-nationals, this distance itself was a crime against humanity, a reason for protest, for revolutions; not that the pilots felt it so, probably infinitely preferring being themselves to being me, whom they almost certainly regarded as a tool of the North Vietnamese Communists, a tool shaped by Eastern education, money, advantages. And if they thought that, they were right in a sense, for to be against the Vietnamese war was an economic privilege enjoyed chiefly by the middle and professional classes. It was largely owing to privilege that I could feel more at home talking French with Dr. Ton That Tung, say, on medical and philosophical subjects than making lame conversation in English with those wary cagey pilots about hobbies, church, family, and the American primary elections.

As it happened, the men I felt most immediately at home with in the North were all from Annam (now renamed Central Vietnam, which makes it sound like a featureless administrative unit): Dr. Tung, Pham Van Dong, Colonel Ha Van Lau of the War Crimes Commission, and the fatherly "Permanent Member" in Hoa Binh Province, although, being of peasant origin, he spoke only Vietnamese. Ho Chi Minh came from Annam, too, of a minor mandarin family; many revolutionaries were formed there, in the shadow of the Emperor's court, and went to school together at Hue University. The Annamites are not well liked by the other Vietnamese, or so I was told in the South. They are the Tuscans of the country, while the people of Tonkin are the Milanese, and the Cochin Chinese are the Neapolitans or Sicilians. Annam, like Tuscany, is looked upon by its neighbors as a basket of crabs—difficult, self-sufficient, proud, provincial, obstinately "local," frugal, tradition-bound, vain of its past.

But these qualities, mostly rural and conservative, are in fact typical of the whole North Vietnamese style of making a new world, embodied in Mr. Phan's "Personally I hate anything artificial," in the tenderness of the intelligentsia for the peasantry and for what the Florentines call the *popolo minuto* (barbers, tailors, small craftsmen), in the sense Hanoi, like Florence, gives of being a large village, where the notables take the air in the evening on the main street. For example, on the night of April 3, when Hanoi gave its answer to Johnson, on coming home from the theater, we found standing in front of the hotel a group consisting of the Minister of Health with his daughter, the small, informally dressed Chief Justice of the Supreme Court, and Colonel Ha Van Lau. They had probably been attending some "friendly dinner" in the hotel (the North Vietnamese expression for an intimate banquet) and had lingered on the sidewalk chatting. When they saw us, they waited to hear what we Americans thought of Hanoi's answer, which was handed to us in mimeograph by a smiling and excited Mr. Phan, and were frankly pleased by the verdict: *"Très intelligent."*

The feeling that Vietnam is a close community or family is sometimes quite strong in Hanoi, as when our guides of the Peace Committee appeared all dressed up in their best suits one afternoon because we were going to visit the National Liberation Front and that was like visiting your most important relations. "We always wear our best clothes when we visit them," they explained, as my companion rushed upstairs to change out of his corduroys. "To do them honor because they are in the front lines and we are in the rear." And at the NLF Delegation, as if to mark the shade of distinction, we were given dressed-up party refreshments: a chocolate liqueur and oranges instead of the usual tea or beer and bananas. Everybody in the North seemed to remember, with irony, General Nguyen Cao Ky, the black sheep of the family. An official in the Foreign Ministry dryly recalled him enrolled in a band of school children at an Independence Day celebration, waving his little bouquet and noisily chanting: "No one loves Ho Chi Minh more than the children!" That is the sort of performance one's relations, cruelly, never forget.

I began to wonder what role the Lao Dong Party played in this network of relationships. "May I ask, what proportion of you in the hospital are Party members?" I said to Dr. Ton That Tung. He burst into loud laughter. They had never counted, he said. Party membership had no significance here. I could see that the question had given offense, which was mystifying since in other socialist countries I knew—Poland and Hungary— curiosity on this subject was treated as normal, and anybody was glad to tell you who was a member of the Party and who wasn't, just as a matter of interest. In fact, though fond of describing himself as a "Communist"—"I am of royal blood and a Communist!" was a joke he repeated at our farewell "friendly dinner"—Dr. Ton That Tung, as I heard later, was not a Party member, and there was no secret about it. Then how had my question been indiscreet? When I told the story to a foreign diplomat, he was puzzled. It was true, he said, that Party membership did not play much of a role here, in comparison with other Communist countries. But maybe just for that reason it was looked on as a private matter, of no concern to outsiders. In any case, the words "Role of Lao Dong Party?" remained blankly in my notebook. I did not want to risk offending again.

For me, the local ethos was clearest in the figure of Pham Van Dong, who received us on a Sunday morning on the front stoop of the presidential palace (formerly the residence of the French governor general), wearing a freshly ironed North Vietnamese army jacket of gray-tan poplin with unbuttoned flap pockets and a collar that showed his still-youthful throat. In the middle of the conference table in the room where our talk took place was a little bunch of roses and carnations from the palace gardens, and when we stood up at last to leave, he slowly picked out a few blooms for each of us, as I have seen an old-lady horticultur-alist do in New England, carefully matching the posy to the char-acter of the receiver, so that you guessed you were having your fortune told in the language of flowers and would have given more than a penny to know what the flowers were saying. Ho Chi Minh used to have the gallant habit of saying it with a single rose to women correspondents; Nora Beloff of *The Observer* remembers the red rose he chose for her at the Fontainebleau Conference. Such courtly manners have an element of impulsive theater, which is not to say that they are rehearsed.

Pham Van Dong is a man of magnetic allure, thin, with deep-set brilliant eyes, crisp short electric gray hair, full rueful lips drawn tight over the teeth. The passion and directness of his delivery matched something fiery, but also melancholy, in those coaly eyes. An emotional, impressionable man, I thought, and at the same time highly intellectual. He had an odd grave mannerism of repeating the final word in a sentence, as though savoring it on his tongue, especially when it had a bitter taste. *"J'ai été roulé, roulé,"* he said, speaking of Geneva, meaning that he had been "stung" like a countryman at a horse fair. During our conversation, which lasted two hours, he used none of the prevailing political clichés and did not waste time on long preambles recapitulating facts or arguments already known to all parties. He came at once to the point. When he intended to evade a question, he made that almost teasingly plain, as when I asked him about the counter-revolutionary laws just promulgated—why now? "Till now, being a new state, we have been very busy," he said. "We have just got around to putting those laws on the statute books." As happens with frank people, he inspired openness in his questioner. Had I thought of it that morning, I could have asked him, for instance, about the Lao Dong Party. Unfortunately, his general lack of hesitation in speaking his mind put most of our talk off the record. In the driveway, as we were leaving, he took account of his indiscretions and asked us, with slight concern, not to repeat certain remarks. Later I got a message passed through his secretary reminding me of four points—really four and a half —that it would be better not to mention. The reader need not fear he is missing state secrets, only the kind of thing we all say and hope will not "get back" to third parties, by which I do not mean Russia or China; neither was referred to that morning. In fact, Russia and China were never at any time referred to in my presence in the North except as distant occurrences in geography, history, art, cuisine.

During the conversation, an aide came in to whisper that there was a pre-alert. "If you don't mind," the Prime Minister said, "we will stay here in my office." I did not mind at all; indeed I felt honored to be included in a contempt for danger so strong and evident that it made me feel safe. To this fastidious man, I thought, bombs were a low-grade intrusion into the political scene, which he conceived, like the ancients, as a vast proscenium. Besides, it was unlikely that "we" would strike the presidential palace at this juncture; in twenty-four hours, Johnson's voice would be heard from the White House, putting an end to the raids on Hanoi. . . . Impossible, of course, to have known that, yet, looking back, I am sure we all sensed that day, had been sensing for a week, that some change was coming, although that evening, as if to deceive our radar, there were three real alerts in quick succession, about ten minutes apart, which sent us to the shelter for the last times.

That morning, with Pham Van Dong, we talked about *l'après-guerre*, whether it would be possible in peacetime for North Vietnam to pursue the original socialist path the war had opened. This—not negotiations, a formality; not an atomic war, which he brushed aside—was the great item on the agenda of the Vietnamese people. Foreign observers interested in varieties of socialism had been quick to notice on trips about the countryside the effects of geographical decentralization on the political structure. More autonomy on the province and district levels and more worker participation in the decisions of factories and cooperatives. What would happen afterward? Pham Van Dong, as I now realize, was perhaps not wholly pleased by the attention enthusiastic foreigners were turning on the phenomenon. This is a touchy area in the whole socialist world. It is a question how much decentralization, *i.e.*, democratization, a Marxist economy can permit itself without regression to capitalist modes. The Yugoslav model of worker management is denounced by orthodox Marxist-Leninists as a sly return to bourgeois practices: competition, the need to show a profit, even advertising. Nor is it certain that the conservatives are wrong in their suspicion that direct democracy—village and factory councils—will "inevitably" lead to anarchy, in the pejorative sense of chaos, or, if not, to a market economy unpleasantly resembling capitalism.

To see North Vietnam as the scene of such an experiment is not an altogether entrancing prospect for the leadership. What if the enemy, capitalism, repulsed by air and foiled by land in the sister South, should creep in the back way, insinuating itself into the very organs of the people's rule: provincial and district committees, factory and co-operative directorates? Then all the sacrifices of the war would have been in vain—a point missed by libertarian well-wishers eager for further change. Yet the progress made in decentralization under the spur of the war offers a challenge to continue in that direction, counting precisely on the nation's spirit of sacrifice and self-discipline. There is also the old tradition of hamlet self-government, summed up in the saying, frequently repeated by foreigners, "The Emperor's rule stops at the hamlet gate," or—a variant— "at the bamboo hedge."

Hanoi listens to these urgings and declines to commit itself. Ever since the judicial murders and popular uprisings of 1956, resulting from the harsh agrarian reform laws, Vietnamese socialist planning has been based on an idea of limit. This is the originality, emphasized by Pham Van Dong, of the Vietnamese "way." By refusing outside help in the form of troops, they have succeeded in limiting the war. Fearful of a population explosion, they have limited births (they are experimenting with a plant juice formerly brewed by witches in the "ethnic" regions and which appears to work something like the Pill); thanks to the bombing, they have been able to reverse modern demographic trends and actually reduce the population of cities. New institutions are introduced with care. For instance, hamlet cemeteries, to replace the family grave mounds in the rice fields. "What do you do with the old graves?" I inquired in a rural co-operative. "Dig them up?" The co-operative chief reacted with horror. "Do you think we want a *revolution?*"

The worship of ancestors, less a superstition than a veneration of the past, must not be disturbed; despite the difficulties the old graves make for modern farm machinery plowing and harrowing around them, only the newly dead go to the cemetery. No cultural revolution would be thinkable here, since culture—the accretion of the past—is the guarantor of Vietnamese independence. The delicate position of Pham Van Dong's government is that it is bent on preserving Vietnamese traditions but it is also bent on preserving the sacred tradition of socialism, *i.e.*, watchful central planning. On the one hand, it proceeds with an almost tactile sense (*cf.* Dr. Tung's surgical fingers) of what its people—and their history—will accept or reject. On the other, it insists on what is "good" for them; this is a moral, ascetic government, concerned above all with the *quality* of Vietnamese life.

307

Material scarcity is regarded as a piece of good luck. Fortune was kind when she made Vietnam poor except in skills. I said something anxious about industrialization. To Pham Van Dong, this was a joke. "We are an agricultural nation." "But you keep hearing about 'the industrial North.'" He shook his head and laughed. They made a little steel. "We don't need much heavy industry. That is not a problem for us. Light industry. Workshops." What he seemed to have in mind was a sort of bicycle socialism, as if here, too, there should be a limit, and the bicycle would be a good place to stop. He spoke of our automobile-TV culture as of something distastefully gross and heavy; Vietnamese ethics are permeated with ideas of lightness and swift pliability: bamboo, bicycles, sandals, straw. As though society's burden of goods should be no heavier than what a man can carry on his back. With a full-lipped contempt very like the contempt he showed for danger, he rejected the notion of a socialist consumer society.

At the time, the implications of this were not clear to me; I was only conscious of a feeling of happy agreement, remembering the meeting between Mr. Khrushchev and Mr. Nixon in the model kitchen—the perfect setting for some future infra-red, deep-fryer One Hell from which nobody could escape except possibly to a trailer camp. But it now comes to me that in those words, with that fastidious grimace, he may have been vetoing the very program I had just told him was "dear to my heart": further decentralization for North Vietnam. In Vietnam I perceived—what doubtless I should have known before—that the fear of decentralization and local autonomy evinced by Communist leaders is not necessarily an abject solicitude for their own continuance in power; it is also a fear of human nature as found in their countrymen, on the assumption that modern man is "naturally" a capitalist accumulator, already spotted with that first sin in his mother's womb and ceaselessly beset by marketing temptations: if you let workers run the factories, they will soon be manufacturing Cadillacs because "the consumer wants them."

Yet the Prime Minister may have been implying the reverse: his faith that the Vietnamese people could assume a greater say in production without abating their idealism. The wares of modern consumer society as displayed in the South might well serve as a deterrent for their Northern brothers, like some dreadful emetic mixed with alcohol to cure forever a taste for drinking. The samples of U.S. technology that had been showered on the North were mainly in bomb form, yet the simplest Vietnamese could perhaps see a connection that eludes many American intellectuals between the spray of pellets from the "mother" bomb and the candy hurled at children in the South by friendly G.I.'s, between the pellets and the whole Saran-wrapped output of American industrial society which can no longer (at least this is my conclusion) be separated into beneficial and deleterious, "good" and "bad," but has been homogenized, so that "good"—free elections, say—is high-speed blended with commercial TV, opinion-testing, buttons, streamers, stickers, canned speech-writing, instant campaign biographies, till no issues are finally discernible, having been broken down and distributed in tiny particles throughout the suspended solution, and you wonder whether the purpose of having elections is not simply to market TV time, convention-hall space, hotel suites, campaign buttons, and so on, and to give employment to commentators and pollsters. Since nobody can live in a vacuum, nobody, whatever he thinks, is free to "drop out"; poor blacks rioting carry home whiskey and TV sets.

To the North Vietnamese—and this applies equally to peasant and Prime Minister; "We are a mature people," they are fond of saying—American life appears not just grotesque, but backward, primitive, pitiably undeveloped, probably because of its quality of infantile dependency. A story, surely true, is told in Hanoi of a shot-down pilot who explained to his captors that his sister in the States was a rich *"industrielle,"* she would pay them for chicken and whiskey, if they would let him have them, and if they would let him go, she would pay an indemnity for any personal or property damage he had caused on his missions —he swore it: "My sister's a millionaire!" With such flying models being deposited on their territory, like beings from a protozoic world, Pham Van Dong might trust at least the present generation to be immune to capitalist temptations, which elsewhere seem an inherent danger of revisionist adventures.

It was Luu Quy Ky of the Journalists' Union who told us the sad story of the greedy pilot, early in our stay; the day before we left, at a farewell meeting, he announced that he was going to sum up for us the characteristics of the Vietnamese people. Here they are:

1. *Amour de la patrie.* Love of fatherland.

2. *Esprit laborieux.* Industriousness.

3. *Esprit de solidarité et entre-aide mutuelle.* Spirit of solidarity and mutual aid.

4. *Subtilité et persévérance.* Subtlety and perseverance.

310

5. *Optimisme. Esprit rieur.* Optimism. Gaiety and merriment.

6. *Esprit internationaliste. Pas de chauvinisme.* International-mindedness. No chauvinism.

I spoke earlier about undergoing an identity crisis in the North. This was due no doubt partly to the bombing, which "shook me up," but also to an unspoken feeling of conflict with the North Vietnamese value system, a conflict that grew more and more obscure as I sought to bring it to the light. Some vague assurance of superiority, not personal but generic, had been with me when I arrived; it was the confidence of the American who knows himself to be fair-minded, able to see both sides, disinterested, objective, et cetera, as compared to the single-minded people he is about to visit. To be just to myself and to those who brought me up, I think I do possess those qualities, though perhaps not as much as I imagine. They are the fossil remains of the old America, detached by an ocean from the quarrels of Europe, having no colonial interests compared to the Great Powers, a permanent outsider and hence fitted to judge and bear witness, enjoying a high material standard of living, which ought to exclude any venality or pettiness. That is how the heroes and heroines of Henry James saw themselves and how their author saw them, with amazed pity and terror. Even after World War II, the words "I am an *American citizen,*" pronounced by a New England spinster, could strike fear into the heart of an UNRRA official, as though the old green passport carried full investigative powers into the management of international relief funds.

My own avowed purpose in going to the North was to judge, compare, and report back; my findings, I reasoned, could not be damaging to the North Vietnamese; on the contrary, a straight dose of reality might dispel some of the phobic attitudes that were allowing the war to continue. A sound, sensible purpose, which I have not lost sight of, but which took for granted my supreme authority as an American to determine the truth. I counted on the public to believe me, as it had believed Harrison Salisbury, when all earlier reports had been discounted, as coming from suspicious sources. Yet after a few days with those single-minded North Vietnamese, I found my claim to being a disinterested party starting not exactly to disappear, but to shrink from showing itself, as if ashamed. The Vietnamese, beginning with peasants eagerly showing you where their fields had been bombed, had an earnest, disarming conviction that you would give them total credence. To question facts, figures, catch small discrepancies would be to abuse this open, naïve (from a Western point of view) trust. The same with their certainty of victory, which soon you began to share, to the point at least of hoping they were not wrong and blotting from your mind as disloyal to their struggle any information leading to a different conclusion that you had been getting from the Western press. But more unsettling than this quickening of sympathy—inevitable, humanly speaking, under the circumstances—was a sense that my detachment and novelistic powers of observation were not only inappropriate but also a sort of alibi. The plea of being elsewhere, at my blameless typewriter, when the crime was committed would not stand up any more for an American writer; opposition to the war was not a sufficient credential to permit me to circulate here as a pure recording sensibility noting down impressions, which, however, I was doing and could not help doing, short of jumping out of my skin. It came down to this: if I was an unsuspicious source, worthy of belief, so far as a wide American public was concerned, this meant I was a suspicious character to all who mistrusted that public's standards and morality—including myself. On the other hand, the command (if that is not too strong a word) of an audience was my value to the North Vietnamese, and if I vacated that little seat of judgment I had pre-empted years ago and resigned the duties, perhaps inflated by vanity, that went with it, then I might as well have stayed home.

Everybody knows that you cannot serve God and Mammon, but few can refrain from trying; each counts on being the exception, especially if, as in my case, it is Mammon who seems to be serving *us*, gratuitously, with no collusion on our part. For my generation, Stalinism, which had to be opposed, produced the so-called non-Communist Left, not a movement, not even a sect, but a preference, a political taste shared by an age group resembling a veterans' organization, which had last seen action during the Spanish Civil War. Since the "brand" of radicalism we preferred had no appeal for the masses (only the CIA, as it turned out, was interested), we had no clear alternative but to be "believing" socialists and practicing members of capitalist society. My own socialism consisted in voting for Norman Thomas until he vanished from the ballot and in anarchist and libertarian sympathies; there was a time in the forties when I might genuinely have tried to live in an anarchist utopia. The dream of a New Jerusalem, which would be my private Calvary (since I am not a willing crank), has stayed with me in reverie, merging more and more with the commonplace let's-

313

get-away-from-it-all desert-island fantasies whose seat seems to be in the liver—the longing for a "cure." Hence my questions to Pham Van Dong about decentralization. Meanwhile, like most of the non-Communist Left, I was moving effortlessly into a higher and higher income bracket. The slight discomfort this caused me was outweighed by the freedom from any financial stringencies and the freedom to write exactly what I wished.

That freedom (*cf.* Norman Mailer) is a perquisite of successful U.S. authors. Until I came to Hanoi, I had joyed in the exercise of it as in the performance of some faintly dangerous athletic feat, which continues to surprise the doer each time it is brought off. There were not so many good things to point to in our country, and to be the embodiment, the living proof, of one of them is reassuring: "Watch me, young man, and learn how to do it. In our country, you do not have to sell out to sell." In Hanoi, for the first time in my travels, I found that this freedom and the material evidences of it, in the shape of clothes and possessions, were not regarded as enviable. The number of my suitcases (I have never learned to travel light) may have afforded some slight amusement; that was all. The license to criticize was just another capitalist luxury, a waste product of the system. This of course is true. The fact that you can read about, say, police brutality or industrial pollution in the New York *Times* or even in a local paper is nothing to be especially proud of, unless something concrete results, any more than the fact that you can read both sides about Vietnam and watch it on television. A free press is livelier than a government-controlled one, but access to information that does not lead to action may actually be unhealthy, like any persistent frustration, for a body politic. The illusion of being effective, the sole justification of my presence there, began to waver in North Vietnam the more I called upon it to defend me against the charge of complicity with American ruling circles—a complicity attested by the mirror. All the excess mental baggage I carried, of allusion and quotation, the·"acquirements" of college, study, travel, acquaintance with prominent figures, weighed as heavy as my suitcases, as my unenvied freedom. My objectivity was making me uncomfortable, like a trade mark or shingle advertising a genuine Mary McCarthy product ("Trust Her to Speak Her Mind"). In short, I was not pleased with myself, or with what I somewhat showily represented.

But if I was nothing but a sample of American society—a feeling that grew on me—then I had no subjectivity at all. Yet I was aware of a subject, an "I," asserting itself from time to time, in protest or scruple, a subject I did not dislike. What I was carrying around with me, too, and not as an encumbrance, was a remnant of Christian ethics, applying to my own conduct and to the world at large. A vision of harmony and a universal pardon, with everybody being forgiven and getting married in the end, as at the finale of *The Marriage of Figaro* or a Shakespearean comedy. Whatever jarred or distressed me in North Vietnam—the history lesson on the blackboard in Hung Yen Province, the extirpation of French, the monothematic narrowness of art and literature—had to do with the loss of universals. The private tumults and crises I had been undergoing, trivial as was their occasion (who cared whether I wore that ring made from a shot-down plane or whether I said "puppet" or

315

"Viet Cong"?), involved the omnipresence, the ubiquity of God. *He* cared. Being an unbeliever made no difference. I had swallowed Him too many times as a child at the communion rail, so that He had come to live inside me like a cherry stone growing or like Socrates' unshakable companion and insistent interlocutor: oneself.

What remained from my Catholic training was the idea that it was necessary to be the same person at all times and places. When alone, I must never perform an action (short of taking a bath, etc.) that I would be unwilling to perform in public. This applied, of course, to thoughts, since God could hear you thinking them. It was the same choral vision of unity and concord, on a piping individual scale, that I still wished to see enacted in a free socialist commonwealth, though I had found it only in art, which is probably the only place where it is native. And it was because of such essentially God-fearing scruples that, as I got to know the North Vietnamese better, I grew ashamed to write little observations about them in my notebook, for you ought not to be two people, one downstairs, listening and nodding, and the other scribbling in your room.

The North Vietnamese, very likely, would have had no hesitation in drawing up a full report every evening on my companion and myself. But their ethic is in the service of the state, society, and mine is more selfish, mainly working at my own salvation. There lay the conflict of values, obscure because in practice the results may look similar, since both strive for correction of base or "low" tendencies. Here, however, more analysis is required. Since I have no trace of belief in a future life, what is meant by "my own salvation"? It comes down, I think, to a simple question of comfort. I am concerned with my own comfort, being able "to live with myself," as people used to say. And that, in a nutshell, was why I had come to North Vietnam.

Patriotism, I had surmised, had played a large part in my decision to go, and this was true, as far as it went. I could not bear to see my country disfigure itself so, when I might do something to stop it. It had surprised me to find that I cared enough about America to risk being hit by a U.S. bomb for its sake, having detested flag-waving from the days when we were made to "pledge allegiance" in school every morning. But if I *were* killed, I argued, it might at least convince a few Americans that civilian targets were being aimed at. I was not a military objective. On the other hand, other Americans over their fresh-frozen orange juice would be saying "It served her right."

Possibly yes, for I have come to recognize that I went chiefly for my own peace of mind. To put it as basely as I can, if my country stopped that brutal, brutish onslaught, I would be able once again to enjoy my normal pursuits. Reading, writing, spending money, looking at pictures and cathedrals, entertaining friends. Sleeping. Paying my income tax. I was still doing all those things, except sleeping, pretty much as formerly, but with a disturbed conscience, like a public-relations counsel reminding me that I had a "position" to live up to. If I could only make that hideous war go away, everything would be as before. That, of course, was a mistake. Nothing will be the same again, if only because of the awful self-recognitions, including this one, the war has enforced.

"Vous avez beaucoup de coeur, madame," Pham Van Dong

317

said. He was talking about my little book on South Vietnam; someone had translated extracts into French for him. "You have shown a deep feeling for the Vietnamese people. Feeling and understanding. *Ça m'a touché.*" Guiltily, I wondered (as many of my critics might) whether he did not mean someone else— perhaps Martha Gellhorn? Then it came to me that he must have read the passages about the lepers and the refugees. Did it take a great heart, though, to feel for them? Before we left, he reverted to the theme, as though I had waved it aside too rapidly. I thanked him again. Would I write a book about the North, he wanted to know. It was too early to say, I replied. Perhaps only a couple of articles. It would depend on how much material I had. "I can't make a book out of something that isn't one." I feared he was disappointed. "I would *like* it to be a book," I said.

Later I heard via the grapevine (Hanoi, as I say, is a small world) that the Prime Minister had been much impressed by my honesty in refusing to say that I would be writing a book when in fact I was in doubt about it. *"Oui, oui, il a parlé de cela."* My heart jumped with pleased surprise. This, then, was the universal pardon. I was set free. He had kissed us, each, with emotion when we said good-by, and now I did not have to feel like a Judas, whatever I would write. The North Vietnamese did not expect more of me than what I was. From each according to his abilities, which is the same as saying, in my Father's house, there are many mansions.

It would be pleasing if the story of my visit could stop there. . . . But it has an epilogue. In Phnom Penh, waiting for me at the airport, was the wife of the West German ambassador to Cambodia. On my way through, she had asked me to try to learn something about the fate of Dr. and Mrs. Krainick of the Medical School of Hue University, who had disappeared during the Tết offensive; the rumor had reached Bonn that they had been captured by the Viet Cong and were being held to treat their wounded. Knowing Dr. and Mrs. Krainick, I did not feel this would be too bad. They had treated all patients alike, and it was thanks to Mrs. Krainick in particular, who came to see me impulsively in my bedroom at the house of a U.S. official, that I had learned some of the truth about conditions in Hue. But in case they needed an advocate, I pleaded their cause at some length when we visited the NLF Delegation. As it turned out, this was not necessary. They knew about the Krainicks, had known about them long before the Tết offensive. Good people, yes, and *"plus ou moins sympathiques à nous."* Mr. Tien, the Chief Delegate, had already been making inquiries, and they were not with any Viet Cong unit. According to his information, they had last been seen in the university compound. He feared they might be dead —killed in a bombing raid.

Nevertheless, I still had hope. In the steaming airport, I told the German ambassador's wife exactly what the Front leader had said. She stopped me, shaking her head. "We have just had news. They are dead. Their bodies have been identified." Later I read that the Krainicks and another German doctor had been found in a mass grave, executed by the Viet Cong. Or possibly, other sources suggested, by the North Vietnamese Army, who would not have known about them. Still another theory was that they might have been murdered by Buddhists; the Krainicks were Catholics,* and during the Tết offensive, old

---

* No. Protestants. Their working so closely with the Knights of Malta had made me think they were Catholics too.

319

scores in Hue were settled—going back to the Struggle Movement of 1966—between Buddhists and Catholics.* Certainly the
Krainicks had enemies among the town officials; last year the
story was that Dr. Krainick was not allowed to enter the hospital
laboratory because of his angry complaints about local corruption. There is no way of knowing yet what really happened, and
I feel somewhat suspicious of American stories of mass graves.
And if the Viet Cong summarily buried the Krainicks, does this
prove that it killed them? According to the news story from
Saigon, the other bodies found in the grave were those of Hue
notables—very likely some of their bitterest enemies. Such an
injustice is hard to bear, on the Krainicks' behalf, and worse is
to think that, after all, it *may* have been the Viet Cong who did
it; no army or guerrilla band fails to commit an occasional act
of senseless, stupid butchery. I should prefer to think it was the
Americans, indiscriminately bombing. This would not have
taken the doctor and his wife by surprise or wounded their feelings. After eight years of service in Hue, they must have been
used to seeing civilian victims of American bombs and being
told there was nothing *personal* about it. . . . With the Viet
Cong, it was different; the young Germans working with the
Krainicks had explained to me that they regularly drove the
Red Cross station wagon into VC territory, along roads the
Americans would not venture to take unless heavily armed, in
convoy, and preferably not even then. When I had applauded
their courage, they said it was only common sense: "They know
we help them when they are sick or wounded, so why should they
shoot at us?"

Assuming it was the Viet Cong—or, slightly less terrible, the

---

* Would this include other Christians? Or did the local Vietnamese make the same
mistake I did and assume they were Catholics?

North Vietnamese—I cannot step forward with an excuse. No power has vested me with the authority to condone the murder of civilians. This came easy to a young militant of the New Left, who told me brusquely that people like the Krainicks had no business in Vietnam: they should either have joined the Viet Cong or gone back to Germany. That it was unreal to expect a middle-aged, middle-class German Catholic couple to do *more* than practice charity (a rare and difficult virtue) cut no ice with him. What happened to them was their own fault for trying to be disinterested do-gooders. *"Plus ou moins sympathiques"* was insufficient. Such people, he added, were obsolete.

If they were obsolete, what was the point of killing them? The ideas of that young man are far from the principle of limit governing the North Vietnamese conduct of the war and far from the "correctness" usually shown by the Viet Cong in their dealings with the civilian population. In fact, his way of thinking was close to the views of the American command, which demands that the population take sides; anybody who remains in a hamlet designated Viet Cong is liable to execution from the air. Our position is that they got what was coming to them for sticking around.

The only excuse for the Krainicks' murder is that it happened and cannot be retracted now, whoever did it. Whoever did it has shouldered a crime that time may pardon or events may avenge. Eventually this war will become "ancient history," water over the dam. If time did not exercise that forgiving power, embodied in the principle of amnesty, nobody could live another second. The North Vietnamese, a mature people, as they say, know this, carefully distinguishing the person of the criminal from his crime, treating the fractures of the shot-down pilots with their advanced surgical skills (did Dr. Tung operate in such cases or did he leave it to his assistants?) and conducting them to air-raid shelters, separate but equal, when the sirens blow.

But Johnson and his advisers, perhaps because of the magnitude of their offenses, cannot even yet accept the ineluctable ending of the war and are literally fighting it off. Their maneuvers suggest that they are seeking the impossible: not the general forgetfulness accorded by time—who remembers the French cabinets of the years before Dien Bien Phu?—but exoneration. The hope of this fades, obviously, whenever peace nears. Might makes right is the only history lesson Johnson appears to have learned, and as he approached the brink of peace last April 3,* he grew frightened and drew back. In the months that have passed, as negotiations have stalled and "limited" bombing continues, he has probably got over his scare. What forces can combine again to lead him to the edge and push him over into the pit, as he has assessed it, of destruction? The mere traction of opinion will not do it. Opinion, like Johnson, wavers, as is shown by the fact that no candidate for his office, however favorable to "peace," has been able to face meeting it under its other name, *surrender*. The moral overtones are displeasing to the American public; surrender is a confession of failure. Yet we will be lucky, though we do not see it, if failure, finally, is the only crime we are made to confess to.

---

* This was in the summer of 1968, before the Democratic convention in Chicago, which finally nominated Hubert Humphrey.

MEDINA

S umming up the first week's testimony in the trial of Captain Medina, the New York *Times* quoted an unnamed observer: "It all seems like an exercise in futility." Dated Sunday, August 22, 1971, that was a fair sample of courtroom opinion at Third Army headquarters, Fort McPherson, Georgia, during any week or hour of the trial, which finally ended a month later, on September 22, in Medina's acquittal.

Calley's company commander, aged 34, of Montrose, Colorado, was being court-martialed on three separate charges, the most grave being the third or "additional charge" that "Captain Ernest L. Medina, US Army . . . Fort McPherson, Georgia, then a member of Company C, 1st Battalion, 20th Infantry . . . American Division, did at My Lai (4), Quang Ngai Province, Republic of Vietnam, on or about 16 March 1968, with premeditation, murder an unknown number of unidentified Vietnamese persons, not less than 100, by means of shooting these persons with machine guns, rifles, and other weapons."

The other two charges had to do with the shooting of a woman, the shooting of a child, and two assaults on a prisoner with a rifle, and were distinct from the additional charge in that the acts specified were claimed to have been committed by him personally (or, in the child's case, under his direct order), while the not less than 100 persons were allegedly murdered by him at one remove, that is, by the men in his command with his consent and approval.

Medina acknowledged shooting the woman, pleading what amounted to self-defense (he thought she was reaching for a weapon), acknowledged that he may have been responsible, involuntarily, for the shooting of the child (having counter-manded too late what he supposed may have been his first, confused order: " 'Get him, get him, stop him, stop him, shoot' or 'don't shoot!' ''), acknowledged firing a rifle twice over a prisoner's head but denied that this constituted assault with a deadly weapon. As for the additional charge, he denied it in its entirety, disclaiming, as he had done in the Calley trial, any knowledge or awareness of what his men had been up to that morning. The scattered bodies of non-combatants he saw in and near the village and the twenty to twenty-eight (his estimate) lying on the north-south trail he had attributed to artillery or gunship fire, and some nearby rifle fire he heard after ordering an old man pulled out of a hootch he had assumed was another pig being shot by the troops. If there were fifty to seventy-five bodies in a ditch, he did not see them.

His defense, on the major charge, was essentially an alibi. He had been elsewhere during the big action—except for a short sally, not more than ninety yards, into the village, he had stayed on the perimeter with the command group, near the LZ (the landing zone in a rice field to the west selected for the morning's assault). When he entered the village proper (more correctly, hamlet or sub-hamlet), where he eventually ate lunch, it was pretty much all over, and any sporadic shootings that were still happening were not in his line of vision. But long before he took the stand to aver this point by point, long before the procession of character witnesses swearing that he was a dedicated conscientious officer, the press and courtroom spectators had reached a verdict, which was simply that the trial was boring, a waste of time.

That seemed to be the view, too, of the defendant and his counsel, who yawned, stretched, doodled, slumped, whispered, rolled martyrs' eyes skyward, nudged neighboring ribs, cupped mouths to pass sardonic asides, like a pewful of restless school-boys during a particularly dull and long-drawn-out chapel service. At the defense table, there were big boyish grins of anticipation whenever F. Lee Bailey, the chief civilian defense counsel, rose, shaking off his ennui and settling his collar, to make one of his "innocent" interventions, like the school bad boy, plump and feigning stupidity, who rises to ask a loaded and deferential question: "Sir!"

On the dais at the rear sat the jury—two full colonels, two lieutenant colonels, and a major—in diverse states of glassy fixity or open drowsiness. At the left end, Lt. Col. Bobby Berry-hill, Jr., from Decatur, Georgia, double-chinned, pendulous, with large soft brown eyes and a long nose, napped from time to time but when fully awake seemed the most reflective of the jurors and finally, at the close of the testimony, asked the only penetrating questions put to Medina at any point in the trial. At the other end of the dais, the youngest member, Major Dudley L. Budrich, from Chicago, an airborne ranger, blond, with bangs and weakly drawn cowboy features, sucked his hollow cheek in a rhythmic motion or chewed on a wad of gum and yawned in the same steady cadence, his jaws opening and shutting on their hinges, like a machine beating time. In the center, the foreman, Col. William Proctor, from Dunwoody,

Georgia, wore an unchanging ferocious glare of command behind accusatory glasses, as though compelling the evidence to present arms and salute him. On his left, a black officer, Lt. Col. Clarence Cooke, born in Enterprise, Alabama, leaned back in his chair and looked indulgent, an adult overseeing a child's game. On the foreman's right, Col. Robert E. Nelson, Jr., originally from Eatontown, Georgia, a thin rather handsome blond officer with cold blue eyes, listened with a curling ironic smile that seemed to mark at least a sarcastic attention to the evidence, but newsmen said it was only a facial tic—the result of combat wounds he suffered in the Korean War. Opposite the jury, behind the spectators' seats, the courtroom door was guarded by a young M.P. sitting on a straight chair and generally asleep.

Facing the jury, the prosecution team—Major William G. Eckhardt and his second, Capt. Franklin R. Wurtzel—assigned by the Army to try the case, presented a façade of severity and grim determination. It was the third of the My Lai 4 cases they had prosecuted, and the third they were going to lose, quite evidently. They acted like the lower end of the batting order with two strikes on them and making blustering motions in the box. Or like members of a freshman debating squad assigned to the less popular side of some already lifeless proposition, such as "RESOLVED, that the United States should withdraw from the Kellogg-Briand Pact." Wurtzel was small, slight, and plaintive, with a breathy lisping voice; Eckhardt, tall and loosely hung, held a big meerschaum pipe in the form of a turbaned Turk's head clamped between his teeth and seemed most in his element when administering the oath to witnesses, which he did with great belligerence and in a voice of thunder.

This forcible-feeble pair had a certain ingenuous pathos. Despite their familiarity (one would think) by this time with the My Lai matter, they appeared poorly prepared and were repeatedly taken by surprise by their own witnesses, as well as scolded, guided, and corrected by the judge.

At the long defense table, opposite the judge, were Medina and his two military lawyers, plus Bailey and two rather indistinct members of his law firm, whose chief function seemed to be errand-running. Each time they left the room or returned, it had to be inserted in the record, interrupting the proceedings and giving an air of busyness and humming activity to the defense organization. But Bailey treated everybody as an errand boy ("Capt. Kadish, make the necessary phone"), scarcely stopping short of the judge. His military associate, Mark Kadish, a young lawyer from Brooklyn doing his hitch in the Army, was dark, with a bright eye like a chicken's, soft whitish arms in summer short-sleeved military shirt, and a rather matronly spread of the hips; when not conferring with Medina or making the necessary phone, he sat with folded arms and head tilted back against the wall, stifling yawns if Eckhardt was examining and looking lazily derisive, like a Jewish intellectual drafted into attendance at some cow college. This appearance was deceptive. The assistant military counsel was Capt. John R. Truman, of Independence, Missouri, also doing his hitch in the Army and a grandnephew of the former President. He smiled a good deal, in a thin eager scholarly way, but otherwise contributed little to the defense presentation and appeared shy.

The judge, Col. Kenneth Howard, was another Georgian and a Methodist Sunday-school teacher. Under his baggy black gown, he wore, not a uniform, but a dark suit, white shirt, and a small flowing black tie, and this rather old-fashioned costume distinguished him from the jury in military dress with the obligatory medals and decorations and from military counsel. Mrs. Millie Burchardt, the civilian press officer, said that he prayed for light before every session. Unlike the other participants, he seemed indeed a prayerful man, guided by the conviction that he was presiding over something more than a legal farce or dutiful debating exercise with a foregone conclusion. He was short, round, slow-spoken, with pepper-and-salt hair that matched his sharp dry country wit, often called into exercise by the theatrics of F. Lee Bailey. Although capable of amusement and drollery, he was also capable of sternness at unseemly laughter in the courtroom. He appeared to know less law than Bailey (*e.g.*, it did not sound as if he had a very sure grasp of the differences between testimonial immunity and transactional immunity) and not to be troubled by it. In making his decisions, he would patiently fall back on common sense, dismissing with a wave of his short broad hand the large green books of case material from which Bailey would cite rules and precedents.

Finally, though, he was moved to anger. More and more, as the trial went on, Bailey, hoping (it was said) for a mistrial if he did not secure an acquittal, goaded him as though sensing a weak point and finally, by repeated pressure, locating it. On September 15, the judge flew off the handle: "Don't repeat back to me that the judge is an idiot and doesn't know what he's doing!" This was what Bailey wanted. There was a long argument behind closed doors, which ended with Judge Howard, doubtless repentant of his outburst, reversing a ruling he had made. But by this time the trial was stumbling anyhow to a close. The prosecution had lost its two principal witnesses and been betrayed by a third. Nobody, even those who believed in Medina's guilt, believed there was any chance of his conviction. Two days later, the judge reduced the additional charge to manslaughter.

Col. Howard's weak point, so insistently probed, may have been his professional pride. Courtroom gossips reported that he felt competitive with Col. Kennedy, who had tried the Calley case. So far as one can tell in the absence of a transcript (no official transcript of either trial is available to the public), Col. Howard had no reason, except his evident modesty, to fear that his performance ranked below Reid Kennedy's; rather the contrary, to guess from published bits. But though "competitive" may not be the word for the judge's state of mind, modesty, combined with a desire to do what is right, can make a mild man sensitive to comparisons. And however Col. Howard stacked up against Col. Kennedy, the Medina trial could not stand comparison with the Calley trial.

This was quickly manifest in the attendance. The military courtroom (always described in the newspapers as "small, stuffy" or "tiny, stuffy") had room for only forty-three people in the spectator section, and the press officers handling the trial expected problems. By court order, thirty seats were provided for the press and four for the public—not counting Mrs. Medina and counsels' wives. Priority would be given to reporters for the networks and wire services, the big dailies, *Time, Newsweek*, three courtroom artists in the front row, the local press. To take care of the press, two overflow rooms were set up, with forty-seven headphones, in the Press Center, and a system of drawing for courtroom passes every morning at 8:30 sharp. If the *Daily News* or CBS man did not show up on time, his seat went into the pool. But as it turned out, the big press hall with desks, telephones, and typewriters was usually half empty, and there were plenty of spare passes in the press officer's basket. Some of the media people who were expected did not materialize; some looked in for a day or so and then dropped out. The German weekly *Der Spiegel* installed a telephone and never came, and you could use the *Spiegel* phone to call a Yellow cab from downtown Atlanta. In the courtroom, filling the unclaimed seats of newsmen, were officers' towheaded children, officers' wives and sisters-in-law, an occasional G.I., one day a Delta Air Lines hostess, and nearly every day a tall curly-haired young major with a drawing-board sketching the principals—he was a research doctor doing his military service and an amateur artist of some talent. The overflow press rooms were used by reporters as hideaways, especially after lunch: it was possible to sleep there, turning off the headphones, and also to smoke, despite a "No Smoking" sign and the intermittent slumbrous presence of an M.P., who was supposed to be on guard.

Word had got around fast that this trial was a dud compared to the Calley trial. "The once lurid testimony seemed stale," Homer Bigart wrote in the New York *Times* during the first week. The Medina show was a box-office turkey. There was no Aubrey Daniel, to put it mildly, in the prosecutor's role. There were no drinking parties with the judge or lawyers or defendant. Medina, small, slit-eyed, looking like the bad Indian in a Western, lacked the all-American appeal of Rusty Calley. The only star was the rather tarnished F. Lee Bailey, in his pin-striped suits, giving desultory interviews on the sidewalk—a

benefit performance for the TV crews and photographers stationed in a sort of bandstand outside the courthouse in the
punishing sun. In his low uninflected voice, talking into the
extended mikes and to a circle of scribbling reporters, he
obligingly played to the gallery, promising to call Calley as a
defense witness and confront him with startling, hitherto-un-
disclosed evidence, threatening to bring the White House into
the case—a feint he made three times, with aplomb, as though
he had Richard M. Nixon up his conjuror's sleeve, like the
handkerchief he sometimes slowly drew out in the courtroom
and gently shook open. Calley, in fact, was produced, under
guard, but the White House, like *Der Spiegel*, ignored Bailey
and his client.

The disgusted conviction that the Medina court-martial was
a poor road show of the Calley hit was perhaps understandable
in the circumstances, given the human appetite for novelty and
the fact that a courtroom is a natural stage set on which some
sort of drama is expected to emerge. No doubt, too, there was
something peculiarly American in the general disappointment,
as though a public event that did not "top" a previous one was
a drag, a loser, a cheat. "We've heard it before. Why bore us?"
was the sullen refrain, though it is hard to see how the Medina
trial, even if well conducted by the prosecution, could have
failed to be in many respects a repetition of the Calley trial.
There was the same personnel, returning to tell its story again,
the same bodies on the trail and in the ditch. What did the press
and public want—mint-fresh atrocities, in preference to stale
ones?

The feeling of boredom and futility at Fort McPherson was
aggravated by the fact that concurrently at Fort Meade, Mary-

land, still another road show was performing—the trial of Col. Henderson, with again the same basic cast of characters: the men of Charlie Company, Lt. LaCrosse, Lt. Alaux (artillery), the helicopter pilots Thompson and Colburn, Millians and Culverhouse, the task-force officer Major Calhoun, Major Watke, Col. Luper, and, hovering up in the flies, the *deus ex machina* and chief author of My Lai, Col. Frank Barker, well beyond the reach of the law's long arm, having answered a higher summons three months after My Lai, when he died in a helicopter crash. There was a growing and eerie familiarity about these men, some still in uniform, some not, making their entrances and exits, like members of an all-male stock company, sometimes cast in slightly different parts: a character witness in the Medina trial would be a prosecution witness in the trial of Col. Henderson. You recognized quite a few from their photos in the various books on My Lai and Calley, on sale at national airports; some had changed their appearance, let hair or sideburns grow, added a mustache, making you feel doubly that they were actors in different make-ups.

While waiting, paper cup of coffee and Army doughnut in hand, for the day's testimony in the Medina trial to begin, reporters could look through the morning paper with yesterday's testimony from the Henderson trial. Far fields seemed greener. Their testimony at Fort Meade sounded better than *our* testimony. Why didn't we have Charles West, since they did? How did *their* prosecutor get those tapes (made by Capt. Charlie Lewellen, for his own amusement, of the radio dialogue accompanying the My Lai action) that haven't been played here, for us? (In fact, the tapes were finally introduced into evidence in the Fort McPherson courtroom, but by the defense, rather than the prosecution.) Witnesses were shuttling back and forth between Fort Meade and Fort Mac. At one point, when F. Lee Bailey was announcing Col. Henderson as a defense witness, it looked as if the two trials might homogenize into a single cloudy mixture, which at least would have cut costs to the taxpayer. In the end, Col. Henderson was not brought to the stand in the Medina case, but, nearly two months after his own acquittal, Medina took the stand in the Henderson case, as a defense witness.

Before Calley was arraigned, some of the younger lawyers in JAG (the Judge Advocate General's office) proposed holding a mass trial on the Nuremberg pattern, with all the suspects in the dock together, from Gen. Koster (never brought to the bar, but censured), down to Staff Sgt. Mitchell (acquitted at Fort Hood, Texas) and Sgt. Hutto (acquitted at Fort Mc-Pherson)—a clean sweep. The idea was vetoed, but it might have satisfied, at least visually, a desire for even-handed justice, avoided repetitiousness, and apportioned blame in large, small, and medium slices according to a single measure. The method used, of holding separate trials, with separate juries, combined with high-level administrative decisions to absolve some of the parties without trial, was bound to produce a haphazard result and leave a sense of unfairness. My Lai was a single big crime, committed by many parties, with accessories before and after the fact; whether Lt. Calley was more or less guilty than Gen. Koster need not have been left to the public, in the throes of hysteria and, finally, indifference, to decide.

The Medina trial, theoretically, had an advantage over the Calley trial, in that the whole picture was laid out more clearly than in the Calley case, where the focus was on the ground, on

the erratic character and behavior of a single malformed lieutenant who, though not demented in the legal sense, was plainly
unable to function in the Army or in American society, even
though in his strivings and failure to "make it," he appeared
more horribly typical than, say, his prosecutor, Capt. Aubrey
Daniel. Since he showed no other signs of sadistic inclinations,
his conduct at My Lai defies understanding unless it is seen
as an effort to distinguish himself, win credit—an all-out spurt
in a success-drive. Calley both got the point and missed it about
Vietnam.

In the Medina trial Calley and the first platoon figured small,
for the most part out of sight, in another part of the village;
without the distorting bent of his personality the massacre
can be centered in a wider frame. If you imagine My Lai 4
as a picture, the top layer, at 2,000 feet, is occupied by Gen.
Koster (code name Saber 6) in his helicopter; below him, in
his helicopter, at 1,500 feet, is Col. Henderson (code name
Rawhide 6), the brigade officer; the next layer is occupied by
Lt. Col. Barker (code name Coyote 6) in the command-control
ship, ranging over the whole operation, his brain child, at a
general altitude of 1,000 feet—the unit he has combined to
put it into execution is christened after him: Task Force Barker.
Underneath him are OH 1b gunships, and occupying the lowest
stratum, in a small observation craft, an OH 23 or "bubble
ship," are Hugh Thompson and Larry Colburn. On the ground,
having been airlifted in, preceded by gunship fire and an
artillery "prep" of the village, are Capt. Medina and his command group, in the rice field; Medina is standing on a grave
mound. Proceeding or soon to proceed into the village itself
are Lt. Brooks (deceased), Lt. Calley, the first and second

platoons, Haeberle, a photographer, and Roberts, an Army writer. The third platoon, Lt. Alaux, and the mortar unit have stayed behind, for the present, with Medina. Phu, an interpreter, is there too, to be joined later by Minh, another interpreter and interrogation expert. Also on the ground are the villagers, some eating breakfast. The time is about 7:30.

The helicopters, large and small, rotating above in hierarchical stratification, have a bird's-eye view of the "combat assault"; that, in fact, is what they are there for. What Gen. Koster saw is not known. Col. Henderson denied seeing anything from his air-lane that he could interpret as unusual, and indeed, in his trial, there was much dispute as to his altitude, the prosecution placing him low and the defense, naturally, high—above Gen. Koster.

Soon, though, Thompson and Colburn do see something unusual, circle back, hover, and land—several times. In the gunships, Millians, Culverhouse, and Brian Livingston also discern something wrong. Higher up, in the command helicopters, the regular counterclockwise movement is disturbed, and there seem to be shifts in position. Is this because of the alarm raised by Thompson over his radio or are the ships simply returning to base to refuel?

Back at LZ Dottie, the take-off point and Tactical Operations Center, are dark, bony, hawk-nosed Major Calhoun and pale stout Capt. Kotouc, the F-2 or brigade intelligence officer (acquitted at Fort Mac of maiming a prisoner by cutting off part of his finger; the charge had been reduced from murder). He is responsible for the faulty intelligence that supposedly has prepared the ground for the massacre: *i.e.*, that Charlie Company would find the 48th VC Battalion in the village and that at seven o'clock that morning all the women and children would have gone to market in the town.

At least once, Major Calhoun leaves LZ Dottie and flies over My Lai 4. Col. Barker, at least once, returns to LZ Dottie and talks to Major Watke, the helicopter command officer, in the TOC. Col. Henderson is in and out of the TOC and, according to one witness, lands at the My Lai 4 hamlet, carrying a clipboard, and speaks angrily to Capt. Medina. It is at the time of the Carter Medivac, and a black, Sp4 Gerald Heming, a demolitions man attached to the command group, watches two helicopters alight; one is the dust-off (medical evacuation) chopper, and the other contains Col. Henderson, who gets out and tells Medina something like "These killings have to stop." But this witness loses credibility with the jury on several counts: he is wearing an Afro beard and a fuchsia-and-gold dashiki with a heart pattern, which stand out like a private fantasy against the regulation summer tans and clean shaves of counsel and M.P.'s; he confuses the gold leaf worn by Major Budrich of the jury with a colonel's silver eagle; he has been drinking (four quarts of wine before a chat with Capt. Kadish the previous night, and some more on top of that); he has tried LSD; and he has a high wild screechy equalitarian sense of humor ("How did you recognize Col. Henderson? Did you ever speak to him?" "No." "Then how do you know him as Col. Henderson?" "I see him every morning at the base. He is coming out of *his* hootch, and I am coming out of *my* hootch").

The tall angry officer with the clipboard, sometimes descending from a helicopter, was one of the mysteries of the trial. He appeared several times in the testimony, assuming different forms, like a god in metamorphosis. Sometimes he seemed to be Major Calhoun; a logical guess was Col. Barker. But there is nothing in the record to show that Barker or Calhoun ever landed at My Lai 4. He can scarcely have been Gen. Koster, aloft, at the apex of the action. It is as if, in the reveries of Charlie Company, some such officer *ought* to have appeared from the skies, a stern and righteous commander zeroing in like a thunderbolt to put a stop to the murder orgy.

That dream officer, Moses from Sinai, should of course have been Col. Barker. He was in command; quite early, while airborne, he got (or overheard) word from the bubble ship that civilians were being killed indiscriminately. He seems to have handled this routinely with a transmission to Major Calhoun, asking him to relay the message to Medina. Yet according to Medina's testimony, Col. Barker was in direct touch all along with him, full of eager queries about the VC body count. And another witness described seeing the C-and-C ship hovering low at the far end of the hamlet. A different version says that it was Watke, not Barker, who alerted Calhoun, if alerted is the right word, as well as Barker himself and then, perhaps because no action was taken, Col. Henderson and Gen. Koster. Still another story is that Barker radioed the TOC that he had had a complaint from "higher up"—just as though this was the first he had heard of anything untoward. Meanwhile Thompson in person was at LZ Dottie, reiterating his complaint and pleading that something be done. It must have been around this time that a witness saw Major Watke in the TOC talking angrily to Major Calhoun. Still no action; merely a transmission from Calhoun to Medina hoping that no civilians were getting hurt. No doubt Barker was already composing his official report on the operation as he cruised over the scene: ". . . well planned, well executed, and successful. Friendly casualties were light and the enemy suffered heavily." He gave a KIA count of 128 VC, noted eleven CIA (VC captured in action), and three captured weapons (old American rifles).

These figures included Alpha and Bravo Companies. To Charlie Company, out of the over-all total, he assigned fifteen KIA, all three captured weapons, and one U.S. wounded—Pfc. Carter, who had shot himself in the foot. In reply, Gen. Westmoreland sent his commendations: "Congratulations on the operation for Task Force Barker to officers and men of C-1-2 [Charlie Company] for outstanding action." But you did not need to be a four-star general to read between the lines of Col. Barker's summary: only three weapons captured, with a KIA count of 128 and a CIA of eleven? Then at least 125 unarmed persons must have been killed. Who or what were they? Barker's figures were prima-facie evidence of a wholesale murder of civilians, legible to anybody as calling for an investigation. Instead, Gen. Westmoreland's message had the effect of closing the subject with a snap. John Paul, Medina's radio operator: ". . . we did hear that we were under investigation, but a few days later I heard—this was just a rumor—that Gen. Westmoreland had given us a job-well-done, and it was dropped."

At the time Barker got his job-well-done from the general, stories of the murders were circulating, not only among the troops, but also among local Vietnamese government authorities—already, the afternoon of the massacre, survivors had begun spreading the tale. Probably fearing that some of this unpleasant publicity might have percolated upward, Barker tried in guarded language to take care of the question. Without citing figures, he spoke of "a problem in population control and medical care of those civilians caught in the fires of opposing forces." As he knew by then, if he had not known all along, there had been no cross fire at My Lai 4.

The mystery of how Barker had arrived at his body count only deepened at Fort McPherson, when Medina agreed that he had given the task force commander a KIA figure of sixty-nine for Calley's platoon, fourteen from gunship fire, and one from an unidentified cause—a total of eighty-four. In reducing Medina's KIA to fifteen, Barker perhaps hoped to draw attention away from the activities of Charlie Company.

IN THE MEDINA TRIAL, none of the existing mysteries was cleared up and others were created. Why were witnesses who had strongly inculpated Medina in earlier appearances not called to the stand here? Gary Crossley ("We phoned Medina and told him what the circumstances were [nothing but women and children in the hamlet], and he said just keep going"), Paul Meadlo ("I don't know if the CO gave the order to kill or not, but he was right there when it happened"), Herbert Carter, Charles West, the writer Jay Roberts. Perhaps Eckhardt tried and could not persuade them to testify again; perhaps he mistrusted them and feared they might change their stories. Yet the prosecution did produce one unwilling witness, who came and took the Fifth Amendment, and a number of others who let the side down. Why call Policeman Louis Martin, whose testimony was obviously shaky and who broke down, when the defense got at him, and admitted to having fantasies, and draw the line at the combat correspondent Jay Roberts, who was heard at

Fort Meade and who in the Calley trial was sure that Medina spent two hours in the village—testimony which, if believed, would utterly destroy his alibi?

At Fort McPherson, trails opened by the prosecution would quickly be abandoned, as though it was too much work to hack a way through the contradictions. Instead, an overgrowth of confusion sprang up. Wurtzel's shoulders slumped as he relinquished an unforthcoming witness; Eckhardt turned on his heel. With the multiple references to a running child being shot, you never knew which one was meant, and were there not two but three? Not counting, of course, those shot by Calley and the first platoon.

There were many short recesses, including one when the prosecutor's wife had a baby and one when Col. Nelson of the jury had a death in the family. The short recesses suggested fatigue symptoms: "Let's take a break." It was an over-all fatigue, due not to courtroom pressures (the schedule was light) or the August and early September heat, but to weariness of the subject and the issues. The issues faded, like much-washed dirty linen, and more and more the trial turned on technicalities. On the admissibility of hearsay evidence (allowable as a statement against interest or as leading to an action), on testimonial versus transactional immunity for witnesses pleading the Fifth Amendment (the first offers a witness immunity from prosecution for anything he may *say* on the stand; the second is supposed to cover him for the whole transaction, before, during, and after his testimony), on the admissibility of statements made to a lie-detector expert (ruled allowable) as distinguished from lie-detector findings (not allowable). Over and over, the jury filed out while counsel and the judge argued about points of law.

Obviously points of law have their place in a law court, but here wrangling and bickering over them seemed to be taking more than double the man-hours given to the actual testimony and to require more and longer recesses as the judge pondered them in chambers. Col. Howard's patience created impatience around him.

On points of fact there were similar long and useless contentions. Two Vietnamese interpreters gave depositions for the prosecution in South Vietnam, the GRVN having denied them passports to come to the U.S. and testify. First of all, the defense charged that as a matter of fact the U.S. government had not used all available pressure on the Thieu government to compel the presence of the witnesses in court. The judge said he thought the government had acted in good faith. Bailey, striking an injured pose, announced that he would call for Nixon's personal intervention (Judge Howard, amused: "I don't know the number of the White House. Do you?"). The defense evidently hoped to have the depositions thrown out, or, failing that, to leave the inference to be drawn that the prosecution had its reasons for not wanting Sergeants Minh and Phu in court. To give Nixon and Secretary Rogers time to exercise due pressure on Thieu and also for another reason, having to do with a contempt citation, the court decreed a ten-day recess, which included Labor Day. When the sessions resumed, though nothing had changed, Bailey did not press his objections. Minh's and Phu's depositions were heard.

But not before another wrangle lasting several hours. In their depositions, both Minh and Phu agreed that Minh had asked Capt. Medina, "Why we kill everybody in hamlet and burn all hootches and kill animals?" Or words to that effect. To which Medina had answered something like "Orders" or "That was an order" or "He just carrying out an order." Before the tapes could be heard by the jury, Bailey played a new card. The depositions were inadmissible because there was no clear indication that either man understood English. Laughter in the court. The idea that an ARVN sergeant, graduate of an interpreters' school, did not know even simple English appealed to the Army sense of humor. As the tapes showed, the defense team had already been ugly with the witnesses during the taking of the depositions: in his questions, Capt. Kadish made clear his opinion that Minh, being Vietnamese, would not know the truth from a lie. And to Phu, Kadish: "Do you *know* north from south?" Aside from providing some Caucasian entertainment, Bailey's ploy was a gross waste of the court's time. It was plain that the interpreters knew enough English to recognize the primary word "orders." But the judge sent the jury out, listened to the tapes of the depositions, and came up with "a finding of fact," namely, that "this witness [Minh] on March 16, 1968, could speak English."

Phu, who was the Charlie Company interpreter, went on with the troops when they finally left the hamlet. He testified that in the afternoon they met some civilians in a hamlet fifteen or twenty kilometers away and that Capt. Medina instructed him to tell them to move out. If they were still there "when we go on operation here again . . . they get killed, same like people in last village." Little attention was paid by either side to this part of his evidence, with its implication that Medina did know exactly what had been going on in My Lai 4. But it implied something else as well, something so taken for granted by both sides that whenever it came up, it passed unnoticed: the policy of creating refugees. The deliberate creation of refugees is not regarded by the United States as a war crime, and Medina was not being tried for it. In fact, generating refugees was treated by the court and by the witnesses as completely natural and normal, in contrast to the actions cited in the indictment, which even when felt to be defensible seemed to need excuse as representing a deviation from the usual standards of conduct. In Vietnam, murder of non-combatants and assaults on prisoners, however often they occurred, were not "policy."

The tranquil acceptance of organized brutality by the Army was laid bare with simple candor by Medina as he gave his opening testimony on his briefing of his men the night of March 15. Here and in the Calley trial, testimony had varied as to whether or not he had ordered non-combatants killed ("'. . . destroy everything that moved,'" Martin; "'. . . kill everything in the village that moved,'" Flynn; "'. . . kill everything in the village,'" Stanley; "'. . . kill everything that breathed,'" Lamartina; "'. . . leave nothing living in the area except GI's,'" Kinch; whereas others said that there had been no mention of killing anything but livestock).

At Fort McPherson, Medina was very much at ease as he expanded on the briefing, recollecting the scene with the men gathered around him seated on ammunition bunkers as he drew a map on the sand. "I told them that we had permission, Col. Barker had received permission from the ARVNs, that the village could be destroyed since it was a VC stronghold, to burn the houses down, to kill all the livestock, to cut any of the crops that might feed VC, to cave in the wells and destroy the village. . . .

"I had two questions that I recall being asked. One was, do we shoot women and children? My answer to that was no, use your common sense; you don't shoot women and children. If the individual is trying to hurt you and has a weapon, then you can shoot him. If he is evading and does not stop, fire your warning shot. If he doesn't stop then, you can either fire to wound or to kill the individual.

"The other question was in reference to closing the wells. One individual thought it would be a good idea if we could obtain some poison to poison the water. I told him that we didn't do this, that we didn't want to poison the water supply. . . . I told them just to close the wells by caving in the walls or contaminating them by cutting a banana stalk and putting it in the well." He is sure the story reflects credit on him—patient, fatherly, setting an example of restraint. Above all, *moderate*. He was the same in the field, the next day, when he was eating lunch in the schoolhouse, which had not yet been blown up, with two little Vietnamese girls he had found ("He was feeding them and treating them real nice," Sgt. Calvin Hawkins, a demolitions man). Then, after the meal, he sent them "on their way" (his expression) to Quang Ngai or Son Tinh in the company of an old man, *i.e.*, to an orphanage or, more likely, a refugee camp.

It seems improbable that this wary company commander actually ordered the murder of civilians with 105 juveniles listening, though the tenor of the briefing can be imagined from the fact that it gave rise irrepressibly to the question "Do we kill

346

women and children?" The men were to murder a hamlet; on that point, the instructions were clear. A veil was drawn as to what was to become of the population. They were to be disregarded, just as though they did not exist. The next step, to conduct them from virtual to real non-existence, then became easy.

If this is reflected on, some of the mystery surrounding My Lai may resolve. Starting with the puzzle of why Charlie Company, under-strength, with 105 combat-green troops, was sent in to attack a VC battalion estimated to consist of 250 to 280 men, when the usual ratio considered acceptable by the Army for an assault on a fortified position was two or three U.S. to one enemy. No explanation has ever been vouchsafed by the Army for such a departure from policy, and the silence permits one to theorize that those conducting the operation did *not* expect to find the 48th VC in the hamlet. But then what was the point of the attack?

Assume that the grand design was the physical elimination of the whole network of hamlets and sub-hamlets known as Pinkville, long a VC haven, and assume that the intelligence was the *reverse* of what has been claimed, *i.e.*, that the 48th VC had *withdrawn* from the area, probably for rest and recuperation in the mountains near the Laotian border, leaving behind perhaps a few local guerrillas, who would run away when the troops swept through. The purpose of the action would be to profit from the occasion to dry up the ocean in which the VC fish swam, that is, the peasantry. When the VC units returned, Pinkville in its entirety would be KIA, with not a living soul left to collaborate, not an animal or a grain of rice. The people, if they constituted a problem (tried to "evade"), could be shot;

otherwise they would be told to "move on" to the cities, as refugees.

Of course this would not be the first or the last operation designed on a counter-Maoist principle, to deprive the enemy of his base in the native population and generate a flow of refugees. But in most cases refugees were either generated "accidentally," by aerial bombing or artillery exchanges, or, when forcibly removed by the Army into camps, as in the famous clearing out of the Iron Triangle in 1967, treated with some slight deference to humanitarian concepts—the peasants were allowed to bring food, animals, bedding, utensils, and so on, into the camps prepared for them. What stands out in My Lai 4 is that no provision of any kind was made for the people.

Unusual secrecy, too, surrounded the operation. Medina said this was because of the fear of leaks through the always-unreliable ARVN: the 48th VC might be tipped off and steal away. But if the 48th VC was known to have already withdrawn, other motives for secrecy can be presumed. Col. Barker had permission from the district or province chief—Medina was not sure which—to destroy the hamlet, but this depended no doubt on the supposition that it contained an enemy force. GRVN authorities were not always happy to issue these destruction permits to the Americans, and it would have been rare, if not unheard-of, to give one to "sanitize" an area of mere sympathizers. Had news leaked that a combat assault was being prepared on the My Lai complex, embarrassment might have been created for Task Force Barker. We do not know *when* Col. Barker got his permission; it may have been weeks old, dating from a time when a VC battalion was really based (or believed to be based) in My Lai 4.

The uncommonly vigorous and bitter reaction of the district chief to the atrocity suggests that he perceived that he (or his superior) had been tricked by the Americans. Both this man, an ARVN lieutenant, and the village chief made repeated reports, with figures, of the known dead (440 for the Son My area), so categorical and, in the lieutenant's case, fiery in tone that an American advisor supposed that ". . . it was. a VC chief, the one who reported it. . . ."

If we assume that intelligence of a VC withdrawal gave Barker a long-desired opportunity to move swiftly to clean out Pinkville, it does not seem too farfetched. The whole operation bears the mark of a particular personality, outstanding in an army that was not noted for enterprise, and which corresponds to Medina's description of the Task Force commander—"a very Gung Ho, Special Forces type of officer."

Capt. Kotouc concurred: "Col. Barker planned operations like artillery people talk about targets of opportunity. He operated fast." Besides, the thrill of risk—for the intelligence might have been mistaken—was likely to attract Barker, a former parachute jumper, and, to cite Medina again, "a hard charger."

It is not necessary to think that Barker's program included a massacre of civilians. Perhaps he really believed that a majority of the women and children would have gone to market that morning. Or he *hoped* Kotouc's intelligence on this point was right. And it was important to him and Medina that the men believe it. Of course the old and the sick would be in the hamlet, but this was not mentioned. They would object to the killing of their animals and the burning of their houses and food stocks. Hence "incidents," at the very minimum, could

349

be counted on to occur, unless strong instructions were given to the contrary, and a close supervision exercised.

As far as one can tell from Medina's behavior, the only instruction given him had to do with speed. On the radio and in person, he kept urging his men to hurry up, get on with it, as though he had been ordered to work fast and clear out of there before anybody caught him. This may help explain the fact, repeatedly elicited by Prosecutor Eckhardt, that no medical aid was given to any wounded or dying civilians Medina saw in the course of his rounds that morning. The *only* medical aid given in My Lai 4 was to Pfc. Carter, whose foot was treated before he was medivacked out at about 11:00 A.M.

"No medical aid given," "No medical given," "No, sir, no medical aid," the toneless witnesses all agreed. This was confirmed by Medina, who admitted to having seen thirty-five or more bodies, not counting those he shot himself or saw shot. When pressed to account for this astonishing circumstance, he said he assumed they were all dead, without bothering to check. When he saw the child shot—by mistake, as he claimed—he said to his men, "Let's get out of here," evincing that same strange hurry and forestalling any intervention by the command-group medic. The same with the woman of Charge 1. And yet, as he said himself, "I have given aid to wounded VCs many times." If he was accustomed to treating wounded *enemy*, what, unless an order, could have caused him to withhold treatment from wounded *civilians?*

Aside from the bodies, dead or dying, that he actually saw, there were the complaints of the helicopter crewmen, which, according to his testimony, did not reach him till between 10:30 and 11:00 A.M. Whether this is believed or not, he did get a report from Calley between 7:30 and 9:30, telling him that a helicopter pilot had landed and objected to the way Calley was running his platoon. Medina did not ask what the pilot had not liked, any more than he went himself or sent a medic to investigate after receiving the later report.

Yet, as the court learned from Chief Warrant Officer Thompson's testimony, not all the bodies heaped up and lying about were dead. He found some still alive and medivacked them on his own initiative to Quang Ngai City. Medina's striking lack of curiosity, not to say his callousness, might have had some excuse had the action been contested, had his medics been busy caring for U.S. wounded and dying. There was no shortage of pharmaceuticals: as one medic related, the company had learned at the briefing that they would get extra morphine and ten Syrettes more than they usually carried. In the circumstances one can only guess that Medina, by withholding aid, was obeying an instruction not to let himself be distracted by the population, should any get in the way. He had emphasized in his briefing that this was a vengeance operation for the buddies lost by Charlie Company to snipers, booby traps, and mines, and to sustain that mood in the men, keep them jacked up (his expression), it was important that the commander not show softness toward enemy sympathizers whose homes were being systematically "wasted."

Such a phrase as "Get rid of him," pronounced by Medina of the blind-and-deaf old man in the burning hootch, summed up with precision the orders of the day. Medina explained that his men had misconstrued him: he only meant to get the old man out of the way. But getting rid of the population (a phrase that may well have occurred in his briefing) implied a similar indifference to the methods used to achieve the result. The "individual" who proposed obtaining poison to put into the wells was only carrying an accepted basic idea somewhat further than necessary, like Lt. Calley, who saw a quicker method of cleaning out the hamlet than rounding up people and sending them "on their way."

No EVIDENCE WAS brought out in the trial to show foreknowledge on Medina's part of the true situation in the hamlet, and the story Pfc. Herbert Carter told two reporters has to be discounted, since he was unwilling to come forward and repeat it under oath: the night before My Lai, he claimed, he overheard Col. Barker and Capt. Medina talking; they had "found out there wasn't going to be no enemy there." In the trial, it was assumed that Medina did not make the discovery till the following morning—at a time the prosecution endeavored to place early and the defense, naturally, very late. But Eckhardt did not appear to see the importance of the point and slurred over it in his presentation, even though the facts elicited from Medina indicated extraordinary laxness for a commander who imagined he was in combat.

On landing, he set up his command post near the temporary LZ in the rice field and waited there while the first and second platoons began the sweep through the hamlet. As he explained, it was conventional to hold back the command group (together with elements of the third platoon, which was the destroy unit); if he had gone through in the first sweep, he might have been shot or captured by lurking VC or lost his RTO men —the lifeline to the TOC and the gunships. But he remained there stationary for *one and a half hours*. Though this was not brought out, presumably he could hear shooting and was able to distinguish the sound made by U.S. weapons from the sound made by Russian- or Chinese-supplied VC weapons. The village was reckoned to be about the length of three football fields and the width of one. Had there been 250 to 280 VC firing at Charlie Company and getting fire back, that would have made quite a lot of noise. Instead, he could have heard only U.S. rifles and machine guns turned on animals and villagers, *i.e.*, relative quiet. Yet he did not move till around 9 o'clock, when he made his brief sally of ninety yards into the hamlet and turned back on getting a radio message to go look for a VC with a weapon, off in the other direction, in the rice fields. This was the woman, lying on the dike, that he shot. She had no weapon and, as others testified, was already wounded.

Yet from his post in the rice field, at 8:30 A.M., an hour after touching down, he had issued a cease-fire to conserve ammunition. What made him do that? That was the gist of the question Col. Bobby Berryhill, the sleepy juror, sent up to the judge to give Medina: "When did you determine in your own mind that the action was uncontested?" Medina's answer was evasive. "Well, sir, throughout the morning there was indication that VC with weapons were fleeing, that they were being shot by the gunships, that they were being marked. [No real evidence was ever brought out of VC with weapons being shot. Hugh Thompson thought he saw one trying to run away. Col. Henderson claimed to have seen two bodies with weapons near My Lai 4 and to have marked the place with a smoke bomb. And there were the two or three he apprehended on the highway, descending in his chopper to make the capture, who turned out to be ARVN soldiers.] I had people going out. I didn't

353

enter the village except for 75 meters and then I headed south. I started getting an awareness that something—that it was uncontested as far as the fact that the 48th VC Battalion wasn't there. We expected to have a big fight with them, and I just was not receiving the reports that would indicate that a battalion was in the village, and only that some VC with weapons fleeing had been killed. And this was somewhere between, I guess it went all the way up to close to 10 o'clock, sir; 9:30."

Col. Berryhill followed through with a second question, which the judge rephrased thus: "Did you normally give a stop firing or cease-fire order to conserve ammo in other operations if they were still contested?" The judge perceived what was behind this and hurriedly warned Col. Berryhill that he should not assume a position of advocacy. Col. Berryhill meant that you don't give a cease-fire order if you think the enemy is shooting at you; the cease-fire order, to save ammo, would date Medina's awareness at 8:30, and not at 9:30 or 10:00. But either Medina did not understand the second question as rephrased by the judge or understood it and dodged the implication in his answer by seeming not to get the drift.

Still, Col. Berryhill's point, even when duly appreciated, did not prove that Medina at 8:30 A.M. knew that his men were shooting women and babies. They might have been shooting pigs or water buffalo. But if he knew there were no enemy in the hamlet, why did he not proceed there, to check up on what was going on? His mistrust of Calley is in the record. Again he was evincing a morbid incuriosity. It is as if Capt. Medina desired to know as little as possible about this "combat assault," as if his main wish was to stay on the perimeter of it, while not actually running away.

One can well believe that he was innocent of the premeditated murder of not less than 100 persons, that indeed he took care to be innocent by refraining from investigation. Had he proceeded into the hamlet at 8:30 A.M., he would have been bound to apprise Major Calhoun at the TOC of what he found —no enemy and a whole raft of civilians—and initiated a query as to what to do about it. Do we go ahead and burn the hootches and blow up the brick houses and kill the animals and push all the people out of the village or what? But his job was to conduct a Search-and-Destroy mission. Why pass on information that would just throw a monkey wrench in the works? So he ordered the men to hurry. You could not count on Gen. Koster's reaction when the information reached him; in a moment of anger at the intelligence foul-up he might even rescind the OD.

By staying so long on the outskirts of the hamlet and out of the reach, apparently, of the TOC, Medina saved everybody a headache. When he entered, it was about over: a brick dwelling or two and the schoolhouse remained to be detonated, the hootches and rice stocks were burning, and there were some unavoidable dead, many more perhaps than he expected.

Assuming he stayed away out of circumspection, there remains a curious point to be explained. On landing, at 7:30, he radioed that the LZ was cold. But then, according to his testimony, he got a correction. "No. LZ hot. You are receiving fire." There is no real confirmation of such a transmission. As the judge noted, it is not heard on the tapes made by Capt. Lewellen. Nobody testified to sending it, and the only witness, besides Medina, who claimed to have heard it was Capt. Kotouc, a doubtful source. Medina could not give the code signal that would show where the message came from. Did he invent this phantom transmission to help account for not knowing, as he claimed, till 9:30 or 10:00 in the morning that the action was uncontested? Or did Col. Barker cut in sharply from the C-and-C ship to remind Medina that they *should* be receiving fire?.

A final question arises. If the object was to wipe out the hamlet, why use infantry rather than air power? There could be a number of reasons. The Americal Division, which included Task Force Barker, was short of air power; Barker had to borrow some for the morning's assault. If B-52's were available, their usefulness was limited to area bombing, and there were "friendlies" operating in the region. Next, infantry is cheaper. Then morale. Charlie Company had been taking casualties without seeing any action—disturbing for the men—and this held, though to a lesser extent, for the whole division. Then, just at this time, a little more than a month after Tết and two weeks before Johnson's "abdication," the war had become very unpopular in the United States, and criticism, insofar as it was moral, centered on the bombing policy and the use of napalm. Finally, one of the aims must have been to develop intelligence (since there *were* VC units in the region), which meant taking prisoners. Medina was "developing intelligence" when he played William Tell with the detainee he was interrogating, who had been captured two days after the massacre. Bombers do not take prisoners.

In the event, using infantry was a fatal error. If the hamlet had been wiped out in an air strike, to the bombing crews it would have been just another mission, quickly forgotten. But face-to-face killing of non-combatants sticks in the memory of those who witness it. If civilians have to die, air and artillery

356

fire are felt by the military to be cleaner than point-blank shooting. Reluctance to believe in the men's savagery persisted at Fort McPherson, despite all the "exposure" given the facts in the media. The judge's and the jury's questions showed that they still had a wistful hope of assigning large numbers of the corpses to the artillery prep and the gunships, as though bodies killed by those means somehow died a natural death—true in a sense since random casualties from machine-gun and artillery fire are a "natural" concomitant of war.

Again and again that hope was dashed, and one could not help sympathizing with the judge and Col. Proctor in their disappointment. Though it would have changed nothing for the victims, most of us would prefer to think that those women and babies and old men had died in a raid rather than been singled out, one by one, for slaughter. Logic here is unpersuasive: the deliberate individual killing of unresisting people *is* more repugnant than the same result effected by mechanical means deployed at a distance and without clear perception of who or what is below. Even those who profess to see no distinction in Vietnam between the crime of war and single acts of homicide would be hard put to deny that distance does seem to count in diminishing responsibility. Demonstrators shouting "Hey, hey, LBJ, how many kids did you kill today?" were logically right in viewing Johnson as the final cause, insofar as that could be targeted in one person, but humanly they failed to convince, since he was not the proximate cause and could not even be said to have *intended* the slaughter of Vietnamese children in the sense that Hitler intended the annihilation of the Jews in the gas ovens.

WHATEVER LOGIC SAYS, remoteness from the scene attenuates responsibility unless a clear, almost telescopic intention* can be shown. It is an old philosophic argument, which holds God innocent of the crimes of men; even though, to believers, He is the final cause of the scandal of existence, He does not exactly will it. The question greatly worried Dostoevsky, as well as a number of saints. But whether or not God is absolved, ordinary people have to absolve themselves of countless crimes committed with their complicity. You are eating a hearty meal, while somewhere a baby is starving. As the charitable appeals point out, you might have saved it. But pleading guilty to the charge does not give you license to let an infant perish in a house fire in your building, as though to say "What's the difference? Both babies are dead, aren't they?"

If one and the same person can condemn Calley and still "live with" the B-52 raids in Laos and Cambodia, which he *knows* must be killing an unknown number of peasants on a daily basis, this only means that he is not totally callous. He knows if he stops to think, but mercifully he is not obliged to think twenty-four hours a day. There are knöwledge and inescapable knowledge. Somewhere in between lies the toleration threshold, differing, obviously, in different people. In the air war, the magnitude of the effect produced by the mere everyday pressing of a button or releasing a catch surpasses the imagination of those concerned, which was not the case with Lt. Calley emptying and reloading his rifle or with the men who watched.

Pilots and bombardiers, unless they are captured, do not confront inescapably the murders they commit. Hence they are no more haunted by them, perhaps less, than the President of

* Such an intention, I think, could be descried in the mind of Nixon during the Christmas, 1972, terror bombing of Hanoi and Haiphong. This, in my opinion, unlike any previous U.S. acts in Vietnam, truly deserves comparison with the Nazis, and it is

the United States and his civilian advisors, who sometimes wear a shamefaced or a brazen look. The airmen, like the generals, maybe because they are exercising a profession, are able to remain tolerant of themselves.

Medina's self-tolerance, in contrast to Calley, wriggling worm-like on a hook, was striking throughout his court-martial, which may account for the public disappointment in the trial as spectacle. In his testimony he told of "your old pucker factor going up" as the helicopters neared the LZ, with rocket ships and miniguns firing, but this seems to have been his unique moment of tension and pulsing excitement. On the ground, as the evidence showed, he had used considerable agility in keeping ugly sights and sounds at a distance and contrived to be as remote from the big carnage as somebody in an office building several miles away. When unavoidably he had to pass a body or a pile of bodies, he walked rapidly on, looking to neither the right nor the left, the way one skirts garbage in a big-city street. On the stand, except for technical know-how, he seemed no more "involved" in My Lai than a newspaper reader perusing a famine story from Biafra or Bangladesh. Unless you had seen his photos, you could not have picked him out in the courtroom as the defendant; leafing through the books of case material, he might have been one of his own lawyers.

To expect signs of repentance from a man in the dock is doubtless old-fashioned. Bluebeard, who killed 40 to 200 children, appeared at his trial dressed from crown to toe in white satin as a mark of contrition and expiation, even though, like Eichmann, he distinguished between divine justice and human justice and considered himself innocent before the law. In current America, where scarcely anybody believes in a higher

interesting that this was the only occasion on public record in the air war when some pilot—notably Capt. Michael Heck—refused to fly bombing missions.

law, to try a man for a crime is automatically to set up a defensive process, a hardening and stiffening of the new skin that closes off any entry for penitent thoughts, let alone egress for open admissions of guilt. Still, it was puzzling to see no traces whatever of the crime and its aftermath either in Medina, joking and whispering with counsel, or in the long file of witnesses from Charlie Company marching up to take the stand. It was as if they felt themselves to be permanently on trial and had assumed a defensive posture of unconcerned normality.

THEY HAD BEEN returned to life. Some were students and wore mod hair styles and counter-culture fashions. Others, being still in the service, could not display a sartorial cool but testified with a marked indifference, like transistors playing. Quite a few had become policemen and tended to rings and sideburns. One was in the anti-war movement; one was a pipe-fitter; one was an undertaker; one who had been a brassière salesman at the time of the Calley trial was now a carpet-installer.

Two, according to testimony, had killed young children: Oliver, the carpet-installer, by his own confession; Widmer, a student, who, incriminated by another witness, took the Fifth Amendment. Yet you would never think it to look at them, particularly Widmer, with a long stubborn meditative face, long light-brown hair and mustache, wearing a lavender shirt and red-and-white-striped tie; an occasional shifty dart of the eyes sidewise as he sat in the witness chair declining to answer made him seem less like a military killer than like a defiant hippie. From cheesy-faced Gene Oliver, guilt transpired, like sweat; yet his discomfort, one would have guessed, was caused by the fear of being caught in a lie, rather than by any sense of shame for the act he was finally avowing.

If this fat inactive-looking man, a sharp dresser in a three-piece suit, cowboy boots, and ruby stickpin, was not wholly implausible as a war criminal, it was hard to take his word for it, even under oath. A surprise witness, he swore that it was he who had killed the child whose murder Medina was charged with ("Stop him, stop him, get him," etc.). During previous interrogations, Oliver had been mum on the slaying; in fact the whole account of himself he had given at the Calley trial had undergone radical revision. *Then* he said he had spent one and a half to two hours in the hamlet; *now* it was five minutes. According to his story now, he had killed the running boy on his own initiative, because he was aware of a sudden movement; he had never heard any order from Medina to shoot and of course he did not bother to "check it out," *i.e.*, to establish whether the child was actually dead.

When asked why he had not told the story earlier, he said, "It was something I had to bury"; what made him come forward, finally, was hearing that Medina was charged with premeditated murder on this count. So it was his conscience that drove him to speak, to save somebody he knew to be innocent. Yet he did not act like a person who has had a weight lifted from his spirit. He was highly ill at ease on the stand, now staring defiantly forward like someone who does not expect to be believed, now making a bizarre nervous grimace resembling a half-suppressed belch. During the recess following his testimony, he refused point-blank to be interviewed by the prosecution about his unexpected confession. Several days later, Eckhardt put him back on the stand, to accuse him of telling another witness (a

lie-detector expert) that he intended to kill him and Capt. Wurtzel: "I ask you under oath if you ever expressed a desire to
kill me?" Oliver denied it.

There was something very strange certainly and seemingly
unbalanced about Oliver. At the Calley trial, he had amused
everybody by maintaining—the only witness ever to do so—that
there had been VC fire at My Lai 4: ". . . three AK-47 rounds
whistled over my head." But his confession here at Fort Mc-
Pherson had to be treated more seriously. It was backed up by
another veteran—a Mormon, Michael Terry, also of the third
platoon, a neat student with sideburns and mustache, in a navy-
blue blazer. He heard a shot, he said, and twenty-five meters
away a young boy fell. It was Oliver, five meters off, who had
fired. Then Capt. Medina called out something that Terry's
religious scruples would not permit him to repeat. Under urging, he paraphrased: "Blankety blank, cease fire." As Oliver
told it, what Medina yelled was "It's only a kid," then "God
damn it, cease fire." Terry's careful spatial recollection, his
quiet manner, and scruple about the Second Commandment
made him seem an unusually trustworthy witness, with a clear
painstaking memory. Yet on May 1, 1969, as cross-examination
established, he had had the following exchange with Col. Wil-
son, a CID investigator: "Did you see any direct killing on the
ground?" "I don't remember. If I did, it didn't stick in my
memory." He now said his memory had been refreshed by
Gene Oliver.

Many of the witnesses, but especially those for the defense,
had told different stories when questioned earlier. Had they
changed, along with their testimony? There was Robert Lee,
who led off for the defense; he had been a medic in the first

(Calley's) platoon but had stayed to the rear with Sgt. Cowen. He had seen a few dead bodies that appeared to have been killed by rifle fire but no actual shooting by troops and had had no awareness that groups of defenseless people were being mowed down. By leading off with this witness, who did not meet Medina himself until evening, the defense was trying to show that it was possible for somebody (as Medina was claiming of himself) to spend the whole morning near and in the hamlet without any awareness of a massacre. Very good. But on September 17, 1969 this same witness had told an investigator that "women and children were being massacred, and I wanted no part of it. . . . I realized when I came into the village what was happening." On the subject of when and if he had heard a cease-fire order given, his testimony had also varied: in Oshkosh, Wisconsin, his home, he had told one story to the CID man and another to Capt. Wurtzel. To explain the discrepancies in his statements, he declared that the CID man had interrogated him without respite from around 2:00 P.M. till 11:00 at night; he had not been allowed to call his wife or take a break to eat—"I felt this man was putting words in my mouth." This last may have been true, but the record showed his statement had been taken at 4:40 P.M. When he had been interviewed by the prosecution, he said, in June, 1971, Capt. Wurtzel, instead of writing down his words, had just typed out a statement and given it to him to sign. But Wurtzel got up to state that there had been no typewriter in the examining room that day.

Lee's and Oliver's were among a number of cases where the government had failed to keep pace with the changing testimony of the witnesses and thus was caught flatfooted. The defense was better keyed in to Charlie Company's shifts of mood. But how can these be accounted for? It is true that people tend to tell an interrogator, particularly perhaps if he is an officer, what they think the interrogator wants to hear. It is also true that memory can be refreshed or become confused by later accretions. One may recall hearing a figure pronounced ("The number 300 sticks in my head"), then suspect one may have seen it in a magazine. Yet the lapses and divagations of memory at Fort McPherson seemed to call for some special explanation. Among the prosecution's witnesses, there was not just confusion but monosyllabic obstinacy, hedging, backing off, refusal to state what the prosecutor was evidently counting on hearing, which suggested that a decision to clam up on or alter earlier testimony had been adopted not just by individuals but by a whole group. This may have been arrived at by joint consultation or through a sort of contagion from ideas and attitudes in the air.

WHEN THE MY LAI STORY first broke, there was general shock and horror. World headlines, editorials. Ron Ridenhour's long-concealed letter made him a hero. The Haeberle pictures appeared in *Life*. This created an atmosphere favorable to voluntary confession. Paul Meadlo went on television to avow what he had done. Other servicemen having no connection with Charlie Company confessed to war crimes *they* had committed. In this wave of repentance and belated truth-telling, fantasy no doubt entered, as always. Some men confessed, if not to imaginary crimes, to a greater criminal knowledge and complicity than they may actually have had. Others told of hearing conversations and witnessing incidents that may never have taken place: the angry officer with the clipboard, now descending from a helicopter, now at LZ Dottie giving another officer hell; the Shakespearean night scene of Col. Barker and Medina conspiring in a field tent or trailer and overheard by Pfc. Carter. In such an atmosphere, it is conceivable that a witness like Robert Lee, when talking to the CID, exaggerated his personal awareness of murder in the hamlet; wishing to feel *included*, he may have put words in his *own* mouth. The same with others who were talking eagerly to journalists.

After the Calley verdict, the wave of national remorse rapidly abated or took the new form of remorse for the conviction of Calley. Some of the men who had testified against him doubtless repented having talked, even if what they had said had been true. As the weird scapegoat theory gained currency (a scapegoat, to be one, must be innocent and expiating the crimes of others), hostility to the Army as the *real* criminal mounted. The infantrymen who had "finked" in the Calley trial probably said to themselves that, if they had it to do over, they would be less co-operative with the brass. Their second chance came. Called to testify against Calley's captain, they balked, changed their stories, could not remember, were not sure. Lee Bailey, outlining the defense case, gave an index of the new mood when he spoke in a sarcastic tone of "these so-called atrocities." Did he mean that My Lai did not happen or that it was not an atrocity? His remark drew no objection from Major Eckhardt, no reprimand from the judge; it just slid by, seemingly unnoticed even by newsmen.

Second thoughts came slowly to Policeman Louis Martin, a former radioman with the command group, who had given damaging testimony against Medina, which was weakened, though, by an unsavory past ("juvenile offenses") and by a story about a promotion refused him by Medina. He was a flashy nervous type, wearing a mustache and a yellow tie, who kept moving his tongue in his cheek as he testified, seemingly in quest of some bulky food deposit. He described a group of eight to twelve women and children in a "patio-type area," being guarded by some soldiers when the command group entered the hamlet; as soon as the command group passed, he saw them mowed down. Capt. Medina, he estimated, was ninety feet away. Shortly after giving this testimony, during a court recess, he went to the defense and confessed that he now "thought" it had been "inaccurate and misleading." Begging not to be put back on the stand, he agreed to take a lie-detector test because he "wouldn't like to see anybody get into trouble." He told the polygraph expert, who then testified for the defense, that the group of eight to twelve people he saw shot had possibly never existed: all his life, he revealed, he had had problems with "illusions and delusions."

Quite different was what happened to Michael Bernhardt, billed as the star witness for the prosecution. His record at My Lai 4 was clean: he had kept his rifle pointed at the ground, refusing to take any part in the slaughter. He was a middle-class boy of good appearance, attractive to journalists, to whom he had talked at length even before the Calley trial, and a friend of Ron Ridenhour. Medina had evidently been wary of him, as a youth with ethical hang-ups, way back in the Vietnamese graveyard where the company spent the night. In his letter, Ridenhour quoted "Bernie": " '. . . that evening Medina came up to me and told me not to do anything stupid like write my congressman,' about what happened that day." To the author of one of the Calley books, he described himself as a lifelong Republican with "absolute faith" in his government. With these credentials, he was bound to be listened to and he was said to be not only eager to testify but ready to come down hard on Medina, whom he considered directly responsible for the massacre. When he was announced, finally, on August 25, for the afternoon session, the courtroom was full of anticipation. Pressmen were guessing that he might have something to reveal today that had not been brought out in the Calley trial, and hopes, naturally, ran high.

But he had hardly taken the oath when Bailey was on his feet, demanding that the jury be sent out while the defense brought evidence to challenge his right to be heard. The jury went out, and under Bailey's questioning the stunned young witness wilted. The night before, he had had a conversation with Capt. Kadish; now he sat listening, incredulous, as his words were read back to him: "Didn't you say 'What I know about My Lai 4 is my business'?" "Didn't you tell Capt. Kadish that you had knowingly withheld evidence in connection with Article 32?" The pale fox-faced young man seemed to stagger in his seat. He must have believed that his talk with Kadish was private. Something apparently had given him the assurance that Kadish would not or could not take notes. Or he had been drinking, like the black witness, Sp4 Heming, when Kadish collared *him*. Or on an LSD trip. Could Kadish have stood him a few companionable beers in some off-post roadhouse? Whatever the circumstances, Bernhardt's part in the night's conversation (Kadish's part was not divulged) sounds more as if he had thought he was "rapping" in some counter-culture bull session than being interviewed by an adversary lawyer. What emerged was simple and enormous: the lifelong Republican had turned against established authority.

" 'I have the prerogative as an individual of telling the truth or not.' 'I don't know whether I'll tell all the truth or not tomorrow.' 'I could lie or conceal the truth for a principle of justice.' 'What I *think* it is [the truth] is what is important.' 'I could tell an untruth to preserve not a person but a principle —namely justice.' " Did he remember Kadish asking him "Are you going to exercise that prerogative [of lying] tomorrow?" Hadn't he answered "Be surprised"?

Bernhardt jibbed at some of the wording and sometimes he opened his mouth as if to protest or explain. But the law was too fast for him. He never got a chance to tell what he had really meant, amplify, restore his statements to context, relate (what was evident from his reaction) how Kadish had conned him. He had the alternative of affirming or denying, and the fact that, for the most part, he was unable to deny showed him, alas, to be the opposite of what he had been boastfully claiming, in short to be a person wholly unskilled at lying.

What he had aired the night before were simply "movement" clichés, but to a military court unfamiliar with the language they were devastating. More in horror than in pity, the judge frowned down from the bench at the stricken witness. One of the guards, a young M.P. first lieutenant, shook his dark cropped head in wonder. He had done his basic training under Bernhardt, then a sergeant: "He was such a very gung-ho guy," he told a reporter.

Bailey moved on to anti-war activities. Kadish: "What are you going to tell the jury tomorrow if you are asked if you've taken part in anti-war demonstrations?" Bernhardt: "You'll get no. I've been to meetings." Kadish: "Is this a subversive group?" Bernhardt: "I'll take the Fifth on that." Now Bailey stopped reading and shouted in his own person: "Are your ideas of truth connected with a subversive group?" Bernhardt's "No" could hardly be heard. All the militancy had gone out of him. As Kadish's betrayal was borne in on him, he looked more and more disbelieving, as if he could not credit his senses. Nor could he expect understanding from Major Eckhardt. A short recess was declared, following which the prosecutor, cold and angry, rose: "We wish to withdraw the witness." Bernhardt, with a bitter look, climbed down from the stand and walked out of the courtroom, making, as he went, a finger gesture some called obscene in the direction of Kadish and Medina.

Another prosecutor might have fought for his witness. He might have drawn him out about the "principle" that would justify lying. Had Bernhardt really said that he would feel justified in lying to *this* court or to some hypothetical court, say, a Nazi one? Nobody at Fort Mac would doubt that a World War II soldier or resistance fighter had the right to withhold information by lying or other means from his Gestapo captors. The shock and astonishment in Bernhardt's face as he heard his statements read back suggested that he had made them in some utterly different connection. It was easy to imagine Kadish, playing on his "movement" vanity, leading him on to "rap" about imaginary eventualities: what would Bernhardt's attitude to the truth be if America became Amerika?* If an attempt is made to reconstruct Kadish's side of the dialogue, Bernhardt's statements appear to fall into two categories. First, defensive maneuvers to elude Kadish's efforts to find out what he was

---

* An interview with Michael Bernhardt in the *Sunday Times* (London), July 30, 1972, by Stephen Fay, has borne this out. "He [Bernhardt] was talking to a defence lawyer the night before he was due to describe Medina's action . . . when the conversation turned, casually it seemed, to any theoretical circumstances in which

going to testify tomorrow: "Be surprised." Second, mere rambling generalizations of the vague argumentative kind that young people are prone to, regardless of their political orientation, so long as they picture themselves as somehow nonconformists.

Nothing in Bernhardt's conduct would appear to place him very far to the left. Indeed, had he been a far-out leftist, he would have been bound to take the position that he had nothing to say to a "bourgeois" court. But there he was, willing and eager to testify. The "subversive group," which the defense avoided naming, was probably something more like the Veterans against the War in Vietnam or the Mobilization than like the Weathermen or the PRP.

But if a case could have been argued for him, Major Eckhardt, Turk's-head pipe grimly clamped in his lantern jaw, was not the man to argue it. He dismissed his witness and lost the hope, if he had ever had one, of obtaining a conviction. Whatever Bernhardt might have testified remains unknown.

"I GET THE FEELING somebody is betraying Eckhardt," a young reporter whispered. He could not guess who. "Sloppy staff work" was the explanation generally offered when the prosecution was booby-trapped. It seemed as though they did not trouble to interview their own witnesses before putting them on the stand. Since Eckhardt and Wurtzel had their backs to the spectators' section during the awful undoing of Bernhardt, it was impossible to read their reactions. Already that morning, they had heard their witness Heming admit that the night before he had been gabbing after drinking four quarts of wine. Were they taken aback when he

Bernhardt might perjure himself as a witness. Bernhardt conceded that he might lie for a particularly strongly-held principle of justice.
"F. Lee Bailey, the skilled trial lawyer. . . , seized on the conversation and

turned up in court late, hung over, and wearing a dashiki, which somebody might almost suspect had been supplied by the defense? Perhaps there was no way of controlling that irrepressible witness or monitoring his testimony, so that he would not mix up a major's oak leaf with a colonel's eagle. Yet the prosecution needed him badly; he was one of the few who would swear to seeing civilians shot in Medina's presence—a little boy, probably the one Widmer was accused of shooting, and a woman running through a paddy field.

It was the government's key witnesses—Heming, Bernhardt, Martin—that the defense was able to "get to," outside the courtroom, in private talks. The prosecution never "got to" a defense witness; there were no surprises or reversals on that side. Perhaps there were personality problems. Major Eckhardt gave the impression of being out of sympathy with the men he called on to testify, who were often bearded, long-haired, uncouthly dressed, a procession of drop-outs, whereas Bailey's witnesses all looked as if they had been counseled on "grooming" and the choice of suit and tie.

The reporter who felt Eckhardt was being betrayed had learned that the next witness, Frederick Widmer, had been telling the defense lawyers that he would not give the testimony the government was counting on from him. Maybe Widmer merely meant that he was going to take the Fifth Amendment. It happened one-two-three; in the course of a single day the government's prize exhibits went down like pins in a bowling alley. As soon as Bernhardt was dismissed, Widmer, cigarettes and sunglasses in his breast pocket, was seated in the chair. "I respectfully decline to answer, on grounds of self-incrimination." He was accompanied by counsel, Capt. Gary Myers, a

discredited Bernhardt. The prosecution decided not to question him, even though he was their star witness. 'It wasn't the witness that let the prosecution down,' Bernhardt says angrily. 'I think the prosecution let the witness down.' "

young very handsome blond lawyer serving with JAG who had been assigned to represent him during the Peers Panel hearings and was still by his side now, having flown in from Washington with the Judge Advocate General's permission.

It was a dramatic turnabout. A Pentagon lawyer co-operating with the defense in blocking the testimony of a crucial government witness. Furthermore, what was at stake was a civil-liberties issue. In order to secure his testimony against Capt. Medina, the government was granting Widmer immunity from prosecution for anything he might say in the trial that could tend to incriminate him, *i.e.*, were he to be asked about the child the witness John Smail said he saw him shoot. Capt. Myers, backed up by Bailey, argued that this did not give him sufficient protection in his constitutional rights. Widmer would need not just testimonial but also transactional immunity, to cover the whole My Lai 4 transaction insofar as it affected him.

The government declined to grant transactional immunity, claiming it was unnecessary, and, after listening to arguments, the judge ordered Widmer to testify. When he still refused, the judge cited him for contempt, and the case was sent to federal court, with the Atlanta Civil Liberties Union—strange bedfellow for the Pentagon—joining Capt. Myers in representing Widmer. The judge of the federal court decided in Widmer's favor.

Again, it was impossible to guess whether Eckhardt was prepared for these startling developments or whether they caught him off guard. It seemed clear, from the minute Widmer strode to the witness chair, that he was utterly determined not to testify. But was this because he really feared prosecution (he did not have much to worry about, judging by preceding ac-

quittals, and besides he was out of the Army) or did his stubbornness on the point have some more interesting motive?

As with Michael Bernhardt, the public never knew. In contrast to Fort Benning, security was tight at the Fort McPherson
courthouse. As witnesses stood down, Judge Howard carefully
cautioned them not to discuss their testimony with outsiders. As
far as the press was concerned, the warning seems to have been
100 per cent effective. Counsel for both sides also remained
distant with reporters, like the defendant and his wife—no
social mingling—as though a quarantine had been decreed. Lee
Bailey's only "leaks" were made to mikes and cameras.

In the absence of any indiscretions, it is hard not to relate
Widmer's .unbudging posture to the post-Calley reaction, that
is, to the "scapegoat" outcry. He was not going to be pushed
around by authority, and the discovery of his constitutional
rights gave him a mighty rock to cling to, with Bailey's deft support. But who in this instance was authority? Did not the
judging and punishing arm in some sense represent the people,
as against Medina and those high-ranking military witnesses
who would swear that he was a strong commander, a forceful
leader, a "*professional* soldier"?

Widmer's determination, in any case, was matched by that
of his defender, who appeared in the courtroom like some un-
compromising puritan angel, wearing full regulation uniform
that stood out dark and trim against the summer tans of military
counsel and the M.P.'s on guard. Gary Myers was the Aubrey
Daniel of the Medina case. One could imagine him as belonging
to that idealistic cell of young lawyers in JAG who had argued
for a Nuremberg-style war-crimes trial. That night he was at
the Civil Liberties Union headquarters in Atlanta, where Charles

Morgan, the director, was giving a little press party for Lt. Col. Anthony Herbert, the insubordinate war critic, another Fort Mac client of the ACLU.

ALL THE DRAMA of the Medina trial had been compressed in the single day of August 25, before the Labor Day recess. But it was Calley's appearance, on September 13, that brought out the crowds. That morning, for the first time, tall curly-haired Major Russell, the doctor-artist, had a disappointment. In the drawing he failed to get the little green courtroom pass; too many regular pressmen were on hand. A correspondent even dropped by from the Washington *Post* (which up to then had been content with a stringer), taking the day off from Fort Meade. In the Press Center, waiting for the drawing, were adolescent girls and boys with long fair hair—not just the usual kids and large middle-aged women, like the redhead who turned up most mornings in a robin's-egg-blue textured stretch pants suit, a triple pearl choker and big pearl clip-earrings. It was like a reunion, that morning, for the reporters who had covered the Calley trial and, above all, for the network and wire-service cameramen who had been standing so long on their platform outside the courthouse with so little work to show for it. At last a front-page face. They were waiting with cameras trained as Calley came up the sidewalk, accompanied by his old-time lawyer, George Latimer: "Hi, Rusty." He made a jaunty awkward sign with his right arm, like "Be seeing you on the campus," and that was it. Once in the courthouse, he was not put on the stand. Through his lawyer, he took the Fifth, was seen to shake Medina's hand in the witness room, and was whisked away, back to Fort Benning. The Washington *Post* went back to the Henderson trial.

BAILEY'S ANNOUNCED PURPOSE in convoking Calley was to confront him with testimony from a new witness, Capt. Hicks. One day back in Vietnam (Hicks was prepared to swear), when the two got to swapping war stories, Calley had told him about My Lai and said that Medina was "surprised" by the massacre. Since Calley's defense at his own trial had been that he was acting on Medina's orders, it was natural that, faced with this new evidence, he would plead the Fifth, especially since his case was still on appeal. Bailey fully expected it. Calling him as a witness was a way of laying the ground for introducing Hicks's testimony, which the judge was likely to rule out as hearsay. In fact the judge did so rule but then reversed himself. To bring Calley to court and grandly permit him to go away silent ("There's no need to parade him here": Bailey) was skillful psychological pressure exercised on the judge to relax his view of the hearsay rule.

Calley's narative, *if* he told it to Hicks and *if* it was true, throws a few rays of new light on what happened in My Lai 4 that morning. In Bailey's summary, the massacre was "triggered" by the villagers' reaction to seeing their water buffalo shot. They cheered when the platoon came in (some newsmen understood "jeered"); then the point man shot a water buffalo, and they were quiet. After that, the angry men "opened up." In other words, if the population had continued to cheer, they would not have got killed.

The whole story is a bit perplexing, not least on account of the cheer/jeer confusion. Assuming that My Lai 4 was a VC hamlet (all "Pinkville" was VC territory), it is not likely that the inhabitants would have cheered at the sight of the platoon. Nor would they have jeered necessarily. A sullen silence was the usual reception in such areas. But if the massacre somehow grew out of the wanton killing of the livestock, the troops' behavior becomes minimally understandable. Under their company commander's direct order, they were committing a wicked action, which some might have felt some premonitions of guilt about if their consciences had not been assuaged by the promise that there would be no civilians present. But it was one thing to shoot up the animals, burn the rice stocks, and contaminate the wells in the guaranteed absence of the population, and another to have to do it with the people looking on. The sense of guilt could then turn the guns on the silent watching people. Thus the arch-responsibility goes back to the Medina and Barker briefings, which ordered the cold-blooded annihilation of a village.

At the same time, the question of calling Calley as a witness pointed to a judicial weakness at the heart of the Medina proceedings. In the Medina trial, Calley could be called only as a defense witness, and his answers, were they to exculpate Medina, would incriminate Calley himself further, besides making him liable to a fresh charge—perjury. He could not be called by the government because the choice between his credibility and Medina's had already been made at Fort Benning, when Medina was put on the stand to state that he had given no orders for the killing of civilians. Calley's main defense, that he was acting under orders, was destroyed there by Medina's testimony. The vote to convict Calley was a vote of confidence in Medina's truthfulness and would be bound to play a role in any future trial Medina would face.

Aubrey Daniel anticipated this legal dilemma and elected not to call Medina as a witness for the prosecution. He evidently foresaw that this would hamper the government in trying Medina himself. It was the jury in the Calley case, over Daniel's objections, who demanded to hear Medina. Perhaps those non-legal brains did not understand the consequences for a future prosecutor of what they were doing. But the future prosecutors understood.

Before Medina's court-martial began, the government issued a significant statement: it did not propose to use evidence of what had been said in the defendant's pre-assault briefing in con-structing the case against him. *I.e.*, to prove the charge of premeditated murder, it could not rely on the evidence of the numerous witnesses who, in the Calley case and elsewhere, had sworn that the captain ordered them to kill "everything that breathed," "everything that moved," and so on. Government reliance on these witnesses would have retroactively confirmed Calley, whose lawyers might seize on the issue to demand a new trial for him. But without that evidence the government's case was handicapped to the point of being crippled. The prosecution admitted as much when on the eve of the trial it told reporters that the evidence against Medina was "skimpy."

True, though it was hardly the prosecution's place to pro-claim it. In fact quite a bit of "everything that breathed" testi-mony (also testimony to the contrary) did crop up, but the official case against him, in the murder of not less than 100 persons, rested on his mere awareness of the massacre, and awareness is very difficult to establish. If the government could have shown intent, awareness could be expected to ensue. That is, if I order you to kill everybody in the next room and then come in and find a pile of bodies, it will be hard for me to claim later that I "assumed" they had all committed suicide. But for a juror weighing the evidence in the Medina trial, intent had to follow awareness: no awareness, no intent. The powerlessness of the government to insist on the alleged criminal content of the orders reduced Medina's role at My Lai 4 to that of a chance spectator.

He did nothing to stop the killing until around 11:00 A.M., when he ordered or did not order a cease-fire (testimony on this was conflicting, to put it mildly), he gave no medical aid, he noticed a few dead bodies. Except when shooting the woman and ordering (or not ordering) the boy shot, he behaved like a casual passer-by, and who can prove what a passer-by saw, let alone what conclusions he drew or should have drawn?

It was not enough for the government to place Medina through eyewitness testimony in the vicinity of several killings. It had to be proved that he saw them, which he denied. For a witness to infer that Medina saw them or could have seen them was not proof. At best, it tended to show likelihood. But just here the fallibility of memory, especially in matters of arithmetic, cast doubts: how many meters, how long a time? Even the most affirmative prosecution witnesses could not do better than vaguely estimate distances, and the sum total of all that uncertainty gave the benefit of the doubt to the defendant, to the point where one felt the jury might wonder whether Medina was ever anywhere near the hamlet since nobody was sure of having seen him there at any fixed point of space or time.

The inability of government witnesses to "pinpoint" a given

action was used, naturally, by the defense to impeach their credibility: "How far were you from Capt. Medina? Was it eight feet, ten feet, a hundred yards?" "Was it less than an hour, more than an hour, less than a half hour, less than fifteen minutes? Speak up!" The peremptory fire of questions shook the men on the stand, who usually ended with a frightened "I don't remember," which caused Bailey to nod in satisfaction, as though such an admission nullified all their testimony.

In the military setting, imprecision seemed damnable, and nobody stopped to think that a witness who could crisply state that he was nine and a half meters from the defendant when an old man was pulled out of a hootch and that the time was eleven hours thirty-five minutes might be more of a fantasy artist than one like former Sp4 Heming who disdained the yardstick. "How near was Capt. Medina?" "How *near*? Why, he *standing* right *there* on the trail." As a witness, Heming had the refreshing habit of treating whatever he reported as self-evident, which indeed is how experience seems to everybody when still in its pure state. To common sense, "near" requires no further definition; it is the opposite of "far."

Yet even when such a confident witness could place Medina within sight or earshot of a killing, it only established his location. Consciousness is something else. How can anybody be sure that somebody standing next to him sees what he sees? Has the other turned his head away at the crucial moment, was his view blocked? Still less if the other is several yards ahead or behind. Suppose the effect is cumulative and reason says, "Well, if he missed seeing the old man shot, he must have seen the running woman" or "What about the noise, the M-16 and machine-gun fire, the screaming?" this still is not proof, but speculation. If Medina was to be presumed innocent, the jury had to keep before its mind the possibility that he failed to see what others saw, since nobody *saw* him see it. As for noise, there were the helicopters overhead making a terrible racket.

It could happen that somebody would spend four hours in a small bamboo-shaded hamlet just missing a hundred-odd murders. The jury, bearing this in mind, seemed duty-bound on the basis of the evidence presented to find Medina innocent even if it guessed him to be guilty.

Yet he was not a simple spectator, but the company commander. On the basis of the defense evidence alone any jury could have convicted him of dereliction of duty with little or no debate. His absence from the scene, attested to by himself, and almost total lack of liaison with the green men under him would lay him open to the charge of cowardice, if he really believed the action to be contested. If, on the other hand, he knew almost from the start (as indicated by the cease-fire-to-conserve-ammo) that the action was uncontested, his conduct was delinquent to a bizarre degree, lacking even the excuse of battlefield panic. There was also his admission, already made at the Calley trial, that on the evening of the massacre he slowly grew aware of the truth—more dereliction, since according to the code an officer was bound to report immediately any atrocities that came to his knowledge, and worse, misprision of a felony, since to cover up, he falsified the body count.

Why was he not tried for dereliction, misconduct, and misprision of a felony, as well as war crimes? The question was widely asked, especially after he checked in at the Henderson court-martial and freely testified to having lied to Henderson, the Peers Panel, and the Army Inspector General's office. When the press put the question earlier, during his own trial at Fort Mac, the prosecution's answer was that it was customary to drop the lesser charge in favor of the greater one. In fact, one count against him in the original indictment had been misprision of a felony and this was dropped when the additional charge was decided on. Even so—said some people who would have rather seen Medina in jail than waving an Honorable Discharge diploma at photographers—if the government felt the evidence on the war-crimes charge was "skimpy," why did it not stick with the lesser charge and obtain a conviction, instead of letting him slip out of the Army into Lee Bailey's helicopter plant?

THE IDEA THAT there was a conspiracy to let Medina get home free was sometimes hard to avoid at Fort Mac. To some observers of the trial, the fact that the judge and four out of five of the jurors were native-born Southerners was in itself a suspicious circumstance—almost proof that the government was working for an acquittal, whether or not Eckhardt and Wurtzel were parties to such an understanding or ignorant pawns. Southerners, it was argued, on account of their military traditions, would incline to sympathize with a career officer and see him as a victim of liberal hypocrisy. No My Lai 4 trial, it was pointed out, had taken place at a northern post, where attitudes might be expected to be a little different, even at the officer level. Why try a Montrose, Colorado, man in the Deep South for war crimes committed in Vietnam unless you want to give him a break?

But the preponderance of Southerners, though partly explained by the trial's venue (the Army tries to rotate officers and men back to where they came from, where they have homes and family ties), was not guaranteed by it. In the Calley trial, at nearby Fort Benning, the jury had been split fifty-fifty between Northerners and Southerners, and Judge Kennedy's home town was Spencer, Iowa. As for the venue, Medina had done his officer's training at Fort Benning, so that it was normal that he should be assigned there while awaiting trial. When his duty-station was later changed to Fort Mac, this was because of an administrative decision to group all the cases directly related to My Lai 4 at Third Army headquarters, in the interests of efficiency and to economize on the travel of counsel and witnesses, according to the Army's announcement. Cases indirectly related to My Lai 4, like that of Col. Henderson, were to be grouped at Fort Meade. It seems logical that the headquarters of the Third Army, covering the southeast of the U.S., should have been chosen, but why Calley's case was left at Fort Benning is not clear, unless preparations for it were already far advanced.

The southern cast of the judging body at Fort Mac is best excused by the southern cast of the Army itself. Southerners predominated among the troops in Vietnam, more so perhaps in other ranks and up to the colonel level than at the top. It was a war of crackers and rednecks (including officers), urban blacks, *chicanos* like Medina, poor Italians, Poles, Puerto Ricans. As the biggest under-privileged minority, the South naturally sent the most boys. Charlie Company, testifying in all the black and white varieties of southern speech, was an aural demonstration of that. So it did not seem inappropriate that Prosecutor Eckhardt should be an Ole Miss graduate, that Capt. John Truman should be from Independence, Missouri, that the M.P.'s should be southern and soft-spoken, that even Major Russell, with his drawing-board, should be a Virginian, that most of the newsmen and the two pretty newsgirls, one blonde and one brunette, should be southern too.

It was an easygoing Deep South show, featuring southern hospitality: Judge Howard repeatedly leaning forward (without being asked) to fill Medina's Coke glass with water as he gave his testimony. The South melted into the Army: Col. Bobby Berryhill's name brought back a bevy of colonels in South Vietnam: Col. Derryberry, Col. Culpepper. . . . And like the Army in Vietnam, and to the same degree, Atlanta, downtown, was integrated, on the job level, in motels, hotels, and restaurants. As the site of an earlier war crime—Sherman's march, which had burned the city to the ground—and the birthplace of Coca-Cola, it made a suitable background. No ante-bellum houses, no history-haunted monuments, nothing to see but a Disneyish reconstruction of the Civil War called the Cyclorama and a sunken maze of souvenir shops and Gay Nineties or frontier-type steak houses called the Underground, a tall hollow-centered de-luxe hotel resembling a maximum-security prison, and a "contemporary" FBI building. Downtown Atlanta did not look as if anybody lived there: they just held salesmen's conventions all year round. Somebody indigenous had resumed General Sherman's work and razed the center of the city to construct parking lots, multi-level garages, motels with swimming pools and free ice-dispensers in a simple cadre of insurance-company skyscrapers: Clear and Hold.

So the jury was not rigged, and Judge Howard in his little flowing black tie was a good man and as free from bias as any prosecutor could hope for. There was no conspiracy to hold the trial at Fort Mac rather than Fort Dix or Fort Lewis, Washington. It had just worked out that way, and the outcome would probably have been the same wherever the trial was held. The American public as a whole seemed quite content with Medina's acquittal (of all the telephone calls received at the Press Center following the verdict only one protested) while at the same time feeling cheated by it. Those who cursed the Army for convicting Calley now sneered at the Army for letting Medina off. Though with less assurance, for the fact is that it was public opinion and not the jury that decided. Leaving out the part played by President Nixon in reducing the Calley conviction and the part played by Wallace and the extreme right in heating mass fury, the determination of the left not to consider *anybody* a war criminal short of a three-star general has meant that no three-star general will ever sit on the accused bench. Medina was a transition figure between the war-makers and the "animals" (as the airmen in Vietnam called the infantry), and his acquittal halted a process that might have gone up the ladder of responsibility. If Medina had been in jail, it would have been harder to acquit Col. Henderson. With Henderson in jail . . . The finger would have steadily pointed upward. Had public pressure been maintained, it might not have been left to the Army to decide when enough was enough. If there was a conspiracy, it was a great nationwide breathing together of left, right, and much of the middle to frustrate punishment of the guilty.

STILL, WAS MEDINA *legally* guilty of anything worse than criminal dereliction that day? On the additional charge, after

the defections of Heming, Bernhardt, Widmer, and Policeman
Louis Martin (each in his own fashion, they let the side down),
the government was left with the depositions of Minh and Phu,
and the testimony of former radioman Kinch, now a private
detective, who was sure he heard the captain say: "That's
enough shooting for the day. The party's over." The sole witness, though, who remembered anything similar (" 'It's over.
The firing's over.' Or something like that") tended to weaken
confidence in the accuracy of Kinch's memory rather than cor-
roborate him. Other government witnesses could merely place
Medina "in the area" of the killings, and Smail, a former
rifleman, who said Medina was close by when Widmer shot the
child, added that the captain had "his head down" when it
happened.

Besides the eyewitnesses, there was the testimony of the polygraph expert Brisentine, who said Medina told him that between 9:30 and 10:30 he felt he had lost control of his men.
If it was as early as 9:30 and Medina was then where he said
he was (outside the hamlet), the question arises, how did he
know? And if by some undetermined means he knew, why didn't
he do something? Or was he not where he said he was?

There were a few straws as well supplied by Nick Capezza, a
New York City housing detective, formerly a medic, who kept
pausing in his declarations to ruminate on a cud of gum. He
remembered that when a report came in that a helicopter pilot
had seen wild firing Medina got on the radio to Calley. "He
asked Calley what the f—— was going on." "Had you ever
heard Capt. Medina talk to Calley like that before?" "Usually
in person, not on the radio." Calley, he said, then reported

"about 30" civilians killed in cross fire. Like Heming, Capezza had seen a tall thin officer carrying a clipboard at the landing zone. In the detective's recollection, he was wearing a helmet.

Medina did not cite the "What the f——" transmission. On the first round, in direct examination, he said he had tried to reach Calley after seeing the group of bodies on the trail but had only got his RTO. Under cross-examination, he hedged. "I possibly may have called Lt. Calley and said 'What's going on up there? I just seen a bunch of bodies.'" This was at the time of the Carter medivac, between 10:30 and 11:00. According-ing to Medina, the report from headquarters that a pilot had seen wild firing came later. "And what did you do when you heard that?" "I rogered the transmission and I radioed the platoon leaders to make sure that their people were not shooting indiscriminately and killing noncombatants, sir." It was im-portant to Medina to place the transmission and hence his own first awareness as late as possible in the morning. The same with the cease-fire.

Testimony on all of this, including Medina's own, was ex-tremely contradictory and confusing. Some heard a cease-fire given; some did not; and the estimated times for it varied widely. As for radio contact with Calley, Medina had two or more different recollections. Eckhardt: "Did you not tell Mr. Brisentine that you had no contact with Lt. Calley at all except for one time when you possibly issued a cease-fire after the boy was shot and when you did issue a cease-fire order after a radio communication from Major Calhoun?" "Yes, sir, I believe that's correct. To the best of my recollection that's what I think I told him." "You had not—is that accurate—you had no contact with Lt. Calley other than those two times?" "I could not recall at that time all the transmissions I had with those platoon leaders. I didn't make a log. . . ."

Yet under cross-examination he related in detail two other transmissions with Calley. One was between 7:30 and 9:30 A.M. "There was a report from Lt. Calley that a helicopter pilot had landed, and I asked him what's the matter. And he says 'He don't like the way my platoon—I am running my platoon.' And I says 'What did you tell him?' . . ." Again, somewhere between 8:00 and 8:30 (before or after the other message?), he received from Calley a KIA report of sixty-nine. Eckhardt: "Did you inquire of Lt. Calley whether these were combatants or noncombatants?" "No, sir. They were reported as VC, sir." "Did you inquire of Lt. Calley whether these 69 people were armed or not?" "I asked Lt. Calley to—how many weapons. And he said they were still checking." In all these recollections, he omitted any mention of the "about 30 civilian casualties from crossfire" answer that Capezza said had come from Calley. Possibly (sloppy staff work) Eckhardt had forgotten Capezza's testimony. He did not ask Medina about it during these exchanges, and the opportunity did not return.

THE CASE AGAINST Medina, such as it was, resided largely in the interstices of his own testimony, which was full, as they say, of holes, not necessarily incriminating but leaving room for further explanation. The feeling remained that the full story of My Lai 4 was still to be told, not the details of the massacre but what lay behind it. The strange conduct of Medina, which could not be hidden, was the only clue left lying in plain sight.

But the Army was clearly not interested in raising speculation but in doing its official duty, which was trying Medina. If he had not been tried, questions would have been asked.

Here perhaps lies the motive for the government's decision to attach the additional charge, so elusive of proof, to the bill of particulars against him, even if this involved dropping the lesser charge, easily provable, of misprision of a felony. As has been said, the additional charge, dated April 1, 1970, was a second thought on the part of the Army. One can see the substitution of an unprovable charge for a provable charge as part of a general whitewash, which would leave Medina free and the officer corps with one less convict in its ranks. But one can also see it less as a cunning maneuver to defeat justice than as a normal exercise in public relations.

Some PR-wise colonel in the Third Army command may well have had a brainstorm one morning: "Hey, if we don't try Medina on the big charge, people will ask why! Maybe we'd better stick it in. We won't get a conviction, but our image will look clean." "But, sir, if we do that, we ought to drop the misprision of a felony count. In law it's not customary to try a man for a felony and for misprision of it at the same time. If somebody commits a felony, naturally he endeavors to conceal it, sir." "OK, drop the misprision count. They've got Henderson on that anyway, over at Fort Meade."

Such PR thinking is a mere businesslike reflex in U.S. institutional life and carries no hint to the thinker that he is embarking on a deceitful plot. If challenged, he would reply that he was only working within the accepted system. To avoid raising questions in the public mind is seen as a laudable aim by advertising-conditioned officials who believe in their product— in this case, the U.S. Army.

In an institution like the Army, it is stupid to ask questions and clever to anticipate any that may come from the outside. Nothing could have illustrated that better than the contrast between the helicopter crewmen and Capt. Medina, as brought out at Fort McPherson. If there were American heroes at My Lai, they were the bubble-ship pilot, Chief Warrant Officer (now Capt.) Hugh Thompson, and his door gunner, Lawrence Colburn. The two were later decorated—with a misleading allusion to "cross fire"—for evacuating Vietnamese civilians they saw cowering in a bunker. Thompson and his crew made three rescue lifts, on their own, independently of any orders, and with rifles on the ready to shoot any man of Charlie Company who tried to interfere. As Colburn had related it earlier, Thompson "told us that if any of the Americans opened up on the Vietnamese, we should open up on the Americans. . . . He stood between our troops and the bunker. He was shielding the people with his body." The pilot of a gunship, Dan Millians, and his co-pilot, Jerry Culverhouse, following on Thompson's initiative, also helped in the rescue; they did two lifts.

It was what they had seen from the choppers that prompted their intervention—approximately 150 dead civilians (Millians), fifty to seventy-five Vietnamese in the ditch who "looked wounded," small children, and "I remember one fairly aged male" (Culverhouse), headless babies (Thompson). What was visible to them can hardly have been totally invisible to Barker in his command-control ship, which Millians said he saw hovering just outside the village.

On Thompson's first landing, he tried to get medical assistance for the wounded. "There was some friendlies just east of the ditch. I motioned to one of them to go help the wounded." But nobody moved. The pilot had a slow sad reminiscent way of shaking his head, as though in sighing harmony with his negative answers. Bailey's tactics of harassment he seemed hardly to notice, brushing off the lawyer's sarcasms like an inconsequential swarm of midges. It was the same with the other helicopter crewmen, whose mildness and almost simple-minded sincerity resisted all Bailey's battery of insinuation—quirked eyebrows, outthrust dubious lower lip, sudden changes of pitch. While standing at the lectern, he had a habit, perhaps designed to be frightening, of wrapping his arms around himself like his own python. From one of the gunship pilots, the lawyer's efforts to shake his testimony elicited a big humorous smile. They had all seen pretty much the same things and gave their accounts with a sort of peaceable weariness, as if it would be nice to oblige the defense and remember something different.

It had begun with Thompson's hovering over the hamlet in his OH 23 observation craft. He noticed something peculiar— dead bodies all over the place. It made him wonder, so he circled and hovered some more. "I'd seen some things that at the time I couldn't understand why they'd happened." He shook his head, paused, and repeated in a bemused voice, "*I couldn't understand.*" The bodies in the drainage ditch, "they were not resisting type people." As he circled, he started to reason: they might have been shot by gunships, but the Vietnamese, being used to air attacks, would not take shelter, he thought, in an open ditch. If they had been killed in a cross fire, the G.I.'s would have just left them where they fell, for their own people to pick up later. It was funny the way they were stacked up like that.

Going back in his memory, under the prosecutor's prodding, Thompson kept twisting and pulling down his lower lip, in a lengthy act of reflection. He too was Georgian—from Decatur—blond, slightly adenoidal, slow of speech, and dogged, extremely ordinary, like his predecessor on the stand, Capt. Culverhouse, who resembled a small wood animal. In comparison with some of the sharpies of Charlie Company, the pilots seemed rural, almost retarded.

The uncomprehending Hugh Thompson flew lower, right above the rice crops, to clear up the questions in his mind. He "saw a woman laying on a dike and popped smoke on her" to signal for a medic. (The defense claimed the smoke signal was understood as "VC with weapon"—a message that eventually reached Capt. Medina.) She had a wound in her abdomen. Then "a captain walked right up to the woman." He nudged her with his foot and retracted, walked away, and fired his weapon. She died. Next the pilot landed where he had seen "a black individual with his weapon pointed into the ditch" with the people in it. He had his argument with Calley and took off with some wounded on the first of his rescue lifts. On the last he flew out a small child who looked wounded and was clinging to its dead mother. He took him to Quang Ngai Civilian Hospital. "My fuel was getting real low." At the TOC he reported the killing of civilians. He had already reported the wounded he had marked with smoke for the gunships to pick up.

The next witness, former Sp4 Larry Colburn, was now a student. His testimony was identical with the pilot's except in very small particulars. He said the woman on the dike had her eyes open. She moved them and looked up at the heli-crew. Then, after the smoke-dropping, Medina arrived with the command group. "He turned her over with his foot and shot her." He remembered, yes, that she had flinched. Thompson remembered it too. But neither could be certain whether she flinched after or before the captain shot her. Colburn was slightly more positive than Thompson that the flinch came after the shooting—a reflex movement—but he would not swear to it. He *thought* it was after, and neither Eckhardt nor Bailey could get him to improve on that.

The flinch, described by both crewmen as a twitch or shudder, became in Medina's testimony a sudden movement that caused him to think she was going to throw a grenade at him. That was not how the episode had looked from the air ("As I remember it, he turned her over with his foot and shot her. That was all," Colburn said over and over), but of course from the air they could not see into Medina's state of mind, and Bailey got Colburn to admit that if he had been in the captain's place and had thought she had a grenade, he would probably have done the same thing.

Despite this triumph, the defense seemed irritated by the fact that it could not shake both witnesses' emphatic certainty that *first* the captain had turned the wounded woman over with his foot; this had preceded any twitch, flinch, or movement. Bailey and Kadish may have felt that this sequence, though it did not prove murder, put their client in an unflattering light. If somebody is visibly wounded (the bleeding could be seen from the air), is the first step in first aid to turn her over with your booted foot and start to walk away?

At every point, Medina's conduct, on seeing dead and

392

wounded persons, was diametrically opposite to the conduct of
Thompson and Colburn. Yet unlike Medina, Thompson and
Colburn had no military responsibility for the men at My Lai.
They had no business landing in the middle of what was supposed to be a battle to conduct rescue operations of enemy
civilians—still less to interfere with the way Calley and his
men were handling the operation. And yet they did.

Larry Colburn testified gently and softly, with many pauses
for thought. He seemed, if not unwilling to testify, unwilling to
remember the scene once more. Under Eckhardt's questioning,
he tended to answer in monosyllables. "You saw one boy alive
in the ditch." "Yes." His voice was low, slightly hoarse. "Movement?" "Yes." "Blood?" "Yes." He had softish clean long
hair and a long projecting jaw. When he was asked to describe
the crewmen's efforts to extricate the live child from the heap
of corpses, he volunteered with a sad half-smile: "Specialist
Andreotta [the third crew member], he was covered with blood."

These mild gentle witnesses seemed to rub on the court's
nerves. Eckhardt's co-ordination of questions to their answers
was sometimes so awkward that the judge, impatient, took over
the examination. And Judge Howard was testy with both of
them, doubting the ability of their bubble ship to hover as low
and as long as they said, skeptical about the height of the crop
in the paddy field. Like Eckhardt, he kept forgetting Thompson's
rank ("Mr.—I mean Captain—Thompson") and became openly
derisive about the pilot's refusal to give precise distances.
The position of the woman on the dike led to wrangles: Thompson remembered her lying on her side facing one way, and
Colburn, he *thought*, facing the other but also on her back. The
judge, fed up with Colburn, suddenly had a new idea: maybe

she had been standing on the dike. *"Standing?"* Colburn's voice was incredulous (had the judge forgotten the stomach wound?). Then quietly, *"Oh, no."* Here was an instance of the court's tendency to slip into a dreamy fugue in which everything in the My Lai massacre would turn out to have a natural, military-manual explanation: gunship strafing, artillery fire, a standing woman with a grenade. . . .

WHAT CAME OUT of Thompson's and Colburn's testimony was the inescapable truth of a massacre. More disturbing still, the fact that to a very ordinary intelligence (Thompson's), the sight of the bodies urgently raised questions that to an ordinary intelligence would seem to want serious answers. Thompson's density, his puzzled inability to *"understand,"* were a sort of saving slow-wittedness. The picture of him hovering in his helicopter trying to comprehend gave a simple measure by which to judge others, who from General Koster on down acted like the three wise monkeys: see no evil, hear no evil, speak no evil.

Unlike the disbelieving pilot, they knew the score in Vietnam. It could not puzzle them to find civilian corpses lying around: sometimes the boys got rough. A smart commander did not criticize every little thing. When Ernie Medina saw some bodies, he did not stupidly start *thinking.* He promptly attributed them to gunships or maybe artillery fire—a military response as automatic as a knee jerk and showing excellent co-ordination: if you see something wrong, blame it on some other service and keep going. So the Navy pilots on the U.S.S. *Enterprise,* when told of photographic evidence of bombing of civilian targets in North Vietnam, genially blamed the Army, and no doubt vice versa.

One might ask where Thompson and Colburn had been during their service in Vietnam that they were still able to be shocked by heaps of civilian dead. Did they suppose this was a clean war? Evidently yes, as was shown by Thompson's frantic indignation, his repeated appeals to higher authority to *do* something to stop the slaughter. His disbelief in what his eyes were showing him was companioned by a touching belief in the willingness of his superiors to correct what in his view *had* to be a ghastly mistake. Yet his faith in the officer corps (even though he had just observed captain's bars on the man taking aim at the woman), what others would call his simple-mindedness, again, were saving graces, as it has turned out. Had it not been for the pilots' complaints to Major Watke, which were in fact passed on, the Ridenhour letter, when it was at last sent by Congressman Mendel Rivers to the Army for investigation, would probably have got little attention. But because of Thompson and Colburn, the Army already knew there was corroboration.

Also Thompson was right in imagining he had seen something exceptional. Despite what Americans seem to like to think, the My Lai 4 massacre was different from the haphazard rapes and killings committed by the "animals," from some airmen's playful "gook hunting,"* and the regulation torture of prisoners practiced by officers and NCO's or, more often, watched by them without comment as the ARVN went on with the job. In fact, the only comparable big atrocity yet on record took place the same day, in the same locality, at the My Khe 4 sub-hamlet, where Bravo Company of Task Force Barker killed 90 to 100 civilians. This was the other salient of Operation Muscatine— Search and Destroy. The commotion caused by reports racing

---

* Gen. John W. Donaldson achieved fame as a high-ranking gook hunter who was also under investigation for the My Lai cover-up. Charged by the Army with the

in to the GRVN village chief, for once in advance of VC denunciations, showed that these atrocities went far beyond the level of violence that had grown to be considered routine.

Thompson seems to have been a conventional southern boy with a conventional faith in the war. He was personally ready to wage it beyond the call of duty. That very morning, in his little bubble ship, he had already exceeded his orders—to scout for VC and report them to the gunships. Catching sight of a Vietnamese male running away from the hamlet whom he judged (by the weapon and the uniform) to be a Viet Cong, he pursued him, shot, and missed. This episode is very much to the point. Had Thompson and Colburn been opposed to the war, on moral or political grounds, their reaction and conduct would have had less value as a measure by which to judge the reactions and conduct of Medina. Nobody at that time would have expected a career officer in Vietnam to behave like a Quaker elder or an SDS militant; still, he was expected to conform minimally to the standards of his kind. In contrast to Thompson and Colburn (who was then only nineteen years old), Medina of course failed miserably, and it could be argued that the presence of the two in the courtroom was actually prejudicial to the defendant. That was perhaps why Judge Howard was so unhappy with them.

Yet if Medina's court-martial proved anything, it was that the standard of behavior exemplified by the pilots and crewmen was a dead letter. The Army code of justice under which the trial was being held had become an historical curiosity without anybody's taking official notice of the fact. How else could it happen that officers and former officers enlisted by the defense as *character witnesses*—e.g., Brig. Gen. Lipscomb, Col. Luper,

murder of Vietnamese civilians, he was absolved after a four-month closed hearing. He is now military attaché at the U.S. Embassy in Paris.

Col. Blackledge, Major Calhoun, Capt. Kotouc—had been under investigation for criminal irregularities in connection with My Lai and, in three cases, actually been charged? The god-given thickness of Thompson was not to be aware of this evolution in Army morals. He was culturally retarded, maybe because of a small-town upbringing, which had kept him uninformed of changes in civilian morality as he was growing up—for of course the Army was not evolving in a vacuum. Far from being sealed off from society, the U.S. Army is porous, and those who leave it are readily absorbed into the social tissue. If the career preference of the men of Charlie Company, on getting out of the service, was evidently "policeman" or "detective," that of the retired-officer character witnesses was "salesman." And Medina was praised not just for his professionalism but for his "warmth" of personality—a consumer criterion now widely accepted by Americans (including the counter-culture) as some sort of ethical evaluator. Only a conflict of scheduling spared the court Col. Henderson as a witness to Medina's outstanding character.

DURING THE TRIAL, the men on the stand suffered much harassment for their inability to quote exactly what Medina had said. "Or words to that effect" was the saving formula on which most fell back. An inadequacy with words, shown by nearly everybody connected with the proceedings, came to seem intrinsic to the mentality behind My Lai. Not just bad grammar—"I seen," "She was laying"—which was so common in the mouths of both officers and other ranks that it got to be courthouse standard English. Even F. Lee Bailey, who had some pride of rhetoric, talked about the "woman laying," with a wonderful air of *noblesse oblige.* But the failure of universal education (more than half of the men of Charlie Company were high-school graduates or better) evidenced by simple bad grammar was less depressing than the monotonous and often ignorant use of "educated" phraseology, *e.g.*, the word "infer" taken to mean "imply" or just "indicate": "He inferred to me that we should keep quiet." The worst language-murderers were the lie-detector experts, Brisentine and Harelson ("Medina may have inferred to his men to kill everyone in the village"), who were also fond of the word "transpire" to mean "happen," of such expressions as "Artillery would be placed into the village" (*i.e.*, "would fire on the village"), and of redundant prepositions ("Capt. Medina described to me as to how she was laying").

Brisentine, dark, "keen-eyed," with bristly short gray hair and an incisive widow's peak, wearing a dark-brown suit, well accessorized, and heavy dark-brown horn-rimmed glasses, was obviously anxious to present himself as an educated, eagle-like intellect—a synthesis of confessor and mind surgeon. His words and phrases seemed to have been born in a briefcase, like the compendious one he carried. Instead of "then," he invariably said "at that time"; instead of "before," "prior to," instead of "about," "regarding." The combination of this business-letter diction with unerring faults of grammar made his testimony sometimes so obscure that you had to divine what he meant, as though he were an oracle. This may have been part of the intention.

Harelson was a Middle Westerner with sideburns, dressed in a dark-green suit, who had spent twenty-one years in what he called "the polygraph business." It was he who had extracted Louis Martin's confession to having illusions and delusions. He seemed less concerned than Brisentine with making the razor-sharp impression of a successful prober of souls and came on as a sort of neighborhood practitioner occasionally called in by the cops. Now and then he forgot to say "regarding" and used the simple "about." It sounded as if he had once taken a correspondence course in home psychiatry: "I asked him about his youth background." One reason the trial was boring was that so many of the participants were verbose, boring people.

It was natural, though, that "experts" close to the apparatus of government and police work should talk in an administrative jargon as remote from human speech as possible. What was sadder was to hear this jargon from the infantrymen of Charlie Company: "a patio-type area," "the initial insertion," always "in the area," never "around there" or "in that part of the hamlet." And "an individual" or "the individual," meaning usually a person that the witness does not care to identify more precisely but also, preceded by an adjective, meaning somebody praiseworthy, as in "a very fine individual."

Men who had formed the habit of speaking like a letter from a credit company or a summons to appear in court were oblivious of their remoteness from normal communication. During the reading of the Minh and Phu depositions, it was clear that Eckhardt was not always getting through to the two interpreters. He did not suspect that if he had once said "before" instead of "prior to," they might have had less trouble in understanding his questions. It was Eckhardt, rather than they, who could not speak simple English. Similarly with bald Capt. Kotouc, the company intelligence officer, who had large glazed blue eyes, large protruding ears, and a small protruding red tongue, and who was festooned like an idol with pale-blue braid, maroon braid, combat ribbons, a metal stick like a whistle, the bronze star with V for valor (he was described by G.I.'s as "independent wealthy" and had imported a pool table and color TV for the men serving under him in Vietnam). Stumbling through his testimony, he apologized to the court: "I have a little trouble in the words." Yet this man, who was also deaf, felt qualified to declare that Sgt. Phu's knowledge of English was so defective that he (Kotouc) had to use signs with him.

Judge Howard's speech was surprisingly pure and precise. In the course of the trial he was the only one ever heard to use "infer" correctly ("I infer from your testimony") but also sparingly—he was more inclined to the informal "I gather from what you say." He had a nice command too of the vernacular: speaking of the lunch break, "We have problems, Mr. Bailey, getting everybody et and back." More than once, he scolded Major Eckhardt for inexact reading from a transcript, and it was probably his concern for exactitude of language (which some construed as mere fussiness) that helped one feel that he was concerned with getting at the truth. Or at least that he had *started* with that concern. About two-thirds of the way through, he seemed to give up, resign himself. Nearly every witness, leaving aside the heli-crewmen and some military character witnesses occupied with housekeeping and maintenance at various Army posts, had lied at one time or another, or, as a defense witness put it: "I've made some changes." Medina would be acquitted; the law would be satisfied, and God alone knew the larger truth.

Some of that lies or lay, certainly, in Medina's conscience. But one of the revelations that transpired from My Lai 4 was that the average American had a new conception of conscience.

It was no longer the still small voice speaking up in the night or the gnawing of remorse. When Paul Meadlo told a television audience "I had it on my conscience," he did not mean the murders he had committed. He meant the fact that some of his buddies had been killed by mines (which, by the way, seem to have been laid by South Korean "friendlies," who forgot to take them up, and not by the VC, as the men were taught). The death of his buddies preyed on Meadlo's mind and made him want to kill somebody in revenge.

Meadlo no doubt had a conscience or he would not have gone on television to half confess, half justify his part in the massacre. But in his vocabulary the word he so lamely brought out did not mean that. For him, "conscience" meant bad feelings, something akin to a bad trip. Yet perhaps in his confused soul he meant both: the bad feelings that preceded the crime and thus "caused" it and the bad feelings he got after it.

For the men of Charlie Company as heard at the Medina trial, conscience seemed to be chiefly an organ of self-justification. It did not tell you to refrain from an action but helped you explain what you did, afterward, when questioned. The witnesses talked about casualties inflicted on them by the enemy as though these were atrocities. That is, as though they themselves were *civilians*. One could hear the still-burning resentment and sense of injury in the testimony of Robert Lee, the first defense witness, as he told of a friend being cut right in half by a mine. Anybody might have thought, listening to him, that the VC should have had his friend's death on *its* conscience.

That attitude was the precipitating cause of the massacre. When a man in uniform, with a gun, makes no distinction between himself and a civilian, he will scarcely make a distinction between the military and civilians of the other side. Having been warned, furthermore, that women and children throw grenades (which happened, though not as often as pretended—too dangerous for the thrower), he will lump them all together with guerrillas, not even sorting out babies. Of course in every soldier, especially in every draftee, there is a civilian pleading for recognition, and this subjective feeling of innocent non-participation was fostered in Vietnam by U.S. propaganda, to the point where an outsider might have gathered that Gen. Westmoreland's army was some sort of UN peace-keeping agency. The illusion was encouraged by the use of terms like "pacification," "rural development," "New Life hamlets," and by Johnson's home oratory, in which he presented himself as the arch-non-belligerent.

Calley in his own trial spoke of a pre-My Lai "remorse for losing my men in the mine field, remorse that those men ever had to go to Vietnam, remorse for being in that sort of situation where you are completely helpless." In short, he felt regret for things that were not his fault, and the sad sensation, as in Meadlo's case, was presented as an excuse for mass murder, about which his conscience, so he said, was at ease. More reveal-ing, in its comedy, was his statement to a journalist: "I may be old-fashioned but I don't approve of rape on the battlefield." Calley was apologizing to the journalist for *drawing a line* some-where, that is, for still having a standard or two. He was trying to show his awareness of current permissive trends. This was typical of the killer who saw himself as a peace-movement figure.

Medina at least was more realistic. He profited from the ambiguities of the Calley outcry, which helped preclude his own conviction on the charges brought, as well as on the charge not brought. But at the time of the Peers Panel hearings, he made his position clear in a statement to the press, speaking sharply of "dissident groups in the United States that have probably welcomed the chance to talk to these people [the men of Charlie Company who were making statements to the panel]." Thus, if only for the record, he spurned an alliance with critics of the war. At the time, of course, he could not have guessed that many of those dissidents would be glad to champion him against the Army, which was getting ready to try him. Since then he has cannily stayed quiet. A little victory party was given in Bailey's suite at the Atlanta Airport Hilton to celebrate his acquittal. Eckhardt stayed away, but Wurtzel came, which gave general satisfaction as showing "the brotherly spirit of the Army." Judge Howard and his wife were present. Medina was wearing a shocking-pink shirt, white shoes, and black-and-red-striped bell-bottom trousers.

Now THAT THE CASE is closed, it does no harm to look at it, just once, from the North Vietnamese and VC point of view. Being a "backward" people, they never understood the sympathy for Lt. Calley expressed by so many war critics. For them, it did not follow that if Johnson and Gen. Westmoreland were war criminals, Calley, Medina, the two black sergeants, Meadlo, Oliver, etc. were choiceless victims of the war machine. The North Vietnamese were able to draw a line between the ordinary American soldier at Khe Sanh or Hamburger Hill shooting and being shot at by their troops and an infantry company butchering women, old men, and children. For the ordinary soldier in combat they expressed commiseration—the natural feeling that arises for another human being, whether you "approve" of him or not. But in their eyes, Medina, Calley, and company were not human beings and probably could never become so again, despite the importance given by Buddhist tradition to repentance and regeneration. No fellow-feeling could go out to them; no identification was conceivable.

Were the North Vietnamese and the NLF to win the war, they would undoubtedly try the immediate authors of the massacre, as well as Johnson, Westmoreland, Koster, and any other higher-ups they could catch—few acquittals would result. But if they could not catch Johnson and Westmoreland, they would still try and condemn all the guilty smaller fry they could lay their hands on. To act otherwise in their position would be to imply that because Hitler eluded justice by committing suicide in his bunker and Bormann and Eichmann escaped it would be *unfair* to pick on the smaller Nazis such as Ilse Koch and the lieutenants and executioners at Auschwitz.

Americans at the outset were extremely proud of having put Lt. Calley on trial, boasting that no other country would have done that, which seems true. Yet that boast was a source of anger to the local "counter-culture," which grudges this miserable country any point of pride. The plum was snatched away before it could be feasted on. Doubtless, if Calley had been acquitted, there would have been the same storm (cries of "hypocrisy," "fake justice") from the left that followed his conviction, though the right would have been appeased. The result is now visible. Medina and Henderson off the hook, Calley's sentence reduced, others not tried, several identified and unidentified mass murderers welcomed back into the population. Now any member of the armed forces in Indochina can, if he so desires, slaughter a reasonable number of babies, confident that the public will acquit him, a) because they support the war and the Army or b) because they don't.

The self-persuasion of innocence that accompanied the American soldier on the road to My Lai has its counterpart in the self-persuasion of guilt on the part of many young rebels, which they redistribute, though, to their elders and to the country at large or, more vaguely, the "system." Where the G.I. in Vietnam out on patrol felt he was really a civilian that nobody had the right to snipe at, the counter-culture is convinced that all Americans except themselves are war-makers, *i.e.*, indistinguishable from war criminals.

Such virtuous "indictments" of a whole culture in its ordinary pursuits are politically sterile. The VC and the North Vietnamese are always careful to distinguish "the American people" from "the U.S. imperialist aggressors." By the American people they mean not the proletariat (whose general support of the war they are aware of) but some larger, vaguer entity— America's better self, still found throughout the whole spectrum of classes. The assumption that everybody *has* a better self is indispensable to those working for change. The opposite assumption, of equating individuals with social categories, most of which are treated as criminal *per se*, when it does not lead to Stalinist-style mass liquidations or assassination commandos, conduces to despair and is anyway patently false. If it is not sure that everybody has a better self, history shows that not everybody is ineluctably determined by being a banker or a colonel or a hard hat.

Cynicism about "the system" is a poor guide to political action; it does not matter if the disgusted cynic is 99 per cent right in his estimates. Thus somebody like Michael Bernhardt, who did *not* write to his congressman to denounce the massacre, being too wised-up, apparently, and saturnine about results, was a wholly ineffective figure, unlike his friend Ron Ridenhour, who was naïve enough to send thirty letters, nine registered, to President Nixon, senators, and congressmen, and unlike Hugh Thompson, with his faith, partly misguided, in Major Watke. Charlie Company was well provided with cynics and reflected in an inarticulate way the contempt and hostility felt by most of the youth population toward authority. But the effect was to concur in the massacre and eventually in the cover-up, on the ground that nothing would be done anyway: the brass would see to that.

The same cynical wisdom led many American war critics to assert, in advance, that the Army, by its very nature, was incapable of trying the real criminals in the My Lai case, that Gen. Peers, being a general, was bound to play tricks with the evidence presented to his panel. . . . In short to try to deny them, through foreknowledge, any freedom of action, instead of insisting that they exercise it to the limit. The limit would scarcely have extended as far as Gen. Westmoreland, but at least he might have been demoted.

An allied notion, also dismissive of any idea of personal freedom, was voiced during the uproar following Calley's conviction: that is that Calley, somehow, was a pawn moved around from birth by "the system," which was no doubt true up to a point, but it does not follow that having failed to "make it," he was unable to tell good from evil. As though that faculty was assigned on the basis of worldly achievement or a listing in *Who's Who*; for another view, see the camel and the needle's eye. If

Calley's social conditioning left him no option as to whether to "open up" or not on the people of My Lai 4, then from what source did Michael Bernhardt derive his freedom to keep his rifle pointed at the ground? Where inner freedom is denied, an external force—be it only the grace of God—must govern decisions and choices, formerly thought to be made by the will. Not only do Bernhardt and those few others who refrained deserve no credit, but no blame, in the last analysis, can be assigned to anyone. Since everybody is the net result of something anterior, then (in this way of thinking), everybody is just the idle observer of his own actions. In that case, Johnson, Westmoreland, Koster, Rusk, etc. would have to be acquitted too.

Still, obviously there is a connection between higher policy and those who—let us say on their own initiative—carried out the massacre. Medina was the juncture-point, but how much he knew—or Major Calhoun, at the TOC, knew—of what was in store for the hamlet may never be found out. As has been said, the massacre was detonated by the Search-and-Destroy concept. This was not a wholly military concept, though the military claimed to have invented it. The purpose of creating Free Fire Zones was not just to give the Army an open field and deprive the enemy of cover and sustenance. Behind this was a further intention, which a man of Medina's limited capacities could scarcely have guessed at and which we probably owe to Johnson's White House intellectuals.

To eliminate the ocean in which the Viet Cong fish swam required something more radical than the generation of temporary refugees, who would be housed in camps and eventually, in many cases, drift back to where their rice fields and ancestors' tombs had been. As such, the refugees were mere by-products of military operations and had no larger utility; indeed, they were more of a negative than a positive because of the pestilential conditions they were obliged to live in and the financial drain on the government of the few piasters daily given for their support. Their real usefulness was to implement what can be called a demographic solution to the war. The ultimate (or residual) aim of the Search-and-Destroy operations was to eradicate an entire rural way of life, based on a monoculture—rice—and closed off to modernization. The two little girls and the old man Medina sent on their way to the city were cases in point. The desired sequel was forced urbanization, usually an irreversible process.

By the time of My Lai 4, this was already well advanced, and being deplored by many Army officers, too short-sighted to see beyond the immediate problems—disease, lack of sanitation, lack of housing, corruption of morals—that the influx of homeless peasants into the cities was giving the unsteady Saigon administration. Army officers thought the people would be better resettled in New Life hamlets or whatever those were called at that period. They failed to perceive the long-run benefits, to the U.S., of a demographic shift to the cities. There the peasants, it could be hoped, would adapt to modernization, acquire cravings for consumer goods, enter light industry and commerce, acquire a service point of view. Even, some of them, get rich. The Viet Cong, a pre-capitalist agrarian phenomenon, which had its roots in the fields and in the archaic village communes, would finally fade away.

In short, forced urbanization was a nationwide version of the famous "We had to destroy the town in order to save it" pronounced during the Tết uprising. Some successes have been toted up. During the last Vietnamese election, a shift of votes to Thieu was noted, that corresponded with the shift of the population to the cities. The Viet Cong is still strong in what is left of the countryside.

Now that American main forces have largely withdrawn, Search-and-Destroy operations are no longer conducted; some of those functions have been taken over by the B-52's. But the South Vietnamese administration, picking up the slack, has embarked on its own "resettlement program." According to a Saigon dispatch of January 9, more than 1,500 persons from Quang Tri Province, described as war refugees, have been airlifted to Phoc Tuy Province, southeast of Saigon. The eventual aim, says the dispatch, is to remove 250,000 villagers from the northern provinces (still VC territory) and resettle them in the south. All of them are said to be displaced persons living in refugee camps. In the North Vietnamese version, published October 25 (and disregarded by the Americans, like the first My Lai reports, as enemy propaganda), 2,000 families from Quang Tri Province had already been removed not from camps but from their villages, and the plan calls for the relocation of 2 to 3 million peasants, who are to be forcibly sent south of Saigon from the five northern provinces. The Saigon story quoted the U.S. pacification chief and senior advisor to the South Vietnamese government: "No one's going who doesn't want to go."

As this sequel to Operation Muscatine was unfolding, soon-to-be-former Capt. Medina was appearing on the David Frost show to tell about his new job with Bailey's helicopter plant. Bailey was on the show too: "I think Ernie Medina is the right guy to stick in there to make a little company into a huge giant." Amen.

SONS OF THE
MORNING

W

hat is the purpose of this book?*
Six hundred and eighty-eight
pages of "colorful" narrative that seem to
have been breathlessly dictated to a recording device and,
except for the portions that appeared in magazines, never to
have been touched by an editorial pencil wielded by the author
or anybody else. One keeps asking oneself to what end all these
excited words were assembled, what they add to the already
replete literature on the U.S. and Vietnam. The book is now a
fantastic best seller, yet the author cannot have aimed simply
at the market. He is too sincere, too "concerned," and who
could have foreseen that the time was right for a huge "backgrounder" on our Vietnam involvement, studded, like a ham,
with anecdotes and gossip about historic decisions and high-
status personalities, syrupy with compassionate insights into
the gamesmanship of power?

In fact the book's success is a mystery to this reader, who
was unable to stay awake for more than a few paragraphs at a
go without ferocious application of will power, tea, coffee,
drinks of water, propping open of eyelids, pinches, strolls about
the room. I attribute my stupefied boredom partly to Halberstam's prose, which combines a fluency of cliché with deafness
to idiom and grammatical incomprehensibility. Yet I have
read many dull and badly written books about Vietnam with
no particular effort. If Halberstam's was such a grind to get

* David Halberstam's *The Best and the Brightest*

through, there must be other reasons. A soft, spineless construction: nuggets of research stuck together with a repellent sweetish glue serving as connective? Still, unavoidably, the narrative moves ahead (since events did), even if the persistent regular insertion of biographical flashbacks, like the occurrence of nuts and raisins in some rather doughy hermits, makes the plot thicken more perhaps than was necessary.

But although the slowness of pace, especially on familiar ground, may cause one impatience, that is not the basic problem—one could skip. The basic problem lies in that question of purpose, which keeps arising: the crying lack of any discernible intention. The author has an air of having *something* on his mind, some weighty portentous burden (having to do, somehow, with the shaping of U.S. foreign policy and the selection of personnel), but whatever it is, or was, he is unable to convey to the reader, who comes out of the experience with no clearer notions than he had before on the cause and prevention of Vietnams. And the bewildered demand "Why is he writing this book? What is he trying to say?" may become, in the course of pages, "Why, for God's sake, am I reading it?"

Despite the tone of concern and civic commitment, the book has less to contribute to the public interest (compare *The Pentagon Papers*) than to consumer appetites for unauthorized prowls down the corridors of power. If Halberstam has any message to impart, it is the anguished cry "Can we not learn from history?" But the historian cannot learn much from *him*, since he virtuously declines to give his sources, pleading the right of journalists not to identify their informants. This means that a great deal here is unverifiable. And though one may rely on his general good faith in reporting, his use of language does not inspire trust. For example, he is free with the word "lie," as applied to McNamara and others, but one starts wondering what he means by that and did they lie, really, when on page 408 one reads that Adlai Stevenson "had stood and lied at the UN about things that he did not know," and again on page 410, "It was better for Stevenson to go before the United Nations and lie." But Stevenson, as is semi-plain from the context, was not lying; he was innocently repeating the lies that had been told him.

Books addressed to the public interest are essentially remedial, conducive, it is hoped, to action, for which information and argument are necessary. But Halberstam is concerned with the *reader*, as opposed to the citizen. He is writing for an audience primed for suspenseful happenings, not doers but listeners, with breath duly bated—an apolitical state. I cannot think who will be benefited by *The Best and the Brightest*, who corrected or instructed, and if the book fails to hold the reader's attention, as it so dismally did in my case, another reason may be that the pieties of the avowed purpose, the sighing and deploring, the reiterated "Why?" "Why?" ("What was it about these men, their attitudes, the country, its institutions, and above all the era which had allowed this tragedy to take place?") dampened my vulgar eagerness to learn Mrs. McNamara's nickname ("Marg") or what author John Marquand's author son said to "Lydie" Katzenbach on the Vineyard that spoiled her whole summer.

The Best and the Brightest (Bishop Heber had a better ear; shouldn't it be *The Brightest and the Best*?) belongs at heart to the genre of popular historical fiction, as the writing shows: "Long afterward . . . the older man [Robert Lovett] would remember . . . ," "The great banking-houses," "That cold December day," "In the great drawing rooms of Georgetown," "In the great clubs of Washington and New York," "after the assassination and all the pain," "the great chambers of Europe," "He [Chester Bowles] seemed behind the times; a few long years [sic] it would seem that he was ahead of them," "Perhaps, just perhaps, it need not have been that way."

There are many effects suggestive of leaves fluttering from a calendar in an old movie to indicate the passage of time, and the author is infatuated with a tense I can only describe as the Future Past, as in "the older man would remember." See "Luce's . . . conscience would bother him," "Those years would show," "These stories would surface," "At a dinner party after the Bay of Pigs Bundy would tell friends . . . ," "The very process of choice would mark what the Administration was," "the power and prestige that the McNamara years would bring," "Years later he would sit in Saigon bars . . . ," "He would write of the early Philippine experience . . . ," "his very entry into the Vietnam war would catalyze them and give them muscle previously missing," "But the Saigon years would not be happy ones." Never "Bundy told friends," "The stories surfaced."

The tone is autumnal, soughing, with many "was to be"s, as well as the uncountable "would"s (certainly up in the thousands), signifying a future already plangent when it has not yet happened. And the "might have been"s, rarer but always present by wistful suggestion, chime in with their own melancholy: if only Kennedy had made Bowles his Secretary of State, if only Johnson had listened to George Ball, if only Harriman had been given more power, if only the reliable old China hands had not been languishing in exile. . . . Yet the "if only" music is quite out of key with the dominant Future Past, which persuades the listener that nothing could have been otherwise, since fate had written its tale in advance, foreseeing with Halberstam in a series of flash-forwards that what would be would be.

THAT AWFUL TENSE, seeming to endow the author with prophetic powers, implies that this is a book of revelations. Actually there are few disclosures of the ordinary kind, that is, of facts not generally known. I learned that Kennedy was a very good golfer, much better than Eisenhower, but kept it dark (no doubt fearing a confusion of "images"), that he used an "auto pen" to mimic his signature on letters (whereas Johnson didn't), that behind a locked door in a bathroom he asked Michael Forrestal if he couldn't persuade Harriman to use a hearing aid, that David Bruce's wife cried when Kennedy was nominated in 1960, which helped lose her husband the Secretaryship of State when "it hung in the balance," that Kennedy was appalled by photos showing what napalm had done to people and did not like defoliation either but finally approved the limited use of both, that aboard the *Honey Fitz*, where a party was going on, he turned red with anger as he read Senator Mansfield's private and pessimistic report on his 1962 visit to Vietnam ("Do you expect me to take this at face value?"), that Johnson enjoyed reading FBI files and pretended to drink bourbon when he really drank scotch, that he was loath to start bombing North Vietnam during the Christmas season. . . .

On Rostow: that he proposed putting sugar in the Cuban oil refineries during the missile crisis (taking the thought over from General Lansdale, who in 1954 had gone around Hanoi putting sugar in the gas tanks of trucks), that he gave a party at his home in Cambridge for "Joyce Carey [sic], the famous English novelist," that he played the guitar. . . .

I had not known that General Westmoreland sometimes ate breakfast in his underwear to keep the press in his uniform. I think I had never heard of General Bill Depuy, an "intellectual" and the coinventor, with Westmoreland, of the Search-and-Destroy strategy. Thanks to Halberstam, I was able to place him when he reappeared recently in the news as a prosecution witness in the Ellsberg trial, to give expert testimony that the publication of the Pentagon Papers constituted a danger to national security.

I had forgotten, if I ever knew, the particulars of the Paul Kattenburg story (gloomy in 1963 about Vietnam to the point of suggesting withdrawal, this rising official paid for his accuracy by having his career blasted), of the Lewis Sarris story (essentially the same: wrote a "devastating" study; was passed over repeatedly for promotion), of the David Nes story (same, though what happened to him finally is not told). Add the Colonel Dan Porter story ("brutally frank report" suppressed in 1963; he quits the Army), the story of his superior, one-star General York (pessimistic report suppressed in 1963; whether or not he left the Army unclear).

There is nothing surprising in these detailed personal histories of blighted hopes and rejected expertise; the opposite would be news, on the man-bites-dog principle: a case of somebody being promoted in Washington or Saigon for telling the truth. But they are useful as reminders of a governmental pattern applied to Vietnam up until March 1968, when Clark Clifford, at Defense, listened to the dark assessments of his subordinates and then secured Johnson's attention while managing to keep his job. We knew from *The Pentagon Papers* that CIA analyses of the Vietnam picture were generally quite accurate, but Halberstam, I think, is the first to disclose that early in 1965, while to bomb or not to bomb was still the question, two CIA intelligence estimates of the over-all situation in Vietnam were sent to Washington from the Saigon Embassy with the negative paragraphs deleted: those paragraphs warned that bombing would bring escalation of the war effort from both Hanoi and the Viet Cong.

Such acts of censorship, as anybody familiar with the literature can imagine, had no doubt become almost routine, capable of scandalizing no one. Nor would receipt of the deleted paragraphs have made the slightest difference. Reading this nth confirmation of a sad record, we nod, as we do when we are told of the scaling down of Colonel William Crossen's report on the enemy's capacity for reinforcement. That was the way the big ball was bouncing. But it was a surprise to learn that in the spring of 1963, "Buddhists were told by government troops to disburse." Yes. Likewise that under Kennedy, "High officials were inveighed to study Mao and Lin Piao."

There is a nice new, though not novel, anecdote about Nixon. Back in 1967, on a visit to Saigon, he met an old friend, General Lansdale, then a civilian charged with running the Vietnamese elections that year. Lansdale hoped to have them honest—a notion that did not appeal much to the Embassy, so he turned to Nixon for support. " 'Oh sure, honest, yes, honest, that's right,' Nixon said, 'so long as you win!' With that he winked, drove his elbow into Lansdale's arm, and slapped his own knee." *

There are piquant details about the operations of the Bundy brothers (McGeorge, it appears, while teaching government at Harvard was recruiting for the CIA), about the ambiguous and indeed mysterious attitudes of John McNaughton, McNamara's deputy, who came out so well in *The Pentagon Papers.* There are facts about the early lives, marriages, and social habits of the Kennedy-Johnson bureaucracy. And did you know that Joe McCarthy got the idea, in germ, for his Communist hunt from Father Walsh, the head of Georgetown University's foreign service school? Or that when the Truman government, in 1950, agreed to give military aid to the French in Indochina, it was a trade-off for French agreement to the Schuman Plan, setting up the Coal-and-Steel Community? This allowed the West Germans, regarded as a potential bulwark against Communism, to increase their coal and steel production. There is a good portrait of General Ridgway and a to me amazing and unintentionally Proustian picture of the CIA as having been "the profession of the upper-class élite." But the only important contribution to our knowledge (or suspicions) relates to Johnson and is more of a subtraction than an addition.

---

* Halberstam's source, though he does not give it, is Daniel Ellsberg. The story, as readers have pointed out, appeared in *Papers on the War.*

First on the Tonkin Bay incident. Without Congress's knowledge, Johnson had authorized covert activities against North Vietnam, which included provocative forays in the Tonkin Bay area and bore the code name 34A. As Halberstam tells it, Johnson, though generally aware of the South Vietnamese PT boats' mission, had no information at all as to what was going on when the *Maddox* was fired on. Later, when it was all over, he indicated that he had a shrewd guess: "For all I know, our Navy was shooting at whales out there." But if he was only guessing, the Tonkin Bay incident cannot have been manufactured by him to get his resolution through Congress, *i.e.*, to receive a blank check for continuing the war as it suited him. This is much less than many war critics had suspected.

Johnson was quick to use the incident, which seemed hand-crafted to his purposes, but if he did not contrive it, who did? McNamara and Bundy? Bundy was in charge of covert operations for the White House. The Joint Chiefs? The Navy on its own? CINCPAC? Or did Hanoi help him out by initiating fire? Those covert operations were almost calculated to produce retaliatory action from the North Vietnamese. But Halberstam does not ask a single one of the natural questions that arise. He passes swiftly over the incident, as though the details possessed no intrinsic interest, to take up the sequel: the Goldwater campaign.

But the fact is that Johnson, guilty or innocent of connivance in the episode, immediately took reprisals. He ordered bombing of the North Vietnamese PT bases and the oil depot at Vinh. This happened in August. If he could bomb so promptly, so automatically then, what are we to make of the image

Halberstam offers us of him in the next months as he contemplates Operation Rolling Thunder, the bombing campaign he started in February 1965 and continued, with a few statesmanly pauses, till the end of March 1968? Halberstam asks us to believe that Johnson was reluctant, undecided, listening to George Ball with one ear and the hawks with the other, "fighting a civil war within himself" all through the fall and early winter and not making up his mind to bomb till some time in January and still holding off for a few weeks.

If so, we have to see Johnson in a softer light, absolved of bad faith toward the electorate, which had voted for him that November as the peace candidate: Vietnam was the sacrifice he slowly and unwillingly extorted from himself for the sake of his domestic policy—the Great Society, which otherwise he could not have pushed through Congress. Acting against his instincts, tragically torn, a man "in a trap," "on a toboggan-slide," he was a victim, and his advisers, to a lesser extent, were victims too, "cornered by bad policies on Asia which they had not so much authored as refused to challenge. . . . And so now they bombed." In so far as all this represents an effort at understanding, it is a new approach to Vietnam and seems intended to replace earlier and leftist "simplifications" in which conscious planning and wicked deception were assigned to the principals.

YET THIS KIND of understanding, while it allows for the mixture of motives and the conflicts present, no doubt, in everybody, does not do more here, at best, than elicit sympathy for the actors as they looked to *themselves*, rather than as history may look at them. History, for Halberstam, is cruel, ironic destiny (the adverb "ironically" is much abused by him, made to work overtime in the most inappropriate conditions) ; nobody controls events unless it is the military, who seem to be a supra-force, like destiny itself.

Johnson and Rusk are the chief beneficiaries of the approach. Rusk is revealed as a narrow but intelligent and conscientious man performing his duty despite original reservations about the policy; he is given the prime virtue of loyalty, which Johnson, a fellow-Southerner, valued greatly. Of Johnson, we are told that he arrived at the bombing and the later commitment of troops by a long road of "fateful decisions" whose fatality at each milestone eluded him. His duplicity with Congress, with the press, was an ingrained character trait of the eternal "loner," rather than the instrument of a well-laid policy. His craftiness and concealment sprang from his acute sensitiveness to public relations, so that the public, or his sense of it, dictated his actions. He was sincere when he said that he did not want to send American boys to die for Asian boys, just as, from the bottom of his heart, he had never wanted to bomb.

So Halberstam presents him, "this great elemental man," racked by insecurity, miserably wishing to draw back from decisions that the rest of us thought he was leading us into. If this seems hard to credit, in view of our knowledge, confirmed by Halberstam, that the bombing program was already, so to speak, on Johnson's desk, waiting only for his signature and for final target selection (do we hit the dikes or not?), it gains a little plausibility from the very practice of contingency planning. If all options are regarded as under diligent study, a president, reviewing them on a daily or weekly basis, may continue in the illusion that he has not decided between them; although in reality certain ones have been excluded, they still are on file under "Possible Action Alternatives."

It is quite likely that Johnson up to almost the last minute hoped he would not have to bomb, in the sense that an armed robber hopes that the bank teller will hand over the money and not "oblige" him to shoot him. He must often have wished that the VC would fade away and not "force" him to bomb those other dinks in the North, just as, dismissing all forecasts to the contrary, he then hoped that the bombing would work, so that he would not be "obliged" to send troops. But in law the possession of a gun (rather than a toy pistol) by a robber is taken as prima facie evidence of an intent to murder, and if people are killed during a holdup, he cannot successfully plead lack of premeditation on the theory that using the gun was only an *alternative* that he held in reserve. The detailed preparations for bombing, the pinpointing of targets declare Johnson's inner readiness to commit the crime, and if it is true that he hesitated, letting himself be influenced by George Ball's contention that the bombing would be non-productive, this would be on a par with that same bank robber hesitating to do the job on hearing from a confederate that experience showed that only petty cash was kept in the drawer.

Johnson's vacillation was probably 90 per cent imaginary, a by-product of bureaucratic paper work—the study of memos evidently inducing the contented executive feeling that all avenues leading to a way out have been explored. There was only one way, ever, out of Vietnam, which was out, but we find no suggestion in Halberstam that withdrawal figured as a serious alternative to Operation Rolling Thunder. The choice was between different means of continuing the war. Reference to a "conference table" solution, in so far as it was sincere, was pure reverie —the wishful thought that Hanoi could be brought by negotiations to surrender its objectives and stop inciting the VC to rebel—but mainly it served as a pretext for piously intensifying the war as the sole means of getting Hanoi to sit down and talk.* All this is well known, and there would be no need for insisting on it if Halberstam's picture of an anguished president locked in combat with his conscience did not require some comparison with reality. A man divided in his soul between dispatching combat troops, increasing Special Forces, and trying out one of three bombing "scenarios" is scarcely a figure of Greek tragedy.

Yet Halberstam's design necessitates a big central figure ("There were many Johnsons: this complicated, difficult, sensitive man"), "terrible decisions," and the incessant manufacture of suspense: Rubicons being crossed, traps closing, doors shutting forever. I do not know how many "turning points" are reached in the narrative or how many "crossroads." His determination to view Vietnam as an American tragedy means that the outcome is ineluctable, foreordained (cf. the "would"s and "were to be"s), and also that all those Rubicons should be invisible to those crossing them; nobody ever says, "Well, the die is cast." Since, like the spectator of a Greek tragedy, the

---

* Compare Nixon's Christmas bombing of 1972.

reader knows anyway what the end is going to be, suspense must be created by artistry and inner conflict heightened where little may have existed in real life.

Were Halberstam Shakespeare or Sophocles (an idea that sometimes seems not far from his mind), the real-life dimensions of his figures, the prosaic nature of the "mighty" conflict would hardly be an issue: *Richard III* is not made absurd by historians' agreement that in reality he was quite a decent monarch, any more than *King Lear* would be diminished by greater knowledge of the political structure of the Britain of his time. But, first of all, Vietnam is too disagreeably close to us, one would guess, to serve as source material for tragic art, even in the hands of a gifted dramatic poet (there is something distasteful in the very notion of approaching it as an *American* tragedy, whose protagonist is a great suffering Texan), and second, Halberstam's incapacity to write English brings the question of art to the forefront ("He did not shirk from the test of wills," "It was not just humiliation on Vietnam which was vested upon Humphrey," "Nor was anyone particularly optimistic the bombing would improve South Vietnamese morale," *inter* hundreds of *alia*), where it certainly ought not to be, and finally, given his want of art, the reader is tempted to find ludicrous the whole "tragic" compassionate premise and ask whether these were really the brightest who now are laid so low.

The moment comes when one wants Halberstam to put up or shut up: enough "turning points" and "crossroads," were those decisions ineluctable or not? His tragic muse tells him they were, given "the men, the attitudes, the era," and so on, but we also hear a weak, liberal voice from the prompting box that shrills no, there were other choices: if only Harriman . . . if only Chester Bowles . . . George Ball . . . Kattenburg . . . John Paton Davies. . . . It would be more convincing if we did not have *The Pentagon Papers*. Document 103 lets us have a look at George Ball's counter-proposals to Johnson. The idea of progressive, clear-seeing statesmen who might have directed the policy otherwise than the way it went loses what plausibility it had in Halberstam's overwrought pages: one has only to read through Ball's strongly worded but insubstantial "Compromise Solution" (which proposes that we "continue bombing in the North but avoid the Hanoi-Haiphong area," et cetera) to have doubts about his role as unhappy Good Counselor, Kent to Johnson's Lear.

THE INFLATIONARY tendency of Halberstam's prose affects not just the principal figures but every supernumerary, every prop and piece of scenery: the "great drawing rooms of George-town." Kennedy's "education had been superb." Bill Bundy is "a deeply educated man." The Kennedy team were "all men of towering accomplishment." The swanked-up villain of the piece is the "Eastern élite," defined as the people who knew the right people, in short the New Frontiersmen, with their supposedly awesome social and academic connections.

An earlier example of the type is Acheson, and the first chapters have a populist flavor, as Halberstam tries to establish a relation between a certain arrogant mentality, blue blood, and old finance capital, all of which, together with the legacy of the British Empire, are meant to account for the Cold War.

Since the thought cannot be stretched to cover less well-tailored men in government who were anti-Communist zealots without having gone to Groton, Choate, or St. Paul's, it is soon dropped by the author, leaving us, after the assassination, with nobody but the Bundy brothers as display models of what he has been talking about. If a clear idea can be imputed to the text, though, it is that an élitist strain in our democracy, represented by the "patrician" Bundy brothers, once implanted in Washington and crossed with the "Can-do" mentality represented by McNamara, bred the monster of Vietnam.

It is easy to agree about the odiousness of the Bundy brothers and even to think that, without them, our Vietnam policy might have been less egregiously self-assured, but harder to be impressed, as Halberstam clearly is, by their social and cerebral endowments, and this goes for the whole New Frontier. A minor embarrassment of the book is watching the author show his eager familiarity with the right forks and spoons of the "prestigious" Washington upper bureaucracy, which he accepts at its own valuation and that of the local society page. More important and equally irritating is the assertion that an aristocracy of brains came to Washington with the Kennedys—a notion that was part of the Kennedy advertising and just as believable as the old "for men of distinction . . . Lord Calvert" ads.

A comparison with the New Deal is useful. Without claiming that the best brains of the country functioned as Roosevelt advisers, one can say that some good and independent minds did: Frankfurter, Berle, Tugwell. . . . Kennedy's academic advisers, with the exception of Galbraith (who was also exceptional in giving some sensible advice), far from being "men of towering accomplishment," were mostly pale fish out of university think tanks. Whatever their actual field of knowledge, they were considered to be adepts of political science—a pseudo discipline of "ruthless" thinking about political "realities" that had developed in the universities under Cold War pressure. There were no political scientists, as such, in Roosevelt's appanage.

Rostow (Economic History), who lasted longest, and McGeorge Bundy (Government) were typical, in their different ways, of this new genre of theoretic intellectual all too delighted to be called to the capital to practice. The atmosphere of a court, which continued through Johnson and was unlike anything in Roosevelt's or Truman's time, probably owed a good deal to the presence of these charlatans, regarded as wizards—Bundy, the surgeon, cutting through "to the bone of an issue," a genius at paper work and administration, Rostow, more the general physician, constantly handing out murderous prescriptions and, in Johnson's reign, on night call.

What came to Washington was not brains and birth but packaged ideology, a form of overweening stupidity generated in university departments of Political Science and Government, where the "honed-down intelligence" of a stick like McGeorge Bundy could be viewed with awe. The fact that Arthur Schlesinger, a simple historian with the normal amount of brains, remained *in* the group but not *of* it, a luckily lesser light in "that glittering constellation," was due not so much probably to his personal modesty as to lack of pretensions to owning a brain that functioned like a scientific instrument.

The gross stupidities and overconfidence of the Kennedy-

Johnson advisers, not to mention their moral insensitivity, issued from a sectarian faith in the factuality of the social sciences, which is not by any means the religion of an élite. The use of computers and input from the "scientists" of the Rand Corporation increased the reverence of the faithful for this crass body of beliefs.

In my opinion, Halberstam also inflates the baleful importance of the military. It is true that generals always ask for more, more men, more hardware, and that if you give them an inch they will take a yard, but, aside from a few "intellectuals" like General Maxwell Taylor and the earlier-mentioned General Bill Depuy, they do not seem to have done much more than their job required, which was to look ahead, foresee future needs, and make recommendations to provide for them. This ability to see the next step is just what was lacking in the civilians, if we can accept Halberstam's quagmire metaphor and believe that they floundered ahead with no idea of where they were going.

On the whole, the generals perceived the logic of the Vietnam commitment quite clearly: if you were going to stay there, you would need more men, more hardware, you would have to bomb the North, and the sooner the better, mine Haiphong harbor and not hesitate to hit the dikes. Given the aim, they were right; maybe, given the aim, General Curtis LeMay was right: if victory was what was wanted, Hanoi should have been bombed back to the Stone Age. It was the only way. There was never any indication from the civilians that victory was *not* what was wanted. Compromise was excluded, linked to "surrender," "humiliation," and it may well be that this war could not and still cannot be resolved by compromise, as the present ineffectiveness of the cease-fire and Nixon's repeated threats to renew hostilities seem to show. What Nixon envisioned was a *victorious* stand-down—a cease-fire that could be violated, unilaterally, by Thieu.

Of course the generals were frequently blind to political considerations (the risk of bringing China into the war, the risk of frightening the electorate, of alienating world opinion), but politics was not their job, and anyway, as Nixon found out, the political fallout from invading Cambodia, hitherto off limits, was so slight that he was encouraged to go ahead with most of the generals' other pet projects: the incursion into Laos, the mining, the dikes (though this is denied), intensified air war on population centers. This does not prove, though, that Nixon had become the Pentagon's creature. He had tested the political water, both domestically and internationally, and found the temperature favorable. It was not the generals (far from it) who recommended "Vietnamization" and the "thaws" with China and Russia. And General Lavelle was demoted and relieved of his command for doing what Nixon made policy a few weeks later.

It is true that Johnson's generals were guilty of chronically optimistic forecasts, from the field, of how near victory was, yet these were what Washington was asking for. One wonders why McNamara was so "elated" on hearing from General Harkins in Honolulu in April 1963 that it might all be over by Christmas. Had he got such an estimate at Ford, he would immediately have demanded supporting facts and figures.

It is amazing and to me inexplicable to find McNamara, in

Vietnam, failing to use the same criteria of judgment he had applied with such severity at Ford. Why did he always swallow the military's fudged statistics? Halberstam's explanation (that he did not want to poach on the military's territory) is inadequate: statistics were *his* territory, and he knew how to spot discrepancies. If he thought that what was good for Ford was bad for the country, this meant that somehow, as a cost-efficiency expert, he knew that his country could not bear the expense of the truth. The Vietnam policy required false figures to sustain it, and he was loyal.

The same could be said of the military. In any case, their rosy reports from the field did not accord with their continual demands for more, which ought to have been a warning to the Administration of what its policy implied. Already, in mid 1962, the military was asking Kennedy for napalm, defoliants, jets, and free-fire zones (to dump unused bombs in). This was a prophetic clarification of the true nature of the war. Had Kennedy listened to the generals, rather than to his experts, who were still selling him the doctrine of "limited wars" and the famous counter-insurgency, he might have seen that it was time to get out while he could. Yet among high Administration figures, only Bobby Kennedy finally drew the obvious inference and in a National Security Council meeting the next year suggested that withdrawal should be considered.

The Administration, however, was unwilling to admit, even to itself, an ends-means relation taken for granted by the military. Though the military pushed for the appropriate means to bring about the end, it was not they who had set the goal in the first place and continued to reaffirm it at every public opportunity.

They are certainly guilty of war crimes, both technical violations of the Geneva Convention and moral violation of the laws of humanity: they encouraged and covered up atrocities, knowingly permitted the torture of prisoners and civilians, engaged in area bombing, and freely used anti-personnel projectiles in inhabited regions containing no military targets.

These were crimes they committed in the exercise of their professional capacities (and as soldiers they had the right to refuse participation), but I do not see how they can be charged with sucking us deeper and deeper into the war, when the decisions to go ahead were made by U.S. presidents and with the consent of Congressional majorities, which could at any time have repealed the Tonkin Bay resolution (and finally did, in Nixon's time, without any noticeable effect), however deceptively it was obtained by Johnson and McNamara. Halberstam's way of telling it of course makes Johnson more sympathetic and the story more dramatic, as the trap slowly closes on him and he yields once again to the steady, relentless pressure from the professional warmakers.

BUT WHY DID we get into Vietnam and why are we still there, covertly, with "advisers," when the flag has been furled? It cannot be the Army, Air Force, and the Navy that are pressing to stay in Thailand, Guam, and the Gulf of Tonkin. The Bundy brothers and Rostow have long since departed from Washington, and no "Eastern élite" is determining policy. Actually what we are doing in Vietnam is a mystery, though in the early stages it seemed to require no explanation: we were there to contain Communism, the way we had in Greece and Korea, even if we did not wish to fully repeat the latter experience. In fact, a successful action is never examined in terms of what caused it; the result is seen as the cause. Or, as Halberstam, who has his shrewd insights, puts it when describing some of the early misgivings and how they were mastered: "Why challenge your goals if you are achieving them?" Once the conduct of the war became problematical, questions began to be asked about the worth of the enterprise. Finally, the worth being doubted, causes were sought, and the history of the involvement was traced, as though in the historical sequence lay buried the explanation.

This is Halberstam's view, when he is seeking to write straight history rather than "for color." In the objective mood, he attributes our involvement to a chain of causality: the Cold War and the "loss" of China, then Senator Joe McCarthy and the demoralization of the foreign service, and, behind these linked happenings, the passing of the British Empire, which left the U.S. as the most powerful nation in the world and hence the guarantor of international stability, *i.e.*, of the status quo as it existed at the end of World War II. None of this is new, but that does not mean it is false. Perhaps there *were* those particular multiple causes, foremost among them the Cold War, from which the others derived, since without it the disintegration of the British Empire would not necessarily have made the U.S. put on the uniform of world policeman, nor would the "loss" of China have given rise to panic. Yet Halberstam seems satisfied to talk of "demonology" in connection with Cold War attitudes, as if that summed up the subject. This line is fashionable among younger people today, but it ignores the historical reality of Stalin.

If you ignore the reality of Stalin, it is easy to be smug in retrospect about the source of U.S. errors. But to have feared the advance of Stalinism, for Europe or for Asia, was not irrational or immoral, even though some of the steps taken against it were. One can cite our China policy, for instance, as misguided from the point of view of our own national interest: it would have been wiser to accept the fact of Mao and the People's Republic since it was already evident and had been pointed out many times by Trotsky and others that Stalin feared nothing more than a plurality of revolutions. But we were not sufficiently astute to perceive this realistic possibility, being blinded by moral considerations which were not at that time wholly hypocritical: recognition of Red China looked to most like further accommodation to Stalinism, and those who argued for it (leaving out fellow travelers) did so neither in moral nor in radical terms but in terms of trimming one's sails to the prevailing winds.

Until the Twentieth Congress, the Cold War, in one form or another, if not in all the forms it took, had some legitimacy, and to talk of the Free World was not sheer hysteria. Halberstam writes as though Soviet totalitarianism had been a figment of Senator Joe McCarthy's witch-hunting imagination, and it is like looking for a needle in a haystack to try to find Stalin's name in the text. The index has it listed nine times, yet, strangely, I fail to see it on three of the pages cited: pages 387, 389, 390.

Still there is no doubt that the Cold War and plain anti-Communism (which are not the same) played a big part in getting us into Vietnam. But the Cold War does not account for our persistence there. Anti-Communism continues to provide the moral screen, but on the practical plane nobody in power believes any longer that our purpose there is to counter a "world Communist threat." Some other explanation must be sought.

The North Vietnamese ascribe it to U.S. imperialism, and this explanation is summarily rejected by nearly all Americans, including most of the war's critics. Halberstam does not even mention the possibility that imperialist interests might be one of the motives. Certainly the pursuit of imperialist goals, in the traditional sense of a quest for raw materials and natural resources to be exploited with the use of coolie labor, is not involved here: we are not after their rice and we have destroyed, by bombing and defoliation, most of their rubber plantations. Even if offshore oil should be found in large quantities, as some American prospectuses have indicated, this would not be an adequate inducement; nor would the exploitation of Cam Ranh Bay as a vacation area by real-estate developers (a perfectly plausible American "vision") pay off the cost of the war.

Yet, in a larger sense, I believe that our investments and markets *are* at stake in Vietnam. Vietnam has been fastened on as a symbol of the right of U.S. capital to flow freely throughout the globe and return home. The fact that American investments in Vietnam are negligible and likely to remain so, even if the oil can be successfully dredged or a Mekong Valley

Power Authority created, does not make us insensitive to the revolutionary challenge represented by the Viet Cong. Vietnam is not Chile or Bolivia, yet the defiance of the American will on the part of a "backward" nation cannot be overlooked. The shot heard round the world. That a revolutionary has no country is just as real to capitalists, large and small, as it was to whoever first said it. A Viet Cong "take-over," if it is allowed to happen, deals a blow to the American way of life and free-enterprise mystique, not only because the revolutionary spirit is contagious and may be carried like Asian flu to the Philippines, South America, Africa, but because the very concept of a self-elected alternative to the American pattern is injurious.

Had South Vietnam "gone Communist" overnight, against its will, through a *coup d'état*, it might count for us today less than Albania. Because Albania did not have a choice. The South Vietnamese had a choice, and that shocks. In our eyes, states that have no choice, like Poland, are regarded as reclaimable morally and perhaps even practically in some vaguely imagined circumstance. We are told how Poles love Americans, how they even loved Nixon when he was there, and this fact—or belief—instead of making us anguish over them, pray for their liberation, quite reconciles us to their fate.

A Hungarian friend recently said to me that there was something almost metaphysical in the American deadlock with Vietnam. I think that is true. Our reluctance to leave cannot be accounted for by the sequence of causality that brought us there and it goes beyond simple unwillingness on the part of a series of chief executives to be the "first American president to preside over a defeat." The metaphysical element grows out of our quite material attachment to our beloved system of production and consumption, and truly is a mystery, in the religious sense, as peculiar as the doctrine of the Trinity to those not initiated. That must be why no argument on the matter has ever been listened to and why the refusal to admit that this was a civil war has been so adamant, for the idea that the enemy could be *within* our ally rather than to the north, was unthinkable: nobody in his right mind, while getting American aid, could choose Communism. It also helps explain the savage cruelty of the means used by men who imagined they were decent.

This is not the place to pursue these reflections, which rest on the gloomy sense that Vietnam *was* unavoidable. If this "Vietnam" had been averted, another would have come along. Even assuming that this one will somehow be terminated, I fear that peace, should it come in reality as well as in name, will be only an intermission in a series of confrontations, which the Americans will be unwise, from their point of view, to postpone too long, lest they lose their technological superiority. Indeed, this technological superiority was surely the other and final reason for our willingness to get into Vietnam and stay there. We knew we had the "muscle" (a favorite Halberstam word), and this gave us confidence, even though the nuclear option, the most bulging part of that muscle, had to be kept under wraps.

The technological gap between us and the North Vietnamese constituted, we thought, an advantage which obliged us not to quit. Despite the "unfair" handicap of not being allowed to use tactical atomic arms, we could still display, as if in an exhibition hall, a whole range of advanced weaponry, as well

as "people sensors," computer systems, sophisticated radar—
only missing was McNamara's projected electronic barrier.
The manufacture and maintenance of all this puerile and costly
junk is as much a feature of the American way of life as
Wheaties, the breakfast food of champions, or shopping malls,
and the lack of consumer appreciation by the North Vietnamese
and the VC of this aspect of our high standard of living, their
stubbornness before the evidence of our overwhelming industrial capacity, added another mysterious obstacle to the understanding between peoples that our intervention was bent on
establishing.

SOME OF THIS can be read between the lines of Halberstam's
chronicle. Between the lines there is room for thought. But the
lines themselves with their flashy "styling" and shoddy work-
manship are a continual distraction and sad reminder of the
low standards now accepted in all branches of U.S. production
as the natural corollary of high output. For me, the necessity
of checking against other sources (among them my own memory) imposed by this manifestly colored and unedited narrative
made the book even more tedious than it might have been
had I consented to read it as a fiction "based on" history. I felt
like Ralph Nader, testing and weighing sentences and paragraphs, a state of mind that in the field of book manufacture
few, I realize, will find sympathetic.

Nevertheless, to show what I mean, I shall give a small concluding example. Halberstam makes much of "the way high-
level military destroyed dissenters" and cites very fully the
cases of Kattenburg, Sarris, Colonel Dan Porter, and others

439

who were broken by the treatment or else simply quit. All true, I am sure. But it occurred to me finally to wonder what *had* happened to the one-star General York whose story Halberstam˙drops at the point where it has illustrated his theme. So I looked him up in the 1968–69 *Who's Who* and found ("York, Robert Howard, army officer") that he is serving—or was five years ago—as Commanding General of the XVIII Airborne at Fort Bragg, with the rank of lieutenant-general. In other words, he not only had not been destroyed but had had a promotion.

This inspired me to look up David Nes, the State Department dissenter whose story also breaks off at a point where one would have imagined that he had been ignored, downgraded, by-passed, driven into premature retirement. But no; it turns out that from 1965 on he was serving as Minister in the U.S. Embassy in Cairo, a grade higher than Deputy Chief-of-Mission, which was his post in Saigon when he angered General Harkins by making pessimistic reports. In fact, unless I misread *Who's Who*, he had already been raised to the rank of Minister in Saigon (where he served till 1965) at a time when Halberstam places him back in Washington being given "the strong feeling that no one wanted to touch anyone who had angered the military, that if the military turned on you, you were dead." It is true that when my *Who's Who* went to press he had not reached the rank of Ambassador, although he was fifty-one or -two years old. In career terms, which in my view interest Halberstam excessively, how dead is "dead"?

INDEX

Vietnamese names appear under the first, or given, name rather than under the family name. Thus Ngo Dinh Diem, whose family name is Ngo, is entered under his given name, Diem.